THE ABORTION DEBATE IN THE
UNITED STATES AND CANADA

GARLAND REFERENCE LIBRARY
OF SOCIAL SCIENCE
(VOL. 648)

THE ABORTION DEBATE IN THE UNITED STATES AND CANADA
A Source Book

Maureen Muldoon

GARLAND PUBLISHING, INC. • NEW YORK & LONDON
1991

Library of Congress Cataloging-in-Publication Data

Muldoon, Maureen.
  The abortion debate in the United States and Canada : a source
book / Maureen Muldoon.
    p. cm. — (Garland reference library of social science ; vol.
648)
  Contents: Includes bibliographical references and index.
  ISBN 0-8240-5260-9 (alk. paper)
  1. Abortion—United States—History—Sources. 2. Abortion—
Canada—History—Sources. 3. Pro-choice movement—United States—
History—Sources. 4. Pro-choice movement—Canada—History—
Sources. 5. Pro-life movement—United States—History—Sources.
6. Pro-life movement—Canada—History—Sources. I. Title.
II. Series.
HQ767.5.U5M85   1991
363.4'6'0971—dc20   91-3658
                                                              CIP

Printed on acid-free, 250-year-life paper
Manufactured in the United States of America

**For
Roger Hutchinson**

Contents

TABLES

Acknowledgments

I would like to thank those who gave permission to reproduce material for this book. These are: Congressional Quarterly Inc., 1414 22nd Street N.W., Washington, D.C.; Sociological Abstracts, P.O. Box 22206, San Diego, CA 92122-0206; Gallup Canada, Inc., 180 Bloor Street West, Toronto, Ontario M5S 2V6; and Gallup, USA.

I would especially like to thank Stanley Henshaw and the Guttmacher Institute, 111 Fifth Avenue, New York, New York 10003, for making available the Tables which appear in Chapter One.

Also, I would like to thank all of the organizations and religious demoninations who responded to my request for their statements on abortion. I hope that this source book will further the dialogue on this important issue.

I am deeply grateful to the many people who helped in the completion of this book. My family, friends and colleagues have been supportive, as they have been in all my endeavors. Bill Jackson, Joan Magee and Tad Venkateswarlu of the Leddy Library, University of Windsor, were very helpful in locating material. Wendy Sullivan, Christine Charlebois, Victoria Kett and Ethel Smith provided excellent secretarial support. Dr. Norm King helped in numerous ways, especially in terms of his computer skills. Most importantly, I thank him for his friendship.

Introduction

Over the last twenty-five years or so, the debate on abortion has not moved any closer to resolution in either the United States or Canada. The courts, the legislatures, the pulpits, the classrooms, the hospitals and clinics and the media have provided the forums for this on-going struggle. Two groups of activists have dominated the debate. The opponents of abortion, who are referred to as anti-abortion or pro-life, advocate restrictive policies on abortion while the pro-choice groups direct their attempts to creating a permissive policy that allows a woman to make her own decision. The anti-abortion advocates and the pro-choice advocates alike have learned the skills and developed the strategies to advance their own positions. Whatever legal and public policy gains are made by one side are often countered by moves from their opponents.

There is available a vast amount of material related to the topic of abortion. The genre of the literature varies from academic journal articles to impassioned newsletters and pamphlets with an unambiguous point of view. From the extensive and diverse literature, this book draws a collection of relevant materials primarily representing aspects of the sociological, philosophical, religious and legal aspects of the abortion issue. Its purpose is to serve as a source book for those interested in seeing how the abortion debate has been conducted within the recent past. The book also serves as a reference work for further study.

DEFINITION OF ABORTION

There are various definitions of the term "abortion." A common definition designates as an abortion any termination of pregnancy, beginning from the moment that the ovum is fertilized. If this definition is used, then certain forms of contraception, such as the interuterine devices, are considered to be abortifacient, because they help prevent implantation. However, other definitions are employed as well. The authors of *Induced Abortion: A World Review*, for example, describe an "abortion" as the termination of pregnancy after implantation of the blastocyst in the endometrium and before the fetus has obtained viability. Viability is reached when the fetus is capable of surviving, with appropriate life support, in an independent extrauterine life.[1]

There are two major categories of abortions. Induced abortions are those initiated voluntarily with the intention of terminating the pregnancy. All other abortions are called spontaneous, even when they result from causes such as injury or fever. Often, the term miscarriage is used to refer to spontaneous abortions.

THE ABORTION DEBATE
IN THE UNITED STATES AND CANADA

In trying to grapple with many of the questions that arise with regard to abortion, it is important to be aware of certain basic facts: who gets abortions, what are their ages and marital status, where are abortions performed, how many are performed and what is the risk to the pregnant woman of morbidity or death. The first section of Chapter 1, using the statistics compiled by the Guttmacher Institute, presents much of the demographic information regarding the practice of abortion in recent years in the United States and Canada.

Chapter 1 also covers recent research on the sociological aspects of abortion. The studies of these researchers cover a wide range of exploration into the social determinants of attitudes and practices regarding abortion. These include such factors as the perspectives of women undergoing prenatal diagnosis, the outlooks of mothers of congenitally impaired children, and perceptions of motherhood. Other research examines an illegal abortion collective and the bombing of abortion clinics.

The final section of Chapter 1 indicates recent opinions as to the circumstances in which abortion should or should not be legal, as revealed in Gallup polls in the United States and Canada. Results from other polls taken since 1975 are included as well.

The philosophical questions contained in the abortion debate are really at the heart of the issue. One of the most fundamental determinations that must be made in the current debate is the point at which there is a human person who is the subject of moral and legal rights. There is little agreement between the opponents of abortion and the supporters of choice on this matter. It cannot be settled by any scientific evidence. There is a spectrum of positions as to when there is a human person. These are based on the physical and social development of the "unborn" or the "conceptus" from the stage of fertilized ovum, to birth, and on into infancy and early childhood. Other philosophical positions hold that it is some property possessed by a person--such as having self-consciousness or the capacity for language--that determines the recognition of moral and legal rights. The fetus may be considered an actual person by the proponents of one position, while another will view the fetus as a potential person. The implications of holding a particular position on the status of the "unborn" determine what kind of public policy regulating abortion is considered acceptable. Some authors argue, however, that considerations other than the status of the "unborn" as a bearer of rights or claims are involved in making moral decisions regarding abortion. Arguments have been made against late abortion, for example, even within the view that the fetus is a nonperson without rights.

Chapter 2, then, introduces some of the important philosophical questions that need to be addressed in the abortion debate. A number of articles that can now be considered as "classic" are presented in abstract form. Most of these articles are easily available in anthologies on abortion or bioethics. The bibliography contains references to the current debate as well as historically important material.

Closely related to the philosophical issues on abortion are the theological questions. Often these are discussed together, and, for some authors, it is difficult to make a sharp distinction between the philosophical and theological discussion. Some reference material that deals with the religious questions has been included in Chapter 2.

The influence of religious belief is strongly evident in the abortion debate. Chapter 3 is the compilation of a number of official policy statements on abortion from religious groups in Canada and the United States. Most of the statements are from Christian denominations. The invitation was made to other traditions, besides Christian, to have their position included. One Jewish group did send in their position. Another Jewish response indicated that it was impossible to speak uniformly on behalf of their members.

The statements generally include their determination of the status of the "unborn," with an explanation of the Scriptural and theological foundations for the position. The proper view of sexuality and marriage and of the role of women and the family are often affirmed in the statements. Directives for endorsing and/or lobbying for an acceptable public policy are usually set forth as well. A lengthy bibliography follows at the end of this chapter.

The most public aspect of the abortion debate has taken place through the different types of advocacy that have been employed. Local and federal governments, the courts, hospital boards, women's health clinics, professional associations, schools, churches and other community centers have been the sites for advocates to promote their position, be they abortion opponents or pro-choice supporters. In both the United States and Canada, a number of leaders and organizations have emerged to actively campaign for changes in the existing abortion policy.

Chapter 4 acknowledges some of the key figures and groups in the abortion debate. It is impossible to mention all of the groups involved. Some are caucuses of large political parties and others are dissenters who oppose the view of their religious denominations. Some groups may have indirect affiliation with a religious denomination or some other community organization, while others may have formed specifically to fight the abortion cause in view of their own position.

Chapter 5 describes the abortion debate in the United States and Canada as it has unfolded through decisions made in the courts and legislatures. In 1973, *Roe v. Wade* began a new chapter that touched every aspect of the abortion debate. Using the trimester framework, the United States Supreme Court ruled that it was an infringement of the woman's right of privacy for the state to interfere with her decision for an abortion within the first trimester of pregnancy. Politically, there have been attempts to amend the Constitution in order to acknowledge the fetus as a person and thus to prohibit abortion. Amendments have been introduced to limit the use of Medicaid funds for abortions for indigent women. Individual states have tried to limit abortions by employing a number of strategies such as requiring parental consent and placing special stringent requirements on the facility where abortions are to be performed. The Supreme Court decision in *Webster v. Reproductive Health Services* in 1989 ruled in favor of three out of four provisions of the 1986 Missouri abortion law. As a result, abortions will be more closely regulated and more difficult to obtain. The trimester framework employed in *Roe* was discarded. The *Webster* decision is the most serious threat to *Roe*. A number of states have attempted to enact very restrictive abortion laws since the 1989 ruling.

In Canada, many notable events have happened with regard to the practice of abortion since the 1969 Omnibus Bill, which allowed therapeutic abortions when the pregnancy threatened the "life or health" of the woman. This determination was to be made by a therapeutic abortion committee within an accredited hospital. In 1988, the Supreme Court of Canada ruled in *R. v. Morgentaler* that the 1969 Omnibus Bill infringed upon a number of the rights guaranteed to all, including pregnant women, and was therefore unconstitutional. In 1989, the federal government tabled a bill to recriminalize abortion. As of 1990, it has passed through the House of Commons and is still in need of Senate approval. Abortion will be available if a medical practitioner is of the opinion that continuing the pregnancy will threaten the life or health of the woman. Physicians become the gatekeepers. It is believed that the effect of the bill, not necessarily intended, will be to limit access to abortions, because physicians will not want their opinions challenged in court, as abortion opponents have threatened to do. In 1989, there were two well-publicized cases, one in Ontario and the other in Quebec, where male friends of pregnant women unsuccessfully attempted to prevent them from seeking an abortion.

Chapter 5 includes excerpts of the actual Court decisions: *Roe v. Wade* and *Webster v. Reproductive Health Services* pertaining to the United States and *R. v. Morgentaler* for Canada. Bill C-43 is included as well. This is the bill, passed by the Canadian Parliament and awaiting Senate approval, which will recriminalize abortion. Current legal and bibliographic references follow at the end of Chapter 5.

In sum, this is a source book on the abortion debate as it has been carried out in recent years. It seeks to represent the diversity of opinion and attitude as it has found expression in the academy, the churches, the courts, and various groups within Canadian and American society. It is hoped that such a work will provide a basis for information and reflection for those who are concerned with this important issue. Two recent bibliographic sources on the abortion issue are: Joan Nordquest, editor, *Reproductive Rights: A Bibliography* (Santa Cruz, CA: Reference and Research Services, 1988); and by Gary E. Skolnick, *Abortion: Index of Modern Information with Bibliography* (Washington, DC: ABBE Publishers Association, 1988).

Notes

1. Christopher Tietze and Stanley Henshaw, *Induced Abortion: A World Review 1986*, 6th edition (New York: The Alan Guttmacher Institute, 1986), 1.

The Abortion Debate in the
United States and Canada

Chapter One

Demographics, Sociological Research and Opinions

What is the number of legal abortions performed in the United States and Canada? What are the demographic characteristics of those women seeking abortion? What does current research reveal about the sociological aspects of abortion? What do the opinion polls say about attitudes toward abortion? This chapter presents information regarding abortion practice in the United States and Canada. Such objective data is valuable in order to make well-informed and accurate assessments about the controversial positions and polices on abortion.

1. ABORTION PRACTICE IN THE UNITED STATES AND CANADA[1]

This section contains data on the incidence and demographics of the practice of abortion in the United States and Canada.

Table 1 indicates the number of abortions, the rate per 1000 women and the ratio per 100 known pregnancies. The Centers for Disease Control (CDC) report 15 to 18 percent lower numbers of abortions than the number estimated by the Alan Guttmacher Institute (AGI). The difference is related to the way that the data is collected. The CDC obtains most of its information from state health departments whereas the AGI pursues its data with active outreach.[2]

The CDC reported the relatively low abortion rate of 4.5 in 1970, which was three years before the *Roe v. Wade* decision. From this time, the rate steadily increased. The effect of *Roe* was to leave the choice in continuing or terminating pregnancy in the early stages

3

to the woman. This change can account for the statistics from 1973 to 1974. The CDC reported the rate at 13.51 in 1973 and 16.41 in 1974; the AGI reported the rate of 16.3 in 1973 and 19.3 in 1974. From 1978, however, the rate does not appear to have increased significantly. The CDC rate was 22.7 in 1978 and 23.9 in 1982; the AGI rate was 27.7 in 1978 and 28.0 in 1985.

In Canada, in the period from 1970 to 1988, in accordance with amendments to the *Criminal Code* set out in the Omnibus Bill, 1969, induced abortions had to be carried out with the approval of a hospital's therapeutic abortion committee. The lowest rate was in 1970 at 2.5. However, the rate steadily increased. It levels off between 1978 at 11.3 and 1982 at 11.0. The statistics show a slight decline after 1983 at 10.2 and in 1987 at 10.2. In 1988, the Supreme Court declared that the abortion law violated the *Charter of Rights and Freedoms*. It was struck down. The effects of the Court decision on the abortion rate are not available at this date. The abortion rate in Canada is consistently lower than in the United States.

Table 2 specifies the associated deaths and mortality rate in relation to the number of legal abortions. The statistics show a steady decline. In 1970 in the United States, the mortality rate was 19.0, while in the period from 1980-85, it was 0.6. The most significant drop was during 1970 to 1974, when it fell from 19.0 to 2.9.

The same decline is found in the Canadian statistics. In the period from 1970-75, the mortality rate was 3.6. In the period from 1980-87, the rate was 0.2.

Table 3 notes the percentage distribution of legal abortions by weeks of gestation. The American statistics show an increase in early abortions since 1973. The CDC reported 36.1 percentage distribution at eight weeks or less in 1973, while in 1982, it was 50.6. The AGI estimated 38.2 percentage distribution in 1973 at eight weeks or less, while in 1985, it was 51.5. The CDC numbers in the 9-12 week period were higher in 1973 at 47.3 than in 1982 at 39.1. The AGI indicates the percentage distribution at 9 to 12 weeks at 47.3 in 1973, while in 1985, it was 39.6. It is the same situation with the percentage distribution of abortions at 17 weeks or more. There were more later abortions in 1973. The CDC indicates 9.7 at 17 weeks or more, while it was 5.0 in 1982. The AGI notes 6.5 at 17 weeks or more in 1973, while in 1985, the percentage distribution was 3.7 at 17 weeks or more.

In Canada, the highest percentage distribution of women who obtain legal abortions falls in the 9-12 week period of gestation. The legal requirements necessary to procure an abortion provide some explanation for this situation. Approval for the abortion had to be sought from a hospital's therapeutic abortion committee. This process could have caused a delay in obtaining an abortion. In 1974, the percentage distribution for the 9 to 12 week period was 58.0. In 1987, it declined slightly to 55.3. In 1974, the percentage distribution for 8 weeks or less was 20.8; for 13-16 weeks it was 14.6 and for 17 weeks or more it was 6.6. In 1987, the percentage distribution for women obtaining abortion in 8 or less weeks did increase to 33.2 over the 1973 figure; for 13-16 it was weeks was 8.0; and for 17 weeks or more it was 3.5.

Table 4 indicates the percentage distribution of abortion patients by type of facility in which the abortion procedure was carried out and the length of hospital stay. In the United States, there is a sharp increase in the number of abortions performed in the non-hospital setting. In 1973 the percentage distribution was 48.0 while in 1982 it was 82.0. Table 4 also shows that there was a decrease in the length of stay in hospitals during the period from 1973 to 1982.

In Canada, in the period from 1974 to 1983, the statistics indicate that legal abortions were not performed outside of the hospitals, except in Quebec. However, information on clinic abortions in Quebec is not provided. In 1985, the percentage distribution of abortions performed outside of a hospital was 14.5. In 1983, Dr. Henry Morgentaler opened an abortion clinic in Toronto. Later, clinics in other cities have been opened as well.

In Table 5, the percentage distribution of legal abortions, their rate and ratio, in view of women's age is shown. In terms of the abortion rate by women's age in both Canada and the United States, the highest rates were in the 18-19 age group. In the United States, in 1985, the abortion rate was 63.0 for this 18-19 age group; it was 52.3 for the 20-24 week age group. The abortion rate declined with each age group, so that the rate was 2.9 for women who were forty or over. Similarly, in 1987 in Canada, the abortion rate for women in the 18-19 age group was 21.0; in the 20-24 age group, it was 18.5. For women 40 or over, the abortion rate was 2.9.

Table 6 notes the percentage distribution of women who obtain legal abortions in view of their marital status. The statistics show that the majority of women who procure an abortion are not married. The AGI notes that women who have never married, who were previously married, including those who were separated, accounted for an 83.3 percentage distribution of the legal abortions in 1985 in the United States. Of the married women, 16.7 was the percentage distribution.

In Canada, the women obtaining legal abortions who never married made up 67.3 percentage distribution; previously married women, including separated women, made up 8.2 percentage distribution; and married women made up 24.5 percentage distribution, according to the AGI.

Table 7 specifies the percentage distribution of women who obtain legal abortions and the ratio per 100 known pregnancies. In the United States, parity refers to prior live births. From 1972 until 1985, the percentage distribution of women obtaining legal abortions follows a similar pattern as shown in the 1985 statistics. It was 54.9 when there were no prior live births. The percentage distribution subsequently declined with the numbers of prior live births: 22.0 when there was 1 prior live birth; 15.1 when there was 2 prior live births. At 5 or more percentage live births, the percentage distribution was 1.0.

In Canada, parity refers to prior deliveries. It appears that the highest percentage distribution of women obtaining legal abortions takes place when there are no prior deliveries. According to the AGI, in 1987 it was 58.4 percentage distribution when there had been no prior deliveries; 19.9 for one prior delivery; 4.9 for three prior deliveries; and 0.4 for 5 or more prior deliveries, as indicated by the AGI.

Table 8 indicates the number of repeat abortions. It indicates the percentage distribution of legal abortions by the number of prior induced abortions. In both the United States and Canada, the highest percentage distribution is with the first abortion and subsequently declined with the number of prior abortions, as indicated by the AGI. In 1985 in the United States, the percentage distribution was 59.5 when there were no prior abortions. It was 26.2 when there was one prior abortion; 9.4 when there was 2 prior abortions and when there was three or more prior abortions, it was 5.0.

In Canada in 1987, the percentage distribution when there were no prior abortions was 78.0. It was 17.4 when there was one prior abortion; 3.6 when there was 2 prior abortions; and when there were three or more prior abortions, the percentage distribution was 1.1.

INCIDENCE OF ABORTION

TABLE 1. Number of Abortions, Abortion Rate per 1,000 Women aged 15-44, Abortion Ratio per 100 Known Pregnancies* and Total Abortion Rate.**

United States	No.	Rate	Ratio	Total Rate
Reported to the CDC				
1970[3]	193,500	4.5	5.0	-
1971	485,800	11.11	2.5	-
1972	586,800	13.21	5.5	-
1973	615,800	13.51	6.5	-
1974	763,500	16.41	9.3	-
1975	854,900	18.0	21.5	-
1976	988,300	20.3	23.2	-
1977	1,079,400	21.7	24.7	-
1978	1,157,800	22.7	25.5	-
1979	1,251,900	24.1	26.1	-
1980	1,297,600	24.5	26.3	-
1981	1,300,800	24.2	26.2	-
1982[4]	1,304,000	23.9	26.2	-
Reported to the AGI				
1973[5]	744,600	16.3	19.3	-
1974	898,600	19.3	22.0	-
1975	1,034,200	21.7	24.9	-
1976	1,179,300	24.2	26.5	-
1977	1,316,700	26.5	28.6	-
1978	1,409,600	27.7	29.2	-
1979	1,497,700	28.8	29.6	-
1980	1,553,900	29.3	30.0	-
1981	1,577,300	29.3	30.1	-
1982	1,573,900	28.8	30.0	-
1983[6]	1,515,000	27.4	29.4	-
1985[7]	1,588,600	28.0	29.7	797

Canada[8]

	No.	Rate	Ratio	Total Rate
1970	11,200	2.5	2.9	-
1971	30,900	6.6	7.7	-
1972	38,900	8.2	10.1	-
1973	43,200	8.9	11.3	-
1974	48,100	9.6	12.0	-
1975	49,300	9.6	11.8	-
1975 All†[9]	59,000	11.4	13.7	-
1976	54,500	10.3	13.2	-
1977	57,600	10.6	13.8	-
1978	62,300	11.3	14.6	-
1979	65,000	11.6	15.0	-
1980	65,900	11.4	15.0	-
1981	65,100	11.1	14.9	-
1982	66,300	11.1	15.0	-
1982 All†[10]	77,500	13.0	13.7	-
1983	61,800	10.2	14.2	-
1984	62,300	10.2	(14.2)	-
1987[11]	63,600	10.2	14.7	299
1987 All†	74,800	12.1	16.6	u

----

*   Known pregnancies are defined as legal abortions plus live births. Births have not been lagged by six months because the necessary birth data are unavailable for most countries.

**   The number of abortions that would be experienced by 1,000 women during their reproductive lifetime, given age-specific abortion rates.

†   Including abortions obtained in Canadian clinics and in the United States.

CDC   Centers for Disease Control
AGI   Alan Guttmacher Institute

u   unavailable
(-)   not included in the 1986 AGI statistics.

TABLE 2. Number of Legal Abortions (in 000s), Number of Associated Deaths and Mortality Rate (95% confidence intervals) per 100,000 Legal Abortions.

	Abortions	Deaths	Mortality Rates	
United States				
1970[12]	193.5	36[13]	19.0	(13-25)
1971	485.8	54	11.0	(8.2-14)
1972	586.8	24[14]	4.1	(2.5-5.7)
1973	744.6	25	3.4	(2.0-4.7)
1974	898.6	26	2.9	(0.4-1.5)
1975	1,034.0	29	2.8	(1.8-3.8)
1976	1,179.3	11	0.9	(0.4-1.5)
1977	1,316.7	17	1.3	(0.7-1.9)
1978	1,409.6	9	0.6	(0.3-1.2)
1979[15]	1,497.7	18	1.2	(0.6-1.8)
1980-85[16]	5,445.9	54	0.6	(0.4-0.7)
Canada				
1970-75[17]	221.0	8[18]	3.6	(1.6-7.1)
1976-83	502.9	1	0.2	(0.0-1.1)
1980-1987[19]	511.0	1	0.2	(0.0-1.1)

Note: For sources not indicated, see Table 1.

TABLE 3. Percentage Distribution of Legal Abortions, by Weeks of Gestation.

	≤8	9-12	13-16	≥17	Total
United States[20]					
Reported to the CDC*					
1973	36.1	47.3	6.9	9.7	-
1974	42.6	44.1	5.5	7.8	-
1975	44.6	43.3	5.0	7.1	-
1976	36.1	47.3	6.9	9.7	-
1977	51.2	40.2	3.4	5.2	-
1978	52.2	39.2	4.0	4.6	-
1979	52.1	39.4	4.2	4.3	-
1980	51.7	38.3	5.2	4.8	-
1981	51.2	38.9	5.2	4.7	-
1982	50.6	39.1	5.3	5.0	-
Estimated by the AGI †**					
1973	38.2	47.3	8.0	6.5	-
1974	44.4	43.6	6.6	5.4	-
1975	46.5	42.7	6.0	4.8	-
1976	47.5	42.8	5.5	4.2	-
1977	50.0	41.1	5.2	3.7	-
1978	50.2	40.9	5.8	3.1	-
1979	50.0	41.1	6.0	2.9	-
1980	51.5	39.8	6.0	2.7	-
1981	51.4	39.8	6.1	2.7	-
1982	51.2	39.7	6.1	3.0	-
1985‡[21]	51.5	39.6	5.2	3.7	100.0
Age, 1981, Reported to the CDC**					
14 or less	33.1	44.5	11.8	10.8	-
15-19	40.8	44.6	9.4	5.2	-
20-24	49.8	40.6	6.5	3.1	-
25-29	55.6	36.6	5.4	2.5	-
30-34	58.4	34.9	4.6	2.1	-
35-39	59.2	33.7	5.1	2.0	-
40 or more	57.8	34.4	4.8	3.0	-

Canada‡

1974[22]	20.8	58.0	14.6	6.6	-
1975	22.4	58.9	13.3	5.4	-
1976	24.1	59.0	11.8	5.1	-
1977	23.8	60.4	11.0	4.8	-
1978	24.7	59.9	11.1	4.3	-
1979	24.6	61.3	10.3	3.8	-
1980	24.6	61.4	10.4	3.6	-
1981	25.5	61.1	9.9	3.5	-
1982	25.9	61.0	9.7	3.4	-
1983	27.7	60.2	8.8	3.3	-
1984	29.5	58.5	8.6	3.4	-
1987[23]	33.2	55.3	8.0	3.5	100.0

Age (Years), 1982

17 or less	16.6	61.9	15.7	5.8	-
18-19	20.1	62.3	13.1	4.5	-
20-24	24.8	61.9	9.9	3.4	-
25-29	29.5	60.9	7.1	2.4	-
30-34	33.4	59.1	5.9	1.6	-
35-39	34.9	56.2	6.3	2.6	-
40 or more	32.6	57.5	6.5	3.4	-

----

* Midtrimester abortions are reported as 13-15 weeks and 16 weeks or later.

** Abortions at 16 weeks (A_{16}) were estimated by the following formula and transferred from the last to the next-to-last gestation category:

$$A_{16} = 4A_{13-15} \times 3A_{16+1}{}^{1/2}/_{12}$$
$$A_{13-16} = A_{13-15} + A_{16}$$
$$A_{17} = A_{16+} - A_{16.}$$

† Estimates are based on the assumption that one-half of the difference between numbers of the abortions reported to the CDC and the AGI were performed in the non-hospital facilities. These abortions were distributed by weeks of gestation proportionally to all abortions at 12 weeks or earlier reported to the CDC. Estimates are also adjusted for changes from year to year in the number of states reporting to the CDC. Last two categories are 13-15 and ≥16 weeks. [24]

†† Last two categories are 13-15 and ≥16 weeks. [25]

‡ Completed weeks.   Note: For sources not indicated, see Table 1.

TABLE 4. Percentage Distribution of Abortion Patients, by Type of Facility in which Abortion was Performed and Length of Hospital Stay (in Nights).

	Non-Hospital	Hospital 0	1	2	3	4	≥5
United States							
1973[26]	48.0	------------52.0-----------------					
1974	53.0	------------47.0-----------------					
1975	60.0	------------40.0-----------------					
1976	65.0	------------35.0-----------------					
1977	70.0	------------30.0-----------------					
1978	75.0	------------25.0-----------------					
1979	77.0	------------23.0-----------------					
1980	78.0	12.0	--------10.0-----------------				
1981	81.0	11.0	-------- 8.0-----------------				
1982	82.0	12.0	-------- 6.0-----------------				

	Non-Hospital	All	0	1	2	3	4	Total
1985[27]	86.9	13.1	10.3	2.8*	u	u	u	100.0

	Non-Hospital	0	1	2	3	4	≥5
Canada							
1974**[28]	0.0	29.5	27.9	21.7	8.4	12.5	
1975	0.0	34.9	26.8	21.6	7.9	---8.8---	
1976	0.0	37.9	28.8	19.7	6.9	---6.7---	
1977	0.0	47.9	22.2	18.8	5.9	---5.2---	
1978	0.0	53.4	21.6	15.4	5.1	---4.5---	
1979	0.0	57.4	21.0	14.5	4.0	---3.1---	
1980	0.0	59.7	21.4	12.6	3.6	---2.6---	
1981	0.0	64.2	20.9	10.1	2.8	1.0	1.2
1982	0.0	67.8	19.4	8.7	2.4	0.8	0.9
1983	0.0	72.5	16.5	7.4	2.1	0.8	0.8

	Non-Hospital	All	0	1	2	3	≥4	Total
1985[29]	14.5	85.5	65.8	12.9	4.5	1.3	0.9	100.0

----

* Distribution is for ≥1 nights.
** Excludes clinic abortions performed in Quebec.
 u unavailable   Note:For sources not indicated, see Table 1.

TABLE 5. Percentage Distribution of Legal Abortions, Abortion Rate and Abortion Ratio, by Woman's Age.

	All	≥14	15-17	18-19	≤19	20-24	25-29	30-34	35-39	≥40

% Distribution

United States[30]

Reported to the CDC

	All	≥14	15-17	18-19	≤19	20-24	25-29	30-34	35-39	≥40
1972	32.6					32.5	17.1	9.8	5.7	2.3
1973	32.7					32.0	17.7	9.9	5.5	2.2
1974	32.7					31.7	18.1	10.0	5.4	2.1
1975	33.1					31.9	18.3	9.7	5.0	2.0
1976	32.1					33.3	18.7	9.3	4.8	1.8
1977	30.8					34.5	18.7	9.5	4.7	1.8
1978	30.0					35.0	18.9	9.7	4.8	1.6
1979	30.0					35.4	19.1	9.6	4.5	1.4
1980	29.2					35.5	19.6	9.9	4.4	1.4
1981	28.0					35.3	20.1	10.6	4.5	1.5
1982	27.1					35.1	20.8	10.7	4.8	1.5

Estimated by the AGI*

	All	≥14	15-17	18-19	≤19	20-24	25-29	30-34	35-39	≥40
1973	32.8					32.3	17.4	9.7	5.5	2.3
1974	32.5					31.9	18.1	10.0	5.4	2.1
1975	32.9					32.1	18.2	9.7	5.1	2.0
1976	32.1					33.3	18.7	9.3	4.8	1.8
1977	31.3					34.2	18.7	9.4	4.7	1.7
1978	30.8					34.7	18.9	9.5	4.6	1.5
1979	30.8					30.8	19.0	9.5	4.3	1.3
1980	29.6					35.4	19.6	9.8	4.3	1.3
1981	28.5					35.2	20.0	10.6	4.4	1.3
1982	27.5					35.0	20.7	10.7	4.7	1.4
1985[31]	26.2	1.1	10.4	14.7		34.5	21.2	11.4	5.4	1.3

----

* Adjusted for changes from year to year in the number of states reporting to the CDC.

	All	≥14	15-17	18-19	≤19 20-24	25-29	30-34	35-39	≥40
Canada									
1974[32]	31.5				29.3	18.5	10.7	6.7	3.3
1975	31.3				29.1	19.5	10.6	6.5	3.0
1976	30.7				29.6	19.8	10.9	6.1	2.9
1977	30.8				30.3	19.4	11.2	5.8	2.5
1978	30.4				31.0	19.2	11.3	5.7	2.4
1979	30.5				31.4	19.3	11.3	5.4	2.1
1980	29.7				31.8	19.6	11.6	5.3	2.0
1981	28.3				32.3	19.9	12.0	5.5	2.0
1982	26.8				32.8	20.4	12.2	5.9	1.9
1983	24.9				33.3	20.8	12.6	6.4	2.0
1984	23.6				33.5	21.4	12.7	6.9	2.0
1985[33]	22.3	0.6	9.3	12.3	31.7	22.4	13.9	7.4	2.2

Rate**

	All ≥14	15-17	18-19	≤19	20-24	25-29	30-34	35-39	≥40	Total
United States†										
1973[34]	23.9				26.2	16.9	10.9	7.1	2.9	437
1974	28.2				30.4	19.6	13.0	8.4	3.3	519
1975	32.5				34.3	21.8	14.0	8.9	3.6	576
1976	35.8				39.6	24.1	15.0	9.3	3.7	638
1977	39.0				44.3	26.9	15.7	9.8	3.9	698
1978	41.1				47.2	28.4	16.4	9.8	3.6	732
1979	43.9				49.9	29.6	16.5	9.4	3.4	764
1980	44.4				51.4	30.8	17.1	9.3	3.5	782
1981	44.8				51.1	31.4	17.7	9.5	3.4	790
1982	44.3				51.2	31.5	17.7	9.3	3.3	787
1985[35]	45.7	4.8	30.7	63.0	52.3	30.9	17.8	9.7	2.9	28.0
Canada										
1974[36]	13.6				14.1	9.7	7.1	5.2	2.3	260
1975	13.7				13.8	10.0	6.8	4.9	2.4	258
1976	14.6				15.1	10.9	7.4	5.0	2.5	278
1977	15.3				15.9	11.2	7.5	4.9	2.4	286
1978	16.3				17.2	11.9	7.8	5.0	2.4	303
1979	17.0				18.1	12.2	7.9	4.8	2.1	311
1980	16.9				18.2	12.1	7.9	4.6	2.1	308
1981	16.3				18.0	11.9	7.7	4.4	1.9	301
1982	16.2				18.5	12.0	7.9	4.5	1.9	305
1983	14.7				17.3	11.2	7.5	4.4	1.7	284
1984	14.7				17.6	11.5	7.5	4.5	1.7	288
1987[37]	15.2	1.2	10.6	21.0	18.5	12.0	7.8	4.6	1.6	10.2

** For women under age 15, rate is computed per 1,000 women aged 13-14; for those under 20, rate is computed per 1,000 15-19: for 40 or more, rate is computed per 1,000 40-44.

† Rates based on numbers of abortions reported to the AGI and age distributions reported to the CDC.
All ≥14 15-17 18-19 ≤19

Ratio††

	All	≥14	15-17	18-19	≤19	20-24	25-29	30-34	35-39	≥40
United States‡										
1973[38]	25.6				17.6	13.2	18.7	28.3	39.7	
1974	29.0				20.0	15.4	21.7	32.8	44.4	
1975	33.4				22.8	17.2	23.5	35.4	48.6	
1976	35.8				25.0	18.6	23.1	36.6	50.2	
1977	38.4				27.6	20.2	23.7	38.5	52.5	
1978	39.6				28.7	20.8	23.5	38.6	51.6	
1979	40.7				29.4	21.1	23.0	37.3	50.4	
1980	41.2				30.1	21.8	23.3	37.2	51.7	
1981	41.2				30.4	22.0	23.9	35.7	51.3	
1982	41.2				30.6	22.3	23.9	34.2	51.4	
1985[39]	42.1	45.7	43.2	41.0	31.5	22.0	21.8	32.2	49.4	29.7
Canada										
1975[40]	23.7				10.0	7.0	10.5	22.0	37.2	
1976	25.8				11.2	7.9	11.1	23.1	41.7	
1977	27.6				12.0	8.1	11.1	23.7	42.8	
1978	30.1				13.2	8.4	11.4	25.0	43.9	
1979	31.9				14.0	8.6	11.4	24.2	43.3	
1980	32.2				14.2	8.6	11.3	23.1	43.4	
1981	32.0				14.5	8.6	11.3	21.9	42.3	
1982	32.5				15.1	8.8	11.3	21.6	43.6	
1983	31.5				14.7	8.2	10.5	20.7	42.7	
1984	31.0				15.1	8.3	10.3	21.2	43.0	
1987[41]	33.4	42.7	38.2	29.7	16.8	8.8	10.3	19.9	39.8	14.7

----

†† Ratio of abortion per 100 known pregnancies (defined as legal abortions plus live births, both adjusted to age of woman at time of conception). For the United States, live births six months later were used to match times of conception for pregnancies ending in birth and pregnancies ending in abortion.

‡ Ratios based on numbers of abortions reported to the AGI and age distributions reported to the CDC.

CDC Centers for Disease Control

AGI Alan Guttmacher Institute

Note: For sources not indicated, see Table 1.

TABLE 6. Percentage Distribution of Women who Obtain Legal Abortions, by Marital Status

	Currently Married	Previously Married	Never Married	Total
United States[42]				
Reported to the CDC				
1972	29.7	--------70.3------		
1973	27.4	--------72.6------		
1974	29.7	--------70.3------		
1975	27.4	--------72.6------		
1976	24.6	--------75.4------		
1977	24.3	--------75.7------		
1978	26.4	--------73.6------		
1979	24.7	--------75.3------		
1980	23.1	--------76.9------		
1981	22.1	--------77.9------		
1982	22.6	--------77.4------		
Estimated by the AGI*				
1973	29.0	--------71.0------		
1974	27.6	--------27.6------		
1975	26.3	--------73.7------		
1976	24.6	--------75.4------		
1977	22.8	--------77.2------		
1978	23.5	--------76.5------		
1979	21.5	--------78.5------		
1980	20.6	--------20.6------		
1981	18.9	--------81.1------		
1982	19.1	--------80.9------		
1985[43]**†	16.7	83.3	u	100.0

----

  * Adjusted for changes from year to year in the number of states reporting to the CDC.
  ** Never married included with previously married.
  † Separated women are included with previously married.

	Currently Married	Previously Married	Never Married	Total
Canada† ††				
1974[44]	32.2	9.6	58.2	
1975	32.3	9.3	58.4	
1976	31.7	9.9	58.4	
1977	30.1	9.7	60.2	
1978	28.4	10.2	61.4	
1979	26.0	9.9	64.1	
1980	25.0	9.8	65.2	
1981	24.6	9.6	65.8	
1982	25.0	9.7	65.3	
1983	24.4	9.4	66.2	
1984	23.9	9.5	66.6	
1987[45]	24.5	8.2	67.3	100.0

----

† Separated women are included with previously married.
†† Women in informal unions are included with currently married.

CDC Centers For Disease Control
AGI Alan Guttmacher Institute
Note: For sources not indicated, see Table 1.

TABLE 7. Percentage Distribution of Women who Obtain Legal Abortions and Ratio per 100 Known Pregnancies, by Parity.

Measure Parity	0	1	2	3	4	≥5	Total

% Distribution

United States*[46]

Reported to the CDC

	0	1	2	3	4	≥5
1972	49.4	18.2	13.3	8.7	5.0	5.5
1973	48.6	18.8	14.2	8.7	4.8	4.9
1974	47.8	19.6	14.9	8.7	4.5	4.5
1975	47.1	20.2	15.5	8.7	4.3	4.2
1976	47.7	20.7	15.4	8.7	4.1	3.8
1977	53.4	19.1	14.3	7.0	3.3	2.9
1978	56.6	19.2	14.1	5.9	---4.2---	
1979	58.1	19.1	13.8	5.5	---3.5---	
1980	58.4	19.4	13.7	5.3	---3.2---	
1981	58.3	19.7	13.7	5.3	---3.0---	
1982	57.8	20.3	13.9	5.1	---2.9---	

Estimated by the AGI**

	0	1	2	3	4	≥5	Total
1973	55.2	15.4	13.9	8.1	3.9	3.5	
1974	53.7	17.3	14.5	8.7	3.6	3.1	
1975	52.4	18.8	15.1	7.5	3.3	2.9	
1976	53.4	19.4	14.9	6.9	2.9	2.5	
1977	56.4	18.9	14.2	6.1	2.5	1.9	
1978	56.6	19.2	14.1	5.9	---4.2---		
1979	58.0	19.2	13.8	5.5	---3.5---		
1980	57.9	19.6	13.9	5.3	---3.3---		
1981	57.8	19.8	13.9	5.4	---3.1---		
1982	57.3	20.4	14.1	5.2	---3.0---		
1985[47]	54.9	22.0	15.1	5.4	1.7	1.0	100.0

----

* Prior Live Births
** Adjusted for changes from year to year in the number of states reporting to the CDC.

Measure Parity

	0	1	2	3	4	≥5	Total
Canada†							
1974[48]	58.0	14.4	14.4	7.4	3.3	2.5	
1975	58.5	14.6	14.8	7.1	2.9	2.1	
1976	58.9	15.3	15.0	6.5	2.5	1.8	
1977	60.3	15.9	14.3	5.9	2.2	1.4	
1978	61.2	16.1	14.2	5.6	1.9	1.0	
1979	63.1	15.8	13.6	5.0	1.6	0.9	
1980	63.6	16.0	13.4	4.8	1.4	0.8	
1981	63.3	16.3	13.9	4.5	1.3	0.7	
1982	63.1	16.8	13.7	4.5	1.3	0.6	
1983	62.2	17.4	14.1	4.5	1.2	0.5	
1984	61.1	18.0	14.4	4.6	1.3	0.5	
1987[49]	58.4	19.9	15.2	4.9	1.2	0.4	100.0

----

† Prior Deliveries

Ratio

Measure Parity	0	1	2	3	4	≥5	Total
United States[50]††							
1973	24.0	10.6	19.1	23.5	23.6	18.4	
1974	26.4	13.3	22.5	27.4	27.2	21.4	
1975	29.1	16.3	25.7	29.7	29.6	24.9	
1976	31.3	17.8	26.7	30.1	29.7	25.7	
1977	34.8	19.0	27.4	29.7	29.8	24.6	
1978	35.5	19.8	27.8	29.9	30.1	25.2	
1979	36.2	20.1	27.8	28.9	28.1	23.2	
1980	36.6	20.8	28.4	28.8	27.4	22.4	
1981	36.8	20.8	28.4	29.0	27.1	22.0	
1982	36.6	21.1	28.4	28.1	26.1	20.9	
1985[51]	35.8	21.9	28.8	28.1	25.2	20.0	29.7
Canada[52]							
1975	15.9	5.7	13.0	17.8	20.3	14.5	
1976	16.8	6.3	14.0	18.6	20.7	16.2	
1977	17.7	6.9	14.2	18.7	21.2	15.1	
1978	19.0	7.4	14.7	19.1	20.9	13.8	
1979	20.0	7.5	14.5	18.0	19.6	14.1	
1980	19.9	7.6	14.4	17.4	18.6	13.3	
1981	19.6	7.7	14.8	16.0	16.7	11.6	
1982	19.8	8.0	14.7	16.7	16.5	10.0	
1983	18.6	7.6	14.1	15.5	14.8	9.5	
1984	18.6	7.8	14.3	15.8	15.6	9.2	
1987[53]†	18.9	8.7	15.1	16.5	14.6	8.1	14.7

----

† Prior Deliveries
†† Ratios are based on numbers of abortions reported to the CDC.

CDC Centers For Disease Control
AGI Alan Guttmacher Institute
Note: For sources not indicated, see Table 1.

TABLE 8. Percentage Distribution of Legal Abortions, by Number of Prior Induced Abortions

	Number of Prior Abortions				
	0	1	2	≥3	Total
United States[54]					
Reported to the CDC					
1974	86.8	11.3	1.5	0.4	
1975	81.9	14.9	2.5	0.7	
1976	79.9	16.6	2.6	0.9	
1977	76.8	18.3	3.4	1.5	
1978	70.8	22.1	5.3	1.8	
1979	69.0	23.0	5.9	2.1	
1980	67.6	23.5	6.6	2.3	
1981	65.3	24.3	7.5	2.9	
1982	63.7	24.9	8.2	3.2	
Estimated by the AGI*					
1974	84.8	12.5	1.9	0.8	
1975	79.5	16.5	2.9	1.1	
1976	77.3	18.1	3.4	1.2	
1977	73.9	20.6	4.1	1.4	
1978	70.7	22.5	5.0	1.8	
1979	68.4	23.5	5.8	2.3	
1980	67.1	24.0	6.3	2.6	
1981	64.9	24.7	7.1	3.3	
1982	63.2	25.3	7.8	3.7	
1985[55]	59.5	26.2	9.4	5.0	100.0
Age, 1981[56]					
≤19	80.5	16.5	2.5	0.5	
20-24	60.0	27.9	8.7	3.4	
25-29	51.9	29.7	12.1	6.3	
30-34	53.4	27.1	11.8	7.6	
35-39	56.6	25.7	10.8	6.8	
≥40	62.1	21.7	9.4	6.7	

----

*   Adjusted for changes from year to year in the number of states reporting to the CDC.

	Number of Prior Abortions				
	0	1	2	≥3	Total

Canada

	0	1	2	≥3	Total
1974[57]	92.1	7.0	0.7	0.2	
1975	91.2	7.8	0.8	0.2	
1976	89.7	9.1	1.0	0.2	
1977	88.4	10.1	1.2	0.3	
1978	86.7	11.3	1.6	0.4	
1979	85.7	12.2	1.7	0.4	
1980	84.4	13.1	2.0	0.5	
1981	83.3	14.0	2.2	0.5	
1982	82.0	14.9	2.5	0.6	
1983	80.6	15.8	2.8	0.8	
1984	79.9	16.1	3.0	0.9	
1987[58]	78.0	17.4	3.6	1.1	100.0

Age, 1982

	0	1	2	≥3
≤19	92.0	7.5	0.5	0.0
20-24	81.0	16.5	2.2	0.3
25-29	75.6	19.6	3.8	1.0
30-34	74.7	19.2	4.4	1.6
≥35	79.6	14.5	4.2	1.6

CDC Centers For Disease Control
AGI Alan Guttmacher Institute

Note:For sources not indicated, see Table 1.

2. CURRENT SOCIOLOGICAL RESEARCH

The sociological aspects of abortion have been subject to a wide range of studies. This research includes such topics as: those who have abortions; the determinants of pro-life and pro-choice attitudes; the attitudes of congenitally impaired children; feminist abortion collectives; the bombing of abortion clinics, to name a few. The selection of recent abstracts from *Sociological Abstracts* represents this variety of research.

Badagliacco, Joanne Marie (Columbia University, New York NY 10027), "Who Has Abortions: Determinants of Abortion Choice among American Women," *Dissertation Abstracts International, A: The Humanities and Social Sciences*, 1988, 49, 3, Sept, 630-A. Available from UMI, Ann Arbor, MI, Order No. DA8809323.

This item is reprinted with the permission of Sociological Abstracts, Inc. and may not be reproduced without its prior permission.

Badagliacco, Joanne Marie (Columbia University, New York NY 10027), "Does Motherhood Matter in Abortion Choice among American Women?", Conference Abstract Supplement, *Sociological Abstracts*, December 1989.

Although abortion is one of the most prevalent means of fertility control worldwide, there is no comprehensive theory to explain why some women choose abortion while others do not. Addressing the issue of who has abortions and what variables affect that decision among United States women, two comparison groups are analyzed-- those who were childless and those who were mothers at the time of the pregnancy in question-using data from the National Survey of Family Growth, Cycle II (1976) and multivariate statistical techniques. The literature concerning fertility decision making and abortion decisions is critically reviewed, and a status set hypothesis is presented as an explanation for abortion decision differences. Among the survey Rs, some variables found to directly affect abortion choice include whether the woman was childless at the time of her pregnancy (motherhood), if she was attending school, whether abortion was legal at that time, race/ethnicity, the availability of abortion facilities, and religiosity. (Copyright 1989, Sociological Abstracts, Inc., all rights reserved.)

This item is reprinted with the permission of Sociological Abstracts, Inc., and may not be reproduced without its prior permission.

Bart, Pauline B. (University of Illinois, Chicago 60680), "Seizing the Means of Reproduction: An Illegal Feminist Abortion Collective--How and Why It Worked," *Qualitative Sociology*, 1987, 10, 4, Winter, 339-357.

An illegal feminist abortion collective in Chicago, Ill, called The Service, is described, through whose efforts 11,000 abortions were performed between 1969 and 1973, when abortion was legalized. An analysis of interview data from 32 members of this lay group indicates how and why the collective was so effective in providing what is usually an MD-controlled medical procedure. After describing the structure of the organization and the process by which women obtained the abortion, including preabortion counseling and postabortion follow-up, two sets of reasons for the collective's effectiveness are presented: the first five reasons deal with the organization's social and historical context, illegality, charismatic leaders, member satisfaction, and financial self-sufficiency; the next nine deal with factors that made The Service a relatively typical democratic collective organization. The most important factor was its lack of concern for organizational survival per se. 19 References. Modified Homotopic Abstract.

This item is reprinted with the permission of Sociological Abstracts, Inc. and may not be reproduced without its prior permission.

Breslau, Naomi (Department of Psychiatry Case Western Reserve University, Cleveland OH 44106), "Abortion of Defective Fetuses: Attitudes of Mothers of Congenitally Impaired Children," *Journal of Marriage and the Family*, 1987, 49, 4, Nov, 839-845.

A sample of mothers of children with cystic fibrosis, cerebral palsy, myelodysplasia, and multiple physical handicaps (N=310) was compared to a probability sample of mothers of children free of disabilities (N=357) on their attitudes toward the availability of legal abortion. In interviews, mothers were asked whether or not they approve of abortion for six reasons, among them the strong probability of a defective fetus. The responses of mothers of congenitally disabled children were indistinguishable from those of controls. The specific characteristics of her child's disability (e.g., mental retardation) were unrelated to the mother's attitude toward abortion for any of the reasons examined. Whether mothers in either group approved of abortion of defective fetuses was found to be closely related to their attitudes toward abortion for the five other reasons. 8 Tables, 16 References. Homotopic Abstract.

Brody, Charles J. & Plunkett, Mark (Department of Sociology Tulane University, New Orleans LA 70118), "Trends in Abortion Attitudes: Evidence from Response Consistency Effects. Conference Abstracts Supplement," *Sociological Abstracts*, December, 1989.

Examination of responses to six General Social Survey questions on abortion indicates a slight overall decline in public support for legal abortion under all circumstances between 1973 and 1987. Analysis of the multivariate response structure of these items using the latent class model proposed by Duncan reveals an increasing tendency toward ideological responding on the part of supporters of legalized abortion. These findings suggest a view of the controversy in which a proabortion ideology crystallizes in response to an apparently small (but vocal) ideological antiabortion contingent. (Copyright 1989, Sociological Abstracts, Inc., all rights reserved.)

Costa, Frances, Jessor, Richard and Donovan, John E. (Institute of Behavioral Science University of Colorado, Boulder 80309), "Psychosocial Correlates and Antecedents of Abortion: An Exploratory Study," *Population and Environment*, 1987, 9, 1, Spring, 3-22.

Longitudinal questionnaire data collected in the United States between 1969 and 1984 are used to examine the relation between young adult women's abortion experience and a variety of antecedent and subsequent personality, perceived environment, and behaviour variables. About 25% of the women in 2 separate samples (N=215 high school and 99 college females) reported that they had had an abortion. Bivariate analyses show that young adult women who have had an abortion are characterized by greater psychosocial unconventionality. Similar differences along an underlying dimension of conventionality-unconventionality distinguish--antecedent to the abortion experience--women who would later have an abortion from those who would not. The findings are consistent with the expectations of problem-behaviour theory (Jessor, R., and Jessor, S.L., *Problem Behavior and Psychosocial Development: A Longitudinal Study of Youth* (New York, NY: Academic Press, 1977). 2 Tables, 14 References. Modified Homotopic Abstract. (Copyright 1988, Sociological Abstracts, Inc., all rights reserved).

Frankel, Susan L. (U New Hampshire, Durham 03824), "Abortion Policy Implementation: Understanding the Availability of Abortion Services in the United States," *Dissertation Abstracts International, A: The Humanities and Social Sciences*, 1989, 50, 3, Sept. 795-A. Available from UMI, Ann Arbor, MI. Order No. DA8907439.

Gillespie, Michael W., Ten Vergert, Elisabeth M. and Klingma, Johannes (Department of Psychology University of Alberta, Edmonton T6G 2E1), "Secular Trends in Abortion Attitudes: 1975-1980-1985," *The Journal of Psychology*, 1988, 122, 4, July, 323-341.

The attitudes toward abortion of respondents to the National Opinion Research Center's General Social Survey (GSS) for the years 1975, 1980, and 1985 (Σ N = 3,940) are compared. R. J. Mokken's and C. Lewis's method of scale analysis, a stochastic extension of Guttman scaling ("A Nonparametric Approach to the Analysis of Dichotomous Item Responses," *Applied Psychological Measurement*, 1982, 417-430), is used to examine whether the 6 abortion items used in the surveys measure 1 or 2 dimensions. It is concluded that the 6 items are unidimensional and, therefore, create a single scale to measure the changes in abortion attitudes across the three periods. Analysis reveal no change from 1975-1980, but a significant, though small, drop in approval from 1980-1985. 1 Table, 2 Appendixes, 44 References. Modified Homotopic Abstract. (Copyright 1989, Sociological Abstracts, Inc., all rights reserved.)

Gillespie, Michael, Ten Vergert, Elisabeth M. and Klingma, Johannes (Department of Sociology University of Alberta, Edmonton T6G 2E9), "Using Mokken Methods to Develop Robust Cross-National Scales: American and West German Attitudes toward Abortion," *Social Indicators Research*, 1988, 20, 2, Apr, 181-203.

R. J. Mokken's method (*A Theory and Procedure of Scale Analysis*, The Hague, The Netherlands: Mouton, 1971) and test (with Lewis, C., "A Nonparametric Approach to the Analysis of Dichotomous Item Responses," *Applied Psychological Measurement*, 1982, 6,

417-430) are presented as tools for cross-national research on attitudes. The procedure is applied in an analysis of responses to 7 abortion items in national surveys of Americans and West Germans (Σ N = 4, 497). These items form a unidimensional scale in both countries with 4 items constituting a scale that is robust across the 2 populations. Implications for the development of Rasch and LISREL models are discussed. 4 Tables, 1 Figure, 2 Appendixes, 32 References. Modified Homotopic Abstract. (Copyright 1989, Sociological Abstracts, Inc., all rights reserved.)

Holmes, Dorothy Gallon (North Carolina State University, Raleigh 27650), "A Path Analytic Model of Attitudes toward Discretionary and Medical/Rape Abortions," *Dissertation Abstracts International, A: The Humanities and Social Sciences*, 1988, 49, 6, Dec, 1587-A-1588-A. Available from UMI, Ann Arbor, MI. Order No. DA8815507.

Jelen, Ted G. (Illinois Benedictine College, Lisle 60532), "Changes in the Attitudinal Correlations of Opposition to Abortion, 1977-1985," *Journal for the Scientific Study of Religion*, 1988, 27, 2, June, 211-228.

The relative importance of respect for human life and sexual conservatism as rationales for opposition to abortion is examined for 3 religious groups using data from the NORC General Social Surveys for 1977, 1982, and 1985. In general, Catholics, and nonfundamentalist and fundamentalist Protestants tend to oppose abortion because of respect for human life, for the entire period. However, in 1977, Catholics who opposed elective abortion tended to do so out of respect for life, while Protestants who opposed it tended to endorse a sexually conservative rationale. By 1985, all groups, except fundamentalists, opposed elective abortion due to considerations of sexual morality; for fundamentalists, considerations of life and sexual conservatism were of equal importance. 6 Tables, 2 Appendixes, 33 References. Modified Homotopic Abstract. (Copyright 1988, Sociological Abstracts, Inc., all rights reserved.)

Johnson, Stephen D. and Tamney, Joseph B. (Ball State University, Muncie IN 47306), "Factors Related to Inconsistent Life-Views," *Review of Religious Research*, 1988, 30, 1, Sept, 40-46.

It is argued that some segments of the antiabortion population of the United States hold inconsistent life-views; specifically, some people who are against abortion support capital punishment, though both involve taking a life. Data from antiabortion subsamples from the 1983 and 1984 nationwide NORC surveys reveal that 218 of these respondents supported capital punishment, while 108 opposed it. Explanations of the results are proposed. 1 Table, 20 References. Modified Homotopic Abstract. (Copyright 1989, Sociological Abstracts, Inc., all rights reserved.)

Kelly, James R. (Fordham University, Bronx NY 10458), "Residual or Prophetic? The Cultural Fate of Roman Catholic Sexual Ethics of Abortion and Contraception," *Social Thought*, 1986, 12, 2, Spring, 3-18.

A review of findings on the contraception and abortion attitudes and practices of Catholics and others, with focus on Catholic sexual ethics. The data show widespread dissent among Catholics from official teaching, although Catholic practice and opinion remain distinguishable from mainstream United States opinion and practice. There are several reasons for anticipating that these differences will persist: disagreement with Church doctrine has not resulted in widespread disaffiliation; natural family planning methods are officially promoted and have received some medical and feminist endorsement; and Catholic social thought now links issues of sexuality and social justice, making it less plausible to characterize Catholic sexual ethics as morally repressive and arbitrary. 42 References. Author Abstract.

Kolker, Aliza, Burke, B. Meredith & Phillips, Jane Q. (Department of Sociology & Anthropology, George Mason University, Fairfax VA 22030 [Tel: 703-323-2900]), "Attitudes toward Abortion of Women Who Undergo Prenatal Diagnosis." Conference Abstracts Supplement, *Sociological Abstracts*, December, 1989. Complete paper available from Sociological Abstracts Document Delivery Service prepaid.

Attitudes about abortion of women who had undergone ammocentesis or chorionic villus sampling (CVS) in Washington, DC, and San Francisco, Calif, are examined via a survey (N=120) and in-depth interviews (N=23 patients and 10 genetic counselors) using an abortion attitudes scale adapted from the General Social Survey (GSS). CVS users were found to have higher education and income than amniocentesis users, but there were no significant differences in abortion attitudes between the two groups. Both groups were found to be far more liberal on abortion rights than the general population, as indicated by the GSS. Most GSSRs believe abortion should be permitted only if the pregnancy resulted from rape or threatens the mother's life, while Rs to this study support abortion on demand. Despite their strong commitment to freedom of choice, however, they find abortion for sex selection unacceptable, value highly the present (or recent) pregnancy, and are disturbed by the possibility of having to terminate it in case an abnormality is diagnosed. In short, the meaning of abortion is socially constructed on the basis not only of ideological worldview but of personal experience with pregnancy and motherhood. (Copyright 1989, Sociological Abstracts, Inc., all rights reserved.)

Marmon, Sharon and Palley, Howard A. (Department of Political Science University of Delaware, Newark 19716), "The Decade after *Roe versus Wade*; Ideology, Political Cleavage, and the Policy Process," *Research in Politics and Society*, 1986, 2, 181-209.

After briefly outlining the history of abortion policy in the United States, two major 1973 United States Supreme Court rulings on this issue--*Roe v. Wade* and *Doe v. Bolton*--are reviewed, along with other significant federal court actions and public policy/opinion changes that have occurred in their aftermath. Results of several nationwide Public Opinion polls conducted between 1965 and 1982 indicate general support for women's right to abortion, though with many qualifications; demographic factors related to abortion attitudes are identified, and an ideological drift in attitudes between major religious groups is noted. The characteristics and organizational strategies of abortion issue activists--the prochoice and prolife groups --are compared, and the politics of abortion rights is demonstrated via a review of recent legislative and bureaucratic activities. 5 Tables, 64 References. K. Hyatt. (Copyright 1989, Sociological Abstracts, Inc., all rights reserved.)

McCutcheon, Allan L. (University of Delaware, Newark 19711), "Sexual Morality, Pro-Life Values, and Attitudes toward Abortion: A Simultaneous Latent Structure Analysis for 1978-1983," *Sociological Methods and Research*, 1987, 16, 2, Nov, 256-275.

A simultaneous latent class analysis of data from the 1978 and 1983 General Social Surveys (N=2,910 respondents) is used to clarify the current controversy over whether opposition to abortion reflects a conservative sexual morality or prolife values. Results indicate that the prolife and prochoice dichotomy represents an incomplete characterization of the United States public--a third group, characterized by a conservative sexual morality and opposition to discretionary abortion, but not to nondiscretionary abortion, must also be included in the classification. The evidence indicates that from 1978 to 1983, this sexually conservative group decreased from 33% to 25% of the United States adult population, the prochoice increased to approximately 50%, and the prolife class remained stable at approximately 25%. 3 Tables, 26 References. Modified Homotopic Abstract.

McDonough, Josefina Figueira (School Social Work Michigan State University, East Lansing 48824), "Abortion: In Search of Pluralistic Criteria of Social Justice." Conference Abstracts Supplement. *Sociological Abstracts*, August, 1988.

For those concerned with issues of social justice and the distribution of rights, the abortion debate should be evaluated from a conflict of rights perspective: mothers' vs fetuses' rights, and women's vs men's rights. After examining the premises on which the definition of each of these conflicts is based, data from a national survey are used to explore the merits of the conflict of rights formulation. Evidence of lack of support for fetus personhood renders the mother-fetus conflict invalid. Findings concerning gender conflict suggest that group self-interest might be associated with position in the abortion debate; however, religiosity and education emerge as the major predictors of opinion on abortion.

Medoff, Marshall H. (Dept Economics California State U, Long Beach 90840), "Constituencies, Ideology, and the Demand for Abortion Legislation," *Public Choice*, 1989, 60, 2, Feb, 185-191.

Using results of the United States Senate vote on the 1983 proposed Hatch/Eagleton Amendment, which would have reversed the Supreme Court's decision to legalize abortion, 1980 census data, church membership statistics, and data on state ratification of the Equal Rights Amendment, a model was developed to identify the various constituencies that may be significant in determining whether a state would continue to allow legal abortions. Results indicate that women in white-collar occupations and non-whites support legal abortions, while evangelical Christians do not. There also exists a direct relationship between the liberal ideology of a state and its political support of legal abortions. It is concluded that, if the determination of legal status of abortions were to revert to the states, 19 states would almost certainly continue to allow abortions, and probably 5 other states as well. However, 18 states would almost certainly abolish legal abortions and 8 other states are unlikely to continue to allow legal abortions. 1 Table, 16 References, Modified AA (Copyright 1990, Sociological Abstracts, Inc., all rights reserved.)

Nice, David C. (University of Georgia, Athens 30602), "Abortion Clinic Bombings as Political Violence," *American Journal of Political Science*, 1988, 32, 1, Feb, 178-195.

A state-level analysis of abortion clinic bombings as a form of political protest, with primary emphasis on the difference between the 42 states that had no bombings and the 8 that did. Analysis of published statistical data from varied sources reveals that abortion clinic bombings occur in states that have weaker social controls, higher abortion rates, and greater acceptance of violence toward women. Hypotheses attributing political violence to economic conditions are not supported by the data. 8 Tables, 62 References. Modified Homotopic Abstract. (Copyright 1988, Sociological Abstracts, Inc., 1988, all rights reserved.)

This item is reprinted with the permission of Sociological Abstracts, Inc. and may not be reproduced without its prior permission.

Plutzer, Eric (Washington U, Saint Louis MO 63130), "Attitudes Toward Abortion: A Study of the Social and Ideological Bases of Public Opinion," *Dissertation Abstracts International, A: The Humanities and Social Sciences*, 1987, 47, 12(1), June, 4514-A.

This item is reprinted with permission of Sociological Abstracts, Inc. and may not be reproduced without its prior permission.

Sadler, Martha L., "The Social Determinants of Attitudes toward Abortion," *Sociological Viewpoints*, 1985, 1, 1, 23-40.

The impact of various attitudinal and demographic variables on approval of abortion in 7 different circumstances is explored via a secondary analysis of interview data obtained from 1,598 United States adults as part of the 1983 National Opinion Research Center survey. Results indicate that educational level, religion, and church attendance have a significant influence on abortion attitudes, while age and gender are of relatively little importance. 8 Tables, 18 References. Modified HA (copyright 1989, Sociological Abstracts, Inc., all rights reserved.)

Scott, Jacqueline and Schuman, Howard (Survey Research Center University Michigan, Ann Arbor 48106), "Attitude Strength and Social Action in the Abortion Dispute," *American Sociological Review*, 1988, 53, 5, Oct, 785-793.

Several predictions about who feels most strongly concerning the legalization of abortion are tested using national survey data. It is predicted that if those who hold a mixed stance about abortion are excluded, the remaining consistent supporters and opponents of abortion should show equal strength of feelings with regard to their respective positions. Findings do not support this prediction: opponents of abortion are far more likely than proponents to regard the abortion issue as important. This finding holds true when religious affiliation is controlled. It is confirmed that blacks are less likely than whites to show strong feelings on the abortion issue, that among pro-choice supporters, women will give greater importance to the issue than men. 3 Tables, 30 References. Modified Homotopic Abstract. (Copyright 1989, Sociological Abstracts, Inc., all rights reserved.)

This item is reprinted with permission of Sociological Abstracts, Inc. and may not be reproduced without its prior permission.

Staggenborg, Suzanne (Indiana University, Bloomington 47405), "Life-Style Preferences and Social Movement Recruitment: Illustrations from the Abortion Conflict," *Social Science Quarterly*, 1987, 68, 4, Dec, 779-797.

Interview data obtained from 9 pro- and 14 antiabortion activists in a major city are used to examine the organizational bases that intervene between macrolevel changes and individual motivations to defend lifestyles. It appears that lifestyle movements are likely to mobilize when common lifestyle preferences lead to the participation of structurally available persons in institutions and organizations and when movement organizations use recruitment strategies that take advantage of these interaction sites. 48 References. Modified

Homotopic Abstract. (Copyright 1988, Sociological Abstracts, Inc., all rights reserved.)

Staggenborg, Suzanne (Dept Sociology Indiana University, Bloomington 47405), "The Consequences of Professionalization and Formalization in the Pro-Choice Movement," *American Sociological Review*, 1988, 53, 4, Aug, 585-605.

Resource mobilization theorists have argued that professionalized social movements emerge as more sources of funding become available for activists who make careers out of being movement leaders. Organizational case histories from the prochoice (abortion rights) movement, based on documentary and interview (N=50) data collected in 6 national and 7 state or local organizations, are analyzed to explore the consequences of professional leadership and formal structure in social movements. Five general propositions are drawn from the analysis: (1) nonprofessional movement activists do not initiate movements and create new tactics--the roles of movement "professional" and movement "entrepreneur" are distinct; (2) professional movement leaders tend to formalize the organizations they lead; (3) formalized social movement organizations (SMOs) help maintain social movements when environmental conditions make mobilization difficult; (4) professional leaders and formalized SMOs stimulate the use of institutionalized tactics; and (5) professionalization and formalization facilitate coalition work. 6 Tables, 41 References. Modified Homotopic Abstract. (Copyright 1989, Sociological Abstracts, Inc., all rights reserved.)

Staggenborg, Suzanne (Dept of Sociology Indiana U, Bloomington 47405), "Organizational and Environmental Influences on the Development of the Pro-Choice Movement," *Social Forces*, 1989, 68, 1, Sept, 204-240.

A revised version of SA 35:3/87S19810/ASA/1987/4527. (Copyright 1990, Sociological Abstracts, Inc., all rights reserved.)

Szafran, Robert F. and Clagett, Arthur F. (Stephen F. Austin State University, Nacogdoches TX 75962), "Variable Predictors of Attitudes toward the Legalization of Abortion," *Social Indicators Research*, 1988, 20, 3, June, 271-290.

Research on abortion attitudes reported by Judith Blake and Jorge H. del Pinal ("Predicting Polar Attitudes toward Abortion in the United States" in Burtchael, James T. (Ed), *Abortion Parley*, Kansas City: Andrews and McMeel, 1980, 28-56) is updated and expanded. After 1978, the last year examined, the United States public's approval of the legalization of abortion initially increased, but then dropped to the lowest level ever recorded by the General Social Survey. Religion, as coded by Blake and del Pinal, and education continue to be strong predictors of abortion attitudes, as are beliefs about premarital sex, divorce, and euthanasia. A major finding is that the same factors that predict abortion attitudes among persons having polar positions on the subject also predict abortion attitudes among the general population. 3 Tables, 2 Figures, 3 References. Modified Homotopic Abstract. (Copyright 1989, Sociological Abstracts Inc., all rights reserved.)

This item is reprinted with permission of Sociological Abstracts, Inc. and may not be reproduced without its prior permission.

Wilcox, Clyde (Dept Government Georgetown U, Washington DC 20057), "Political Action Committees and Abortion: A Longitudinal Analysis," *Women and Politics*, 1989, 9, 1, 1-19.

The formation and behavior of prolife and prochoice organizations are addressed, and the resources and strategies of political action committees (PACs) on both sides of the abortion issue are compared, using longitudinal data from the Federal Election Commission for 1977-1984. Results show that prolife PACs outnumber their prochoice counterparts by a wide margin and raise considerably more money as well. Prochoice groups are more partisan, giving heavily to Democrats, and also give higher proportions of their contributions to incumbents. Many prolife groups have engaged in independent expenditures, a practice not common in prochoice PACs. 4 Tables, 20 References. Modified HA (copyright 1990, Sociological Abstracts, Inc., all rights reserved.)

Wilson, Michele and Lynxwiler, John (Dept Sociology U Alabama, Birmingham 35294), "Abortion Clinic Violence as Terrorism," Terrorism, 1988, 11, 4, 263-273.

Violence against abortion clinics and other activities directed toward patients and staff of abortion facilities have been termed terrorism by the prochoice movement. However, the Federal Bureau of Investigation (FBI) denies that these actions are terrorism. Instances of abortion clinic violence for 1982-1987 were examined, based on indices of media coverage, seeking to determine whether there is a correspondence between these incidents and definitions or models of terrorism. The findings suggest that these incidents do fit the classification of "limited political" or "sub-revolutionary" terrorism. Reasons why the FBI has not considered them so are entertained. One is that current international tensions have resulted in a preoccupation with only certain types of events that for administrative, i.e., jurisdictional, reasons have come to essentialize terrorism. Another explanation, posited by prochoice activists, is that the FBI's decision is a consequence of political influence, the current administration being openly antichoice. 2 Tables, 41 References. Modified HA (Copyright 1989, Sociological Abstracts, Inc., all rights reserved.)

Wreen, Michael (Department of Philosophy, Marquette University, Milwaukee WI 53233), "Abortion: The Extreme Liberal Position," *The Journal of Medicine and Philosophy*, 1987, 12, 3, Aug, 241-265.

The extreme liberal view of abortion argues that neither the fetus, at any state of development, nor the young infant has a right to life. The general argumentative strategy employed by a number of philosophers in arriving at this view is critiqued as a step toward clarifying and expanding on the abortion debate. 22 References. Modified Homotopic Abstract.

This item is reprinted with the permission of Sociological Abstracts, Inc. and may not be reproduced without its prior permission.

3. OPINION POLLS ON ABORTION[59]

American Opinions[60]

The sharpest shift recorded by the Gallup Poll since it began measuring opinions about 15 years ago took place in the percentage of Americans who say abortion should be "legal under any circumstances." The increase is from 24% in 1988 to 31% in April 1990. For those who hold the position that abortion should be "illegal under all circumstances," opinion has declined from 17% in 1988 to 12%. This drop is the lowest point to date. There is a 19-point margin of pro-choice over pro-life attitudes in the April 1990 poll.

Do you think abortions should be legal under any circumstances, legal only under certain circumstances, or illegal in all circumstances?

	Legal under any circumstances	Legal under certain circumstances	Illegal in all circumstances
1990*	31%	53%	12%
1988	24	57	17
1983	23	58	16
1981	23	52	21
1980	25	53	18
1979	22	54	19
1977	22	55	19
1975	21	54	22

Note:"No opinion" omitted.

*The 1990 findings are based on two askings of this question, April 5-8 and 19-22, 1990.

Since the 1989 Supreme Court decision of *Webster v. Reproductive Health Services* which allowed state legislatures a greater measure of control over abortion laws, Idaho and New Hampshire have passed legislation. Because each was subsequently vetoed by the respective state governors, neither will become law. The proposed laws serve as a measure of the potential support that similar bills may generate in other states in the next few years. The following questions were asked by the Gallup Poll News Service, April 5-8, 1990.

As you may know, the state of New Hampshire recently considered a new law which would legalize abortion any time until fetal viability, and after that if the woman's physician determines if it is necessary for the woman's health or life, or if the fetus has a life-threatening abnormality. Would you favor or oppose the state where you live passing this law?

Favor state passing law	53%
Oppose state passing law	36%
No opinion	11%
	100%

As you may know, the state of Idaho recently considered a new law which would make it illegal for any woman to have an abortion except in four cases: 1 - rape reported to the police within seven days of the rape, 2 - incest where the woman is under 18, 3 - where the fetus is deformed, and 4 - where there is a physical threat to the health of the mother. Would you favor or oppose the state where you live passing this law?

```
Favor state passing law  . . . . . . . . . . . . . . . .  42%
Oppose state passing law  . . . . . . . . . . . . . . .  52%
No opinion  . . . . . . . . . . . . . . . . . . . . . .   6%
                                                        100%
```

Canadian Opinions

In Canada, opinions on abortion have remained relatively stable between 1988 and 1990. Noteworthy differences are evident in terms of the geographic location and level of education of the respondent. Opinions regarding specific cases when abortion should be legal were also polled.[61]

The question asked was:

Do you think abortions should be legal under any circumstances, legal only under certain circumstances, or illegal in all circumstances?[62]

Attitudes Concerning Abortion

	Legal under any circumstances	Legal under certain circumstances	Illegal in all circumstances	No opinion
National				
- Dec/89	27%	59%	12%	3%
- Aug/89	26	63	10	2
- Feb/89	27	59	13	2
- Sept/88	20	65	13	2
- June/88	25	59	15	2
- Feb/88	28	55	13	4
- 1983	23	59	17	1
- 1978	16	69	14	1
- 1975	23	60	16	1

Region:

Atlantic	12	74	7	7
Quebec	26	60	10	4
Ontario	32	51	15	2
Prairies	17	69	12	2
B.C.	37	51	9	2
Toronto	46	41	11	3
Montreal	37	49	9	5

Education:

Public	15	63	17	4
High School	24	59	14	3
Comm. Coll.	30	59	7	5
University	35	55	9	2

Religion:

Protestant	29	58	10	3
Catholic	19	63	14	3

Sex:

Male	28	58	10	4
Female	25	60	13	3

The question asked was:

In which of these specific cases would you think an abortion should be legal?

- If there is a strong chance of a serious defect in the baby
- If the woman's health is endangered by the pregnancy
- If agreed upon by a woman and her physician
- If the family has a very low income and cannot afford any more children
- If it is within 5 months of conception
- If it is within 3 months of conception
- If conception is due to rape or incest

Acceptable Circumstances for Abortions

	Jan 1990	Aug 1989	Feb 1989	Sept 1988
If woman's health endangered by pregnancy	82%	84%	80%	78%
If conception due to rape or incest	73	78	73	69
If strong chance of serious defect in baby	69	75	67	64
If agreed upon by woman and doctor	50	55	47	41
If within 3 months of conception	45	49	41	36
If family has very low income	38	39	36	29
If within 5 months of conception	30	31	30	24

Note:Percentages may not add exactly to 100, due to rounding.

In the summer of 1989, two women who sought abortions, Barbara Dodd from Ontario and Chantel Daigle from Quebec, were met with court injunctions to stop them, filed by their boyfriends. These injunctions were eventually struck down.

The question was asked:

Should an abortion be allowed if the woman requests one but the man disagrees?[63]

Whether Abortion Should be Allowed Without the Consent of the Male

	Yes	No	Don't Know
National	57%	31%	12%
Region			
Atlantic	38	45	17
Quebec	67	27	6
Ontario	55	32	13
Prairies	51	35	14
B.C.	62	25	13
Toronto	56	30	15
Montreal	73	22	5
Sex:			
Male	58	29	13
Female	55	34	11
Religion:			
Protestant	59	30	12
Catholic	51	38	12

4. BIBLIOGRAPHY

For related material, see Advocacy, Law and Politics Bibliographies

Adler, Nancy, Henry David, Brenda Major, Susan Roth, Nancy Russo and Gail Wyatt. "Psychological Responses After Abortion." *Science* 248 (April 6, 1990): 41-44.

Boyd, Kenneth, Brendan Callaghan, and Edward Shotter. *Life Before Birth: Consensus in Medical Ethics*. London: S.P.C.K., 1986.

Boyd, M., and D. Gillieson. "Canadian Attitudes on Abortion: Results of The Gallup Polls." *Canadian Studies in Population* 2 (1975): 63.

Brinkerhof, Merlin and Marlene Mackie. "Religion and Gender: A Comparison of Canadian Student Attitudes." *Journal of Marriage and Family* 47 (May 1985): 415-429.

Collins, Anne. *The Big Evasion: Abortion, the Issue That Won't Go Away*. Toronto: Lester and Orpen Dennys, 1985.

Cuneo, Michael W. *Catholics Against the Church: Anti-Abortion Protest in Toronto, 1969-1985*. Toronto: University of Toronto Press, 1989.

------. "Conservative Catholicism in North America: Pro-Life Activism and the Pursuit of the Sacred." *Pro Mundi Vita* 36 (1987): 3-28.

David, Henry P. *Born Unwanted: Developmental Effects of Denied Abortions*. New York: Springer Publishing Co., 1988.

Faden, Ruth R. et al. "Prenatal Screening and Pregnant Women's Attitudes Toward the Abortion of Defective Fetuses." *American Journal of Public Health* 77 (March 1987): 288-290.

Figueira-McDonough, Josefira. "Men and Women as Interest Groups in the Abortion Debate in the United States." *Women's Studies International Forum* 12 (1989): 539-550.

Francome, Colin. *Abortion Freedom: A Worldwide Movement*. Boston: George Allen and Unwin, 1984.

Ginsberg, Faye D. *Contested Lives: The Abortion Debate in an American Community*. Berkeley: University of California Press, 1989.

Handwerker, Penn W. Ed. *Births and Power: Social Change and the Politics of Reproduction*. Boulder: Westview Press, 1990.

Hartnagel, Timothy F., James J. Creechan, and Robert Sullivan. "Public Opinion and the Legalization of Abortion." *Canadian Review of Sociology and Anthropology* 22 (1985): 411-430.

Henshaw, Stanley K. "Induced Abortion: A World Review, 1990." *Family Planning Perspectives* 22 (March-April 1990): 76-89.

Henshaw, Stanley K. and Jane Siverman. "The Characteristics and Prior Contraceptive Use of U.S. Abortion Patients." *Family Planning Perspectives* 20 (July-August 1988): 158-168.

Jelen, Ted G. "Changes in the Attitudinal Correlations of Opposition to Abortion, 1977-1985." *Journal for the Scientific Study of Religion* 27 (June 1988): 211-228.

Joffe, Carole. "The Meaning of the Abortion Conflict." *Contemporary Sociology* 14 (1985): 26-28.

Kelly, James R. "Beyond the Stereotypes: Interviews with Right-to-Life Pioneers." *Commonweal* 105 (November 20, 1981): 654-659.

_____. "The Koop Report and a Better Politics of Abortion." *America* 162 (June 2, 1990): 542-546.

Koop, C. Everett. "The U.S. Surgeon General on the Health Effects of Abortion." *Population and Development Review* 15 (March 1989): 172-175.

Luker, Kristin. *Abortion and the Politics of Motherhood.* Berkeley: University of California Press, 1984.

Markson, Stephen L. "Citizens United for Life: Status Politics, Symbolic Reform and the Anti-Abortion Movement." Unpublished PhD dissertation, University of Massachusetts, 1979.

Mason, Susan E. "The ‹Pro-Family› Ideology of the 1970s." Unpublished PhD dissertation, Columbia University, 1981.

Merton, Andrew H. *Enemies of Choice: The Right to Life Movement and its Threat to Abortion.* Boston: Beacon Press, 1981.

Messer, Ellen and Kathryn May. *Backrooms: Voices from the Illegal Abortion Era.* New York: St. Martin's Press, 1988.

Mohr, James C. *Abortion in America: The Origins and Evolution of National Policy.* New York: Oxford University Press, 1978.

Neitz, Mary Jo. "Family, State, and God: Ideologies of the Right-to-Life Movement." *Sociological Analysis* 42 (1981): 265-276.

Petchesky, Rosalind Pollack. *Abortion and Women's Choice: The State, Sexuality and Reproductive Freedom.* Boston: Northeastern University Press, 1990.

------. "Antiabortion, Antifeminism, and the Rise of the New Right." *Feminist Studies* 7 (Summer 1981): 206-246.

Porter, Ruth and Maeve O'Connor. *Abortion: Medical Progress and Social Implications.* London: Pitman, 1985.

"Public Opinion and the Legalization of Abortion." *Canadian Review of Sociology and Anthropology* 22 (1985): 411-430.

Roe, Kathleen. "Private Troubles and Public Issues: Providing Abortion Amid Competing Definitions." *Social Science and Medicine* 29 (1989): 1191-1198.

Romaniuc, A. *Fertility in Canada: From Baby-boom to Baby-bust.* Ottawa: Ministry of Supply and Services, 1984.

Sachdev, Paul. Ed. *Abortion: Readings and Research.* Toronto: Butterworths, 1981.

Scott, J. and H. Schuman. "Attitude Strength and Social Action in the Abortion Dispute." *American Sociological Review* 53 (1988): 785-793.

Steinor, Gilbert Y. Ed. *The Abortion Dispute and the American System.* Washington DC: Brookings Institute, 1983.

Tribe, Lawrence. *Abortion: Help for the Adult Children of Dysfunctional Families.* New York: Norton, 1990.

Vanderford, Marsha. "Vilification and Social Movements: A Case Study of Pro-Life and Pro-Choice Rhetoric." *Quarterly Journal of Speech* 75 (May 1989): 166-182.

Wright, Lloyd and Robyn Rogers. "Variables Related to Pro-Choice Attitudes Among Undergraduates." *Adolescence* 22 (Fall 1987): 517-524.

Notes

1. The source of the statistics used in this section are taken from two publications of the Alan Guttmacher Institute. For further information on definitions, data sources and statistical methods and for more detailed analysis of the data, refer to Christopher Tietze and Stanley Henshaw, *Induced Abortion: A World Review, 1986* (New York: the Alan Guttmacher Institute, 1986). In this book, measures relating abortions to women (or to a total population) are referred to as rates, whereas measures relating abortions to births or pregnancies are called ratios (8). For the most recent statistics, see Stanley Henshaw, "Induced Abortion: A World Review, 1990," *Family Planning Perspectives* 22:2 (March/April 1990): 76-89. Tables included in this section have been compiled by combining the information from the two Alan Guttmacher Institute sources.

2. Tietze and Henshaw, *Induced Abortion: A World Review, 1986*, 42.

3. United States: Centers for Disease Control. 1985. *Abortion Surveillance 1981*. Atlanta. Also earlier volumes.

4. United States: Centers for Disease Control, 1985. "Abortion Surveillance 1983-83," *CDC Surveillance Summaries* 35, 35:255.

5. S.K. Henshaw and E. Blaine, *Abortion Services in the United States, Each State and Metropolitan Area, 1981-1982* (New York: Alan Guttmacher Institute, 1985).

6. S. Henshaw, "Trends in Abortions and Pregnancies, 1982-84" *Family Planning Perspectives* 18, no. 1 (1986): 34.

7. Henshaw, "Induced Abortion: A World Review, 1990," 78.

8. Canada: Statistics Canada. 1984 *Therapeutic Abortions 1982*. Ottawa. Also earlier volumes. Canada: Statistics Canada. *Therapeutic Abortion 1983 and 1984*. Ottawa. As quoted in Tietze and Henshaw, *Induced Abortion: A World Review, 1986*, 78.

9. Canada: Committee on the Operation of the Abortion Law. 1976. *Report of the Committee on the Operation of the Abortion Law*. Ottawa. An estimated 9,600 Canadian women obtained abortions in the United States in 1975. No clinic abortions were funded by Quebec.

10. Based on an estimate of 5,000 Canadian women obtaining abortions in the United States and 6,200 in Quebec. See, Henshaw et al. 1985. "A Portrait of American Women who Obtain Abortions." *Family Planning Perspectives* 17:2, 90-96.

11. Henshaw, "Induced Abortion: A World Review, 1990," 78.

12. As quoted in Tietze and Henshaw, *Induced Abortion: A World Review, 1986*, 109.
13. 1970-71: Estimated on basis of deaths attributed to legal abortion on death certificate. Tietze and Henshaw, *Induced Abortion: A World Review, 1986*, 109.
14. 1972-81: United States: Centers for Disease Control. 1985. *Abortion Surveillance 1981*. Atlanta. Also earlier volumes.
15. For a further breakdown according to gestation, procedure and facility, see Tietze and Henshaw, *Induced Abortion: A World Review, 1986*, 109.
16. Henshaw, "Induced Abortion: A World Review, 1990," 80.
17. As quoted in Tietze and Henshaw, *Induced Abortion: A World Review, 1986*, 108.
18. Attributed to legal abortion on death certificate.
19. Henshaw, "Induced Abortion: A World Review 1990," 80.
20. As quoted in Tietze and Henshaw, *Induced Abortion: A World Review, 1986*, 80.
21. As quoted in Henshaw, "Induced Abortion: A World Review, 1990," 82.
22. As quoted in Tietze and Henshaw, *Induced Abortion: A World Review, 1986*, 78.
23. As quoted in Henshaw, "Induced Abortion: A World Review, 1990," 82.
24. For estimation methods, see S. K. Henshaw and J. Van Vort in A.R. Kahn et al., "Induced Abortion in a Rural Area of Bangladesh, *Studies in Family Planning*, 17:95, 1986.
25. For estimation methods, see S. K. Henshaw and J. Van Vort in A.R. Kahn et al., "Induced Abortion in a Rural Area of Bangladesh," *Studies in Family Planning*, 17:95, 1986.
26. As quoted in Tietze and Henshaw, *Induced Abortion: A World Review, 1986*, 123.
27. As quoted in Henshaw, "Induced Abortion: A World Review, 1990," 83.
28. As quoted in Tietze and Henshaw, *Induced Abortion: A World Review, 1986*, 122.
29. As quoted in Henshaw, "Induced Abortion: A World Review, 1990," 83.
30. As quoted in Tietze and Henshaw, *Induced Abortion: A World Review, 1986*, 57.
31. As quoted in Henshaw, "Induced Abortion: A World Review, 1990," 85.
32. As quoted in Tietze and Henshaw, *Induced Abortion: A World Review, 1986*, 54.
33. Henshaw, "Induced Abortion: A World Review, 1990," 85.

34. As quoted in Tietze and Henshaw, *Induced Abortion: A World Review, 1986*, 61.
35. As quoted in Henshaw, "Induced Abortion: A World Review, 1990," 85.
36. As quoted in Tietze and Henshaw, *Induced Abortion: A World Review, 1986*, 59.
37. As quoted in Henshaw, "Induced Abortion: A World Review, 1990," 85.
38. As quoted in Tietze and Henshaw, *Induced Abortion: A World Review, 1986*, 68.
39. As quoted in Henshaw, "Induced Abortion: A World Review, 1990," 85.
40. As quoted in Tietze and Henshaw, *Induced Abortion: A World Review, 1986*, 71.
41. As quoted in Henshaw, "Induced Abortion: A World Review, 1990," 85.
42. As quoted in Tietze and Henshaw, *Induced Abortion: A World Review, 1986*, 74.
43. As quoted in Henshaw, "Induced Abortion: A World Review, 1990," 86.
44. As quoted in Tietze and Henshaw, *Induced Abortion: a World Review, 1986*, 73.
45. As quoted in Henshaw, "Induced Abortion: A World Review, 1990," 86.
46. As quoted in Tietze and Henshaw, *Induced Abortion: A World Review, 1986*, 68.
47. As quoted in Henshaw, "Induced Abortion: A World Review: 1990," 87.
48. As quoted in Tietze and Henshaw, *Induced Abortion: A World Review, 1986*, 66.
49. As quoted in Henshaw, "Induced Abortion: A World Review, 1990," 87.
50. As quoted in Tietze and Henshaw, *Induced Abortion: A World Review, 1986*, 72.
51. As quoted in Henshaw, "Induced Abortion: A World Review, 1990," 87.
52. As quoted in Tietze and Henshaw, *Induced Abortion: A World Review, 1986*, 71.
53. As quoted in Henshaw, "Induced Abortion: A World Review, 1990," 87.
54. As quoted in Tietze and Henshaw, *Induced Abortion: A World Review, 1986*, 119.
55. As quoted in Henshaw, "Induced Abortion: A World Review, 1990," 88.

56. K. Prager, "Induced Terminations of Pregnancy: Reporting States. 1981," *Monthly Vital Statistics Report* 34:4, Supplement 2 (1985).

57. As quoted in Tietze and Henshaw, *Induced Abortion: A World Review, 1986,* 118.

58. As quoted in Henshaw, " Induced Abortion: A World Review, 1990," 88.

59. The surveys on abortion questions were conducted by the Gallup Poll News Service, United States on Thursday, April 26, 1990 entitled "Americans Shift Toward Pro-Choice Position" by George Gallup and Frank Newport; and by Gallup Canada, Inc., on Thursday, August 24, 1989 entitled "Majority Believe Woman's Request is Paramount in Abortion Decision," and January 15, 1990 entitled "27% Favor Legalizing Abortion Under Any Circumstances" by Lorne Bozinoff and Peter MacIntosh. They are used with permission of Gallup Poll News Service, United States, and Gallup Canada, Inc., respectively.

60. The results are based on telephone interviews with randomly selected national samples of adults, 18 and older. The first survey was conducted with 1,239, April 5-8, 1990. The second survey was conducted with 1,239 adults, April 19-22, 1990. For results based on samples of this size, one can say with 95% confidence that the error attributable to sampling and other random effects could be plus or minus 3 percentage points. In addition to sampling, question wording and practical difficulties in conducting surveys can introduce error or bias into the findings of public opinion polls.

61. Lorne Bozinoff and Peter MacIntosh, "27% Favor Legalizing Abortion Under Any Circumstances," *Gallup*, January 15, 1990.

62. The January 1990 results were based on 1,020 personal interviews with adults, 18 years and older, conducted December 6-9, 1989. A national sample of this size is accurate within a 4% margin, 19 in 20 times.

63. Lorne Bozinoff and Peter MacIntosh, "Majority Believe Woman's Request is Paramount in Abortion Decision," *Gallup* August 24, 1989.

Chapter Two

Philosophical Perspectives on Abortion

1. Philosophical Discussion on Abortion

The issue of abortion raises philosophical questions at many levels: for the private conscience of individuals, for public policy, and for constitutional law. The key questions concerning the moral justifiability of abortion focus upon the problems of the moral status of the unborn, as well as the resolution of the conflicting rights of the pregnant woman (the right to privacy and the right to reproductive freedom) and the rights of the fetus (right to life, right to be protected, not harmed). Public policy questions concern the legitimacy of government enforcement of a set of moral convictions held by some persons but rejected by others, within a pluralistic society. Other questions consider the moral coherence of ascribing legal rights to "unborn persons."[1] Much of the literature addressing the philosophical aspects of abortion acknowledges and responds to various theological positions as well. Feminist perspectives raise numerous questions about the patriarchal framework of the current abortion debate as well as the issue of abortion itself.

It is not likely that the abortion issue will be settled by philosophical arguments. Kristen Luker, a sociologist, points out that the abortion issue is only the tip of the iceberg. She says that what is at stake is "not only the definition of the embryo, but also two different definitions of the world: Motherhood, the appropriate roles of men and women, and the nature of morality."[2]

The Status of the Unborn

The moral justifiability of abortion depends upon the standing given to the unborn (embryo, fetus) at a given stage of life. This debate on abortion continues without any apparent resolution because there is not any agreement of what constitutes protectable human life or personhood. For many arguments, a critical factor is the moral standing given to a particular stage of fetal development or the possession of certain properties. The fertilized ovum develops through many stages in the process from conception to birth. Rem Edwards and Glenn C. Graber list various stages of fetal development and ask when the prenatal human fetus does have a moral and/or legal standing which requires others to protect its life?[3] These stages of fetal development are:

1. At *conception* when it acquires a complete set of human genes, making it a member of the human species;
2. At *implantation*, 6 to 7 days after conception;
3. At individuation, 14 days after conception. Up to this stage twinning and recombination are possible;
4. When the *heart starts beating*, 3-4 weeks after conception;
5. When the fetus starts *looking human* and *all the organs* are present in a rudimentary stage, at around 6 weeks;
6. When there is a reflex response to pain and tickling stimuli, around 7 weeks;
7. When *brain waves*, emanating from the brain stem, are first detectable, around 8 weeks;
8. When *spontaneous movement* independent of stimulation begins, at 10 weeks;
9. When the *brain has a complete structure*, around 12 weeks;
10. At *quickening*, when the mother first feels the fetus's movement, between 12 and 16 weeks.
11. When there is a *10 percent probability of survival* outside the womb, 20 weeks;
12. At *viability*, when the lungs and other organs are developed sufficiently to support independent life, traditionally from 24 to 28 weeks;
13. When *conscious awareness* occurs, probably with the appearance of distinct sleep versus awake brain wave patterns, at around 28 weeks;
14. When the *eyes are reopened* at around 28 to 30 weeks, after being sealed shut since around 13 weeks;
15. At *normal birth*, around 40 weeks;
16. When *self-consciousness, language use, and rationality* begin, between 1 and 2 years after birth.

These developmental stages are used to establish the status of the unborn in terms of personhood and as a bearer of rights. The official Roman Catholic position maintains that there is a human person, who is a bearer of rights, from the moment of conception. Another view holds that in the first few months of a pregnancy, abortion involves, not a human person, but simply a piece of tissue.[4] Often the fetus is understood as a *potential person*. Then the question of when to draw the line between potential and actual personhood needs to be asked. Edward Langerak draws the line for abortion at the beginning of the second trimester. At this time, the fetus is a potential person, who has a 50-50 chance of developing into a person and whose presence has begun to manifest itself.[5] Jane English concludes that no single criterion can capture the concept of a person. A line simply cannot be drawn.[6]

Other positions hold that the presence of certain properties are required to give standing to fetuses and newborns. These properties include: being a member of the human species; having a capacity for pleasure or pain; having desires or interests; having self-consciousness; having intelligence and rationality; having language capacity; being valued by others.[7] Michael Tooley asserts that fetuses and newborns do not have a right to life because they do not possess a concept of a continuing self.[8] Furthermore, he suggests that adult members of other species may possess properties which endow them with a right to life.

The Spectrum of Positions on Abortion

The conventional approach to categorizing positions on abortion employs the terms: conservative, moderate and liberal. These follow from the determinations made in the questions raised earlier, regarding the stage of fetal development or the properties required to give moral standing to the fetus.

The most extreme conservative position holds that there is a human person who is the bearer of rights, from the moment of conception.[9] The presence of a complete set of human genes, the increasing resemblance of the fetus to a baby, and the mother's experience of the fetus as an "other" provide the needed evidence to support this position. A less extreme conservative position maintains that there is a human person from some early stage, soon after conception. Implantation is an example of this position. Conservatives maintain that abortion is morally wrong because it involves the killing of an innocent human life. The rights of the pregnant woman do not override the rights of the fetus.

At the other end of the spectrum is the extreme liberal view, which claims that only sometime after birth, when certain properties such as language and reasoning ability are apparent, is there a human person. Thus, unborn fetuses are not bearers of rights. The rights of the woman are respected. The less extreme liberal position recognizes personhood and the moral standing which goes along with it at an earlier time, such as viability or birth. After this time, the rights of the unborn must be weighed along with those of the rights of the pregnant woman.

The moderate view holds that it is somewhere between conception and natural birth that the fetus acquires the necessary properties to be recognized as having moral standing. There are various views about what are the necessary properties. In addition, the moral standing of fetuses may be accorded a different priority than that of others, as, for example, the pregnant woman. Instead of being a person, the fetus may be understood as having potential personhood. For this position, abortion in the earlier stages is morally acceptable, because the fetus does not have rights. As the fetus develops, abortion becomes morally problematic, because with the emergence of the necessary properties in the fetus, rights are recognized.

Within the last decade or so, the perspectives of explicitly feminist philosophers and theologians have been brought to bear upon the abortion debate. Not only are their arguments on abortion different, but so too are their philosophical and theological frameworks, in that the experience of women is taken seriously and patriarchal bias is exposed. There are a variety of feminist positions on abortion. Even though some of these positions can be located in the pro-choice and pro-life groups,[10] as conventionally understood, many feminist authors approach the question of abortion in terms of the position of women within the larger social and cultural system.[11] For example, Sandra Harding asserts that "there are important commonalities in prolife and prochoice women's actual needs, perception of their needs, and values. These commonalities are distorted or ignored in the current abortion dispute and often by women on both sides of the dispute."[12] She explains that beneath the surface of the dispute, there is a shared recognition that women are fully human and that the sexual politics of the social order refuses to acknowledge women's fundamental humanity.

The philosophical views held concerning the moral status of the "unborn," the recognition given to such rights as privacy, reproductive freedom, the rights of the "unborn," and the role of women and the family, all provide the basic assumptions underlying various legal public policy approaches with regard to abortion practice. The conservative view, which recognizes personhood or protectable human life in the very early stages, leads to a restrictive policy approach and, consequently, allows for very limited legal access or no access whatsoever, except when the woman's life is at stake. The liberal approach which gives moral and legal status to the fetus very late in the pregnancy, at birth, or some time after birth, and also recognizes certain rights of the pregnant woman, leads to a policy approach which allows access to abortion until late in the pregnancy. This view may also hold that the state has duties in view of the women's rights and may create the conditions favoring easy access to abortion. Moderate views may hold that in the early stages the fetus has no status or very limited status, such that abortion is permissible, especially in view of the rights of the women. But at some point, the fetus develops, or its potential has been realized, to the extent of gaining .moral and legal status, either fully or in some degree. Abortion then becomes morally and/or legally wrong, except in the circumstances where the continued pregnancy may seriously threaten the woman's life or health.

2. PHILOSOPHY ABSTRACTS

Baird, Robert, and Stuart Rosenbaum. *The Ethics of Abortion, Pro-Life vs. Pro-Choice*. Buffalo, New York: Prometheus Books, 1989.

This anthology consists of many of the "classic" philosophical articles on abortion (English, Ramsey, Thompson, Tooley, Warren, to name a few). The legal decisions of *Roe v. Wade* and *Webster v. Reproductive Health Services* are also included.

Burt, Robert. "Fact, Fables and Moral Rules: An Analysis of the Abortion Debate." *New Scholasticism* 62 (Autumn 1988): 400-411.

Burt argues that the prohibition of killing the innocent is not absolute in the Judaic-Christian tradition. He examines the thought of Augustine and Aquinas.

W. B. Bondeson, H. Tristram Englehardt, Jr., S. F. Spicker and D. H. Winship, eds. *Abortion and the Status of the Fetus*. Dordrecht, Holland: D. Reidel Publishing Company, 1984.

This volume grew out of a symposium, "The Concept of Person and Its Implications for the Use of the Fetus in Biomedicine," held at the University of Missouri--Columbia in 1980. It contains articles on abortion and science and public policy, personhood and the concept of viability, women and moral responsibility, and the classical and religious roots of the current controversy.

Callahan, Joan. and Knight, James. *Preventing Birth: Contemporary Methods and Related Moral Concerns.* Salt Lake City: University of Utah Press, 1989.
   The book describes various methods of birth control, including induced abortion. Related moral issues concerning elective abortion and women's legal liability for fetal harm are discussed.

Callahan, Sidney and Daniel Callahan, eds. *Abortion: Understanding Differences.* New York: Plenum Press, 1984.
   The purpose of the book is to enrich the dialogue on abortion. Its intent is to reach some deeper understanding of why people differ on abortion and to gain some insights into how and why individuals weigh and order their values when addressing the abortion issue. The attempt is made to shift from the "tip of the iceberg," which is the public debate on morality and policy, to the broader system of values which serves as a basis for differing abortion stances. The participants, who are predominantly women, were asked "to make explicit their implicit linkages between abortion and the values and views they hold on other fundamental issues" (xvi). The topics covered include social science perspective, abortion and the family, childbearing and childrearing, abortion and women, abortion and culture and the positions held by the two editors/contributors.

Dore, Clement. "Abortion, Some Slippery Slope Arguments and Identity over Time." *Philosophical Studies* 55 (March, 1989): 279-291.
   Dore considers the question of whether there is a cutoff point with respect to the developing fetus, beyond which it becomes seriously wrong to kill it. He argues that there is no cutoff point but that it becomes a prima facie wrong to abort as the fetus comes more and more to resemble a baby who desires continued life.

Edwards, Rem. "Abortion Rights." *National Forum* 69 (Fall 1989): 19, 21, 23-24.
   Edwards provides a number of arguments against the conservative position which holds that there is a person with moral standing from the moment of conception.

English, Jane. "Abortion and the Concept of a Person." *Canadian Journal of Philosophy* 5 (October, 1975): 233-243. This article is reprinted in numerous anthologies.

The author examines the concept of a person and concludes that no single criterion can capture the concept of a person. She then goes on to argue that, even if a fetus is a person, abortion is still justifiable in many cases; and even if a fetus is not a person, killing it can still be wrong in many cases. She concludes that abortion is justifiable early in pregnancy, to avoid modest harms, whether a fetus is a person or not. Abortion late in pregnancy is seldom justifiable except to avoid significant injury or death.

Feinberg, Joel. *The Problem of Abortion*. Second Edition. Belmont, California: Wadsworth, 1984.

This anthology contains many classic articles on abortion, including those by Noonan, Wertheimer, Sumner, Warren, Tooley, English and Thompson.

Hare, R.M. "A Kantian Approach to Abortion." *Social Theory and Practice* 15 (Spring, 1989): 1-14.

Hare leaves aside the ambiguous question "is the fetus a person?", and asks what are the ascertainable properties of the fetus which may make it wrong to kill it. He argues that the property is the fetus's potentiality for growing into a person.

Harrison, Beverly Wildung. *Our Right to Choose: Toward a New Ethic of Abortion*. Boston: Beacon Press, 1983.

Harrison's thesis asserts that an adequate moral approach to abortion cannot be formulated without affirming that women need, as a social good, the capacity to shape their procreative power. A feminist perspective is necessary to formulate this case for procreative choice. She identifies two tasks for the study. First, a critique of the misogynist bias of theological and moral tradition on abortion is undertaken. The second task involves the elaboration of the elements essential to an ethic of procreative choice. The question of what constitutes a sound social policy is addressed. A method of liberation ethics is employed.

Noonan, John T., Jr. ed. "An Almost Absolute Value in History," *The Morality of Abortion: Legal and Historical Perspectives*. Cambridge, MA: Harvard University Press, 1970. Also in *Bioethics*. Rem Edwards and Glen Graber. San Diego: Harcourt Brace Jovanovich, 1988. 598-603.

Noonan takes the position that it is not possible to "draw the line" when it comes to deciding when full human personhood exists. It is present from conception. A being with a complete set of human genes is by definition fully human and is in possession of all human rights.

Petchesky, Rosalind Pollack. *Abortion and Woman's Choice: The State, Sexuality, and Reproductive Freedom.* New York: Longman, 1984.
    Petchesky begins with the premise that reproduction and fertility control must be understood as historically determined and as a socially organized activity. From a feminist perspective, she analyzes the need for safe, legal abortions and then uses this analysis to develop a theory of the social relations of reproduction and a feminist concept of reproductive freedom.

Ramsey, Paul. "The Morality of Abortion." In *Moral Problems: A Collection of Philosophical Essays.* Ed. James Rachels. Second edition. New York: Harper and Row. 37-58. Originally appeared in Daniel Laddy, *Life or Death-Ethics and Options.* Seattle: University of Washington Press, 1971. Also in *The Ethics of Abortion: Pro-Life vs. Pro-Choice*, Baird and Rosenbaum, cited above.
    After presenting the range of opinions regarding the point at which there is a "human," Ramsey says that from an authentic religious point of view none of them matters very much. Human life is sacred, not because of something inherent in man, but because the value of a human life is ultimately grounded in the value that God is placing on it. He asserts that a man's dignity is an overflow from God's dealing with him, and not primarily an anticipation of anything that he will ever be by himself alone. Also, it does not matter what religious formulations are used to support this point including: origin of a human life; man's creation in the image of God; biblical doctrine of God's covenant with his people; or the doctrine of man's ultimate destination. He believes that the erosion of religious regard for nascent life is due to the technological and abortifacient era, which is the contemporary context.

Nancy Rhoden, "The New Neonatal Dilemma: Live Births from Late Abortions." *Georgetown Law Journal* 72 (June, 1984): 1451-1509. Also in *Bioethics*. Rem Edward and Glenn Graber. San Diego: Harcourt Brace Jovanovich, 1988. 556-583.
    Rhoden describes the various abortion techniques and the treatment of premature newborns. She then addresses the question of whether infants born from abortion should be saved. The problems surrounding the meaning of viability are examined.

Smith, Janet E. "Abortion and Moral Development: Listening with Different Ears." *International Philosophical Quarterly* 28 (March 1988): 31-51.

This article critically examines Carol Gilligan's *In a Different Voice*. Smith holds that Gilligan's conclusions are undermined by the fact that she views abortion as a morally acceptable act. As a result, she has failed to ask many pertinent questions of the interviewees. Smith claims that those who hold abortion to be an intrinsically immoral act would "hear" these interviews "with different ears."

Sumner, Wayne. *Abortion and Moral Theory*. Princeton: Princeton University Press, 1981. A revised version of chapter 4 appears as "A Third Way," in Joel Feinburg, *The Problem of Abortion*, cited above.

Sumner defines a third approach to abortion, which combines elements of the liberal view for early abortions with elements of a conservative view for late abortions. He gives his position an intuitive defense by showing that it coheres better than the liberal and conservative views with our considered moral judgments on abortion and closely related issues. He also grounds his approach in a moral theory.

Thomson, Judith Jarvis. "A Defense of Abortion," *Philosophy and Public Affairs* (Fall, 1971): 47-66. This article has been reprinted in numerous anthologies, including Baird and Rosenbaum, *The Ethics of Abortion: Pro-Life vs. Pro-Choice*, and Feinberg, *The Problem of Abortion*, both cited above.

Thomson begins with the premise that the fetus is a person from the moment of conception. She is interested in exploring how one moves from this premise to the conclusion that abortion is morally impermissible. She compares the situation of the pregnant women and the fetus with that of an unconscious famous violin player, hooked up to another person who alone can provide the necessary blood type for the violinist. In the light of this analogy, she considers a number of liberal and conservative views on abortion. These positions include: cases when the continuation of the pregnancy is likely to shorten or threaten the mother's life (because abortion is the direct killing of the fetus, a woman can defend her life against the threat to it by the unborn child, even if doing so involves its death); actions that may be done by a third party; situations where the mother's life is not at stake; the meaning of the right to life (not to be killed unjustly); the responsibility of the pregnant woman for the fetus (being a minimally decent Samaritan).

Tooley, Michael. "Abortion and Infanticide." *Philosophy and Public Affairs* 2 (Fall, 1972): 37-65. This article has been reprinted in numerous anthologies, including Baird and Rosenbaum, *The Ethics of Abortion: Pro-Life vs. Pro-Choice*, cited above.

Tooley asks what properties are necessary to being a person, i.e., to have a serious right to life? He claims that an organism possesses a serious right to life if it possesses the concept of a self as a continuing subject of experiences and other mental states and believes that it is itself a continuing entity. This condition is not satisfied by human fetuses and infants, and thus they do not have a right to life. Unless there are other objections to abortion, it is morally acceptable. However, because it is possible that adult members of other species--cats, dogs and polar bears--do possess properties that endow them with the right to life, our treatment of them may be morally indefensible.

Warren, Mary Ann. "On the Moral and Legal Status of Abortion, with Postscript on Infanticide." *The Monist* 57: (January, 1973): 43-61. Included in Joel Feinberg, *The Problem of Abortion*, cited above. This article also appears in a number of anthologies.

The author considers whether or not it is possible to establish that abortion is morally permissible even if it is assumed that the fetus is an entity with a right-to-life. She argues that in fact this cannot be established conclusively. It is necessary, therefore, to ask whether or not a fetus has the same right to life as a human being.

In response, the author holds the view that a fetus cannot be considered a member of the moral community because it is not a person with full and equal rights. It is personhood, not genetic humanity, which is the basis for membership in this community. The fetus, at whatever stage, does not satisfy the basic criteria of personhood. This criteria consists of consciousness, reasoning, self-motivated activity, capacity to communicate and the presence of self-concepts and self-awareness. The fetus cannot even be given rights on the basis of the resemblances to persons because the fetus is not similar enough nor does the fetus's *potential* personhood override the moral rights of actual people, in this case, the mother's rights.

In the "Postscript," the author argues that her position does not commit her to support infanticide. She explains that even if newborn infants are not persons, they are very close to being persons. They may be wanted by other people for adoption. Also, once born, the existence of the infant no longer jeopardizes the right of the mother to protect her life and health.

Wolf-Devine, Celia. "Abortion and the Feminine Voice." *Public Affairs Quarterly* 3 (July 1989): 81-97.

The author argues that abortion is a masculine response to the problem posed by a unwanted pregnancy. The "feminine voice" generates a strong presumption against abortion as a way of dealing with an unwanted pregnancy.

3. BIBLIOGRAPHY

Anderson, Susan Leigh. "Criticism of Liberal/Feminist Views on Abortion." *Public Affairs Quarterly* 1 (April 1987): 11-16.

Bachelor, Edward. Ed. *Abortion: The Moral Issues.* New York: The Pilgrim Press, 1984. (Anthology)

Barry, Robert. *Medical Ethics: Essays on Abortion and Euthanasia* New York: Lang, 1989.

Becker, Lawrence C. "Human Being: Boundaries of the Concept." *Philosophy and Public Affairs* 4 (1975): 334-359.

Benjamin, Martin. *Splitting the Differences: Compromise and Integrity in Ethics and Politics.* Lawrence: University Press of Kansas, 1990.

Bigelow, John and Robert Pargetter. "Morality, Potential Persons and Abortion." *American Philosophical Quarterly* 25 (April 1988): 173-181.

Bole III, Thomas. "Metaphysical Accounts of the Zygote as a Person and the Veto Power of Facts." *Journal of Medicine and Philosophy* 14 (December 1989): 647-653.

Borchert, Donald and Phillip Jones. "Abortion: Morally Right or Wrong?" *Listening* 22 (Winter 1985): 22-35.

Brandt, Richard B. "The Morality of Abortion." *The Monist* 36 (1972): 691-696.

------. "Hare on Abortion." *Social Theory and Practice* 15 (Spring 1989): 15-24.

Brody, Baruch. *Abortion and the Sanctity of Human Life, A Philosophical View.* Cambridge, MA: The M.I.T. Press, 1973.

------. "Abortion and the Sanctity of Human Life." *American Philosophical Quarterly* 10 (April 1973): 133-140.

Burtchaell, James T. Ed. *Abortion Parley.* Kansas City: Andrews and McMeel, 1980. (Anthology.)

Callahan, Daniel. *Abortion: Law Choice and Morality.* London: Collier-MacMillan, Ltd., 1970.

Callahan, Joan. *"The Silent Scream*: A New Conclusive Argument Against Abortion?" *Philosophy Research Archives* 11 (1986): 181-195.

Carrick, Paul. *Medical Ethics in Antiquity: Philosophical Perspectives on Abortion and Euthanasia.* Dordrecht: Reidel, 1985.

"Case Study: When a Mentally Ill Woman Refuses Abortion." Commentaries by Mary Mahowald and Virginia Abernathy. *Hastings Center Report* 15 (April 1985): 22-23.

"Case Study: The Unwanted Child: Caring For a Fetus Born Alive After an Abortion." *The Hastings Center Report* 6 (October 1976): 10-14.

Chervenak, Frank A. et al. "When Is Termination of Pregnancy During the Third Trimester of Pregnancy Justifiable?" *New England Journal of Medicine* 310 (February 23, 1984): 501-504.

Chopko, Mark, Phillip Harris, and Helen Alvare. "The Price of Abortion Sixteen Years Later." *National Forum* 69 (Fall 1989): 18, 20, 22.

Cohen, Marshall, Thomas Nagel, and Thomas Scanlon. Eds. *Rights and Wrongs of Abortion.* Princeton: Princeton University Press, 1974. (Anthology.)

Collins, Barbara G. "Transforming Abortion Discourse." *Affilia* 2 (Spring 1987): 6-17.

Cudd, Ann. "Sensationalized Philosophy: A Reply to Marquis's "Why Abortion is Immoral." *Journal of Philosophy* 87 (May 1990): 262-264.

Davis, Nancy. "Abortion and Self-Defence." *Philosophy and Public Affairs* 13 (Summer 1984): 175-207.

Devine, Philip E. *The Ethics of Homicide.* Ithaca and London: Cornell University Press, 1978. 46-105.

------. "Relativism, Abortion and Tolerance." *Philosophy and Phenomenological Research* 48 (Summer 1987): 131-138.

Englehardt, H. Tristram, Jr. "The Ontology of Abortion." *Ethics* 8 (1974): 217-234.

------. "Bioethics and the Process of Embodiment." *Perspectives in Biology and Medicine* 18 (1975): 486-500.

------. "Foundations: Why they Provide So Little." *Journal for the British Society for Phenomenology* 20 (May 1989): 170-172.

Englehardt, H. Tristram and Cefalo, Robert. "The Use of Fetal and Anencephalic Tissue for Transplantation." *Journal of Medicine and Philosophy* 14 (February 1989): 25-43.

Erde, Edmunde L. "Studies in the Exploration of Issues in Biomedical Ethics: The Example of Abortion." *Journal of Medicine and Philosophy* 13 (November 1988): 329-347.

------. "Understanding Abortion Via Different Scholarly Methodologies." *Journal of Medical Humanities and Bioethics* 7 (Fall-Winter 1986): 139-147.

------. "Understanding Abortion Via Different Scholarly Methodologies, Part II." *Journal of Medical Humanities and Bioethics* 8 (Spring-Summer 1987): 56-66.

Feinberg, Joel. "Abortion." In *Matters of Life and Death*. Ed. Tom Regan. New York: Random House, 1978. 183-217.

Finnis, John. "The Rights and Wrongs of Abortion: A Reply to Judith Thomson." *Philosophy and Public Affairs* 2 (1973): 117-145.

Fleming, Lorette. "The Moral Status of the Fetus: A Reappraisal." *Bioethics* 1 (January 1987): 15-34.

Foot, Phillippa. "The Problem of Abortion and the Doctrine of Double Effect." *The Oxford Review* 5 (1967): 5-15.

Galvin, Richard Francis. "Noonan's Argument Against Abortion: Probability, Possibility and Potentiality." *Journal of Social Philosophy* 19 (Summer 1988): 80-89.

Gilligan, Carol. *In a Different Voice: Psychological Theory and Women's Development*. Cambridge: Harvard University Press, 1982.

Goodman, Michael. Ed. *What is a Person?* Clifton, NJ: Humana Press, 1988.

Gorovitz, Samuel, "Moral Conflict in Public Policy." *National Forum* 69 (Fall 1989): 31-32.

Glover, Jonathan. *Causing Death and Saving Lives*. Hammondsworth, Middlesex: Penguin Books, 1977. Chapters 9-12.

Granfield, David. *The Abortion Decision*. Garden City, NY: Doubleday Image Books, 1971.

Grisez, Germaine G. *Abortion: The Myths, the Realities, and the Arguments*. New York: Corpus Books, 1970.

Grossman, Richard. "Preventing Pregnancy: A Neglected Option." [Response to "When a Mentally Ill Woman Refuses Abortion," *Hastings Center Report* 15 (April 1985): 22-23] *Hastings Center Report* 16 (April 1986): 44-45.

Guttmacher, Alan F. Ed. *The Case for Legalized Abortion*. Berkeley, CA: Diablo Press, 1967.

Hall Robert, E. Ed. *Abortion in a Changing World*. New York and London: Columbia University Press, 1970. Two Volumes. (Anthology)

Hare, Richard M. "Abortion and the Golden Rule." *Philosophy and Public Affairs* 4 (1975): 201-222.

------. "Abortion: Reply to Brandt." *Social Theory and Practice* 15 (Spring 1989): 25-32.

Hartshorne, Charles. "Concerning Abortion: An Attempt at a Rational View." *Christian Century* 98 (January 21, 1981): 42-45.

Herbenick, Raymond M. "Remarks on Abortion, Abandonment, and Adoption Opportunities." *Philosophy and Public Affairs* 5 (1975): 89-104.

Hilgers, Thomas and Dennis Dennis. Eds. *New Perspectives on Human Abortion.* Frederick, MD: University Press of America, 1981.

John, Helen. "Reflections on Autonomy and Abortion." *Journal of Social Philosophy* 17 (Winter 1986): 3-10.

Kluge, Eike-Henner. *The Practice of Death.* New Haven and London: Yale University Press, 1975. 1-100, 182-209.

Kohl, Marvin. *The Morality of Killing.* Atlantic Highlands, NJ: Humanities Press, 1974. Chapters 3-5.

Kremar, Elmar, "On Killing the Immature." In *Philosophy and Culture.* Vol. 3. Ed. Venant Cauchy. Montreal: Editions Montmorency, 1988. 436-441.

Lake, Randall A. "The Metaethical Framework of Anti-Abortion Rhetoric." *Signs: Journal of Women, Culture and Society* 11 (Spring 1986): 478-499.

Lamb, David. *Down the Slippery Slope: Arguing in Applied Ethics.* London: Croon Helm, 1988.

Langerak, Edward. "Abortion: Listening to the Middle." *Hastings Center Report* 9 (October, 1979): 24-29.

Lombardi, Louis. "The Legal versus the Moral on Abortion." *Journal of Social Philosophy* 17 (Winter 1986): 23-29.

Lycan, William. "Abortion and the Civil Rights of Machines." In *Morality and Universality: Essays on Ethical Universalizability.* Ed. Nelson T. Potter. Dordrecht: Kluwer, 1985. 139-156.

Macklin, Ruth. "Ethics and Human Reproduction: International Perspectives." *Social Problems* 37 (February 1990): 38-50.

Maier, Kelly L. "Pregnant Women: Fetal Containers or People with Rights?" *Affilia* 4 (Summer 1989): 8-20.

Markowitz, Sally. "Abortion and Feminism." *Social Theory and Practice* 16 (Spring 1990): 1-17.

Marquis, Don. "Why Abortion is Immoral." *Journal of Philosophy* 86 (April 1989): 183-202.

Mason, J. K. *Human Life and Medical Practice.* Edinburgh: Edinburgh University Press, 1988.

Meeks, Thomas. "The Economics Efficiency and Equity of Abortion." *Economics and Philosophy* 6 (April 1990): 95-138.

Mehta, Ajit C. "Ethical Issues in Abortion, Amniocentesis and Sterilization." *Journal of Family Welfare* 34 (Spring 1987): 49-53.

McConnell, Terrance. "Permissive Abortion Laws, Religion and Moral Compromise." *Public Affairs Quarterly* 1 (January 1987): 95-109.

McInerney, Peter. "Does a Fetus Already Have a Future-Like-Ours?" *Journal of Philosophy* 87 (May 1990): 264-268.

Murphy, Julien S. "Abortion Rights and Fetal Termination." *Journal of Social Philosophy* 17 (Winter 1986): 11-16.

Noonan, John T., Jr. *A Private Choice: Abortion in America in the Seventies.* New York: Free Press, 1979.

------. Ed. *The Morality of Abortion: Legal and Historical Perspectives.* Cambridge, MA: Harvard University Press, 1970. (Anthology)

Norcross, Alastair. "Killing, Abortion and Contraception: A Reply to Marquis." *Journal of Philosophy* 87 (May 1990): 268-277.

Overall, Christine. *Ethics and Human Reproduction: A Feminist Analysis.* Boston: Allen and Unwin, 1987.

------. "Reproductive Ethics: Feminist and Non-Feminist Approaches." *Canadian Journal of Women and the Law* 1 (1986): 271-278.

------. "Selective Termination of Pregnancy and Women's Reproductive Autonomy." *Hastings Center Report* 20 (May-June 1990): 6-11.

Pahel, Kenneth. "Michael Tooley on Abortion and Potentiality." *Southern Journal of Philosophy* 25 (Spring 1982): 89-107.

Perkins, Robert. Ed. *Abortion.* Cambridge, MA: Schenkman Publishing Co., 1974. (Anthology)

Perry, Clifton. "Methods of Aborting." *Reason Papers* 11 (Spring 1986): 63-67.

Petchesky, Rosalind Pollack. "Reproductive Freedom: Beyond a Woman's Right to Choose." *Signs: Journal of Women, Culture and Society* 5 (Summer 1980): 661-685.

Railsbach, Celeste Condit. "Pro-Life, Pro-Choice: Different Conceptions of Value." *Women's Studies in Communication* 5 (Spring 1982): 16-28.

Ramsey, Paul. *The Ethics of Fetal Research.* New Haven: Yale University Press, 1975.

Robertson, John A. "Extracorporeal Embryos and the Abortion Debate." *Journal of Contemporary Health Law and Policy* 2 (Spring 1986): 53-70.

Rodgers, Sandra. "Fetal Rights and Maternal Rights: Is There a Conflict?" *Canadian Journal of Women and the Law* 1 (1986): 456-469.

Schartz, Stephen, and Tacelli, R. K. "Abortion and Some Philosophers." *Public Affairs Quarterly* 3 (April 1989): 81-98.

Schedler, George. "Will Preserving American Women's Procreative Freedom Conflict with Achieving Equality Between the Sexes?" *Reason Papers* 14 (Spring 1989): 45-58.

Shaw, Margery and A. Edward Doudera. Eds. *Defining Life: Medical, Legal and Ethical Implications.* Ann Arbor: AUPHA Press, 1983. (Anthology)

Sher, George. "Hare, Abortion, and the Golden Rule." *Philosophy and Public Affairs* 6 (1977): 185-190.

------. "Subsidized Abortion: Moral Rights and Moral Compromise." *Philosophy and Public Affairs* 10 (1981): 361-372.

Sider, Ronald J. *Completely Pro-Life: Building a Consistent Stance.* Westmount: Inter-Varsity Press, 1987.

Silverstein, Harry S. "On a Woman's Responsibility for the Fetus." *Social Thought and Practice* (Spring 1987): 103-119.

Singer, Peter. *Practical Ethics.* Cambridge and New York: Cambridge University Press, 1975.

Stone, Jim. "Why Potentiality Matters." *Canadian Journal of Philosophy* 17 (December 1987): 815-829.

Strasser, Mark. "Noonan on Contraception and Abortion: Comments on Noonan's *The Morality of Abortion: Legal and Historical Perspectives.*" *Bioethics* 1 (April 1987): 199-205.

Sumner, L. W. "Abortion." In *Health Care Ethics.* Ed. Donald Van De Veer. Philadelphia: Temple Press, 1982. 162-183.

Tooley, Michael. "Response to Mary Anne Warren's 'Reconsidering the Ethics of Infanticide.'" *Philosophical Books* 26 (January 1985): 9-14.

Tooley, Michael and Laura Purdy. "Is Abortion Murder?" In *Abortion Pro and Con.* Ed. Robert Perkins. Cambridge, MA: 1974.

Waters, Kristen. "Abortion, Technology and Responsibility." *Journal of Social Philosophy* 17 (Winter 1986): 17-22.

Warren, Mary Anne. " The Abortion Issue." In *Health Care Ethics.* Ed. Donald Van De Veer. Philadelphia: Temple Press, 1982. 162-183.

------. "The Abortion Struggle in America." *Bioethics* 9 (October 1989): 320-332.

------. "The Moral Significance of Birth." *Hypatia* 4 (1989): 46-65.

------. "Reconsidering the Ethics of Infanticide." *Philosophical Books* 26 (January 1985): 1-9.

Watt, Helen. "Singer on Abortion: A Utilitarian Critique." *Australasian Journal of Philosophy* 67 (June 1989): 227-229.

Weil, William, and Martin Benjamin. Eds. *Ethical Issues at the Outset of Life.* Boston: Blackwell Science, 1987.

Wennberg, Robert N. *Life in the Balance: Exploring the Abortion Controversy.* Grand Rapids, MI: Eerdmans, 1985.

Wertheimer, Roger. "Understanding the Abortion Argument," *Philosophy and Public Affairs* 1 (1971): 67-95. A shortened version can be found in Joel Feinberg, *The Problem of Abortion*, cited above.

Weston, Anthony. "Drawing Lines: The Abortion Perplexity and the Presuppositions of Applied Ethics." *Monist* 67 (October 1984): 589-604.

Wilcox, John. "Nature as Demonic in Thomson's Defense of Abortion." *New Scholasticism* 63 (Autumn 1989): 463-484.

Wilson, Bryan. "On a Kantian Argument Against Abortion." *Philosophical Studies* 53 (January 1988): 119-130.

Zaitchik, Alan. "Viability and the Morality of Abortion." *Philosophy and Public Affairs* 10 (Winter 1981): 18-26.

Notes

1. Joel Feinberg, *The Problem of Abortion* (Belmont, Calif.: Wadsworth, 1984), 1.
2. Kristen Luker, "Abortion and the Meaning of Life," *Abortion: Understanding Differences*. Eds. Sidney Callahan and Daniel Callahan (New York and London: Plenum Press, 1984), 45.
3. Rem Edwards and Glen Graber, *Bioethics* (Harcourt Brace Jovanovich, 1988), 530-531. They include in their section on abortion an important article on fetal development by Andre Hellegers entitled "Fetal Development," (543-548). It is reprinted from *Theological Studies* 31: 1 (March 1970): 3-9.
4. Thomas Szasz, "The Ethics of Abortion," *Humanist* 26 (1966): 148.
5. Edward Langerak, "Abortion: Listening to the Middle," *The Hastings Center Report* 9 (1979): 24-29.
6. Jane English, "Abortion and the Concept of the Person," *Canadian Journal of Philosophy* 5 (October, 1975): 233-243.
7. This is a slight modification of the list presented in Rem Edwards and Glen Graber, *Bioethics*, 530.
8. See Michael Tooley, *Abortion and Infanticide* (New York: Oxford University Press, 1983).
9. John Finnis, "The Rights and Wrongs of Abortion," *Philosophy and Public Affairs* 2:2 (1973): 117-145.
10. See Sidney Callahan, "Value Choices in Abortion," *Abortion: Understanding Differences* (New York and London: Plenum Press, 1984), 285-301.
11. See Sandra Harding, "Reflections on Abortion, Values, and the Family," and Mary Mahowald, "Abortion and Equality," in *Abortion: Understanding Differences*, Sidney Callahan and Daniel Callahan, eds. (New York and London: Plenum Press, 1984): 203-224 and 177-196. For a feminist theological approach, see Beverly Wildung Harrison, *Our Right to Choose: Toward a New Ethic of Abortion* (Boston: Beacon Press, 1983).
12. Sandra Harding, "Beneath the Surface of the Abortion Debate," 205-206.

Chapter Three

The Positions of Religious Denominations

The fact that the abortion debate has persisted for so long and that positions have been held with such intensity is due in large part to religious belief. The role of religion has been to provide a world view and an understanding of the person and community within that world. Important principles such as the sanctity of life or the necessity of following one's conscience are grounded within a religious tradition. The calculation of consequences will depend largely upon what the religious denomination holds as morally good. Authority is given to a religious position because it is seen as being revealed by God through sacred texts, through recognized interpreters, or through reason and experience aided by faith. Thus, there are deeply rooted bases for positions on abortion, and believers are not easily persuaded differently.

The religious traditions offer a number of positions. Differences can be found among the traditions and even within a particular tradition itself. Individual members may hold dissenting views from the mainline teaching and practice. Some denominations do not have any official statements whereas others have clearly articulated and carefully argued positions.[1]

1. THE RANGE OF POSITIONS WITHIN THE CHRISTIAN TRADITION[2]

The responses received express a variety of positions. Some regard abortion as the taking of a human life and, therefore, equivalent to murder. Some consider the practice of abortion as destructive of the moral consciousness and character of the people of any nation. Other views maintain: that the decision for an abortion always has a tragic dimension but calls for compassion if the right to abortion has been exercised; that the decision for abortion should be made between the woman and her doctor based on her moral and religious insights into life; that abortion can be a responsible moral choice; that abortion may be required to affirm and protect the mother's life and denial of the right to abortion in such situations deprives the person of her fundamental right of human freedom. Reasons to justify abortion may be limited to situations necessary to save the mother's life. They are also advanced for situations when the life or health of the mother is threatened, in cases of rape and incest, for socioeconomic reasons and for contraceptive purposes in certain circumstances. Some positions hold the life of the mother and the life of the fetus to be of equal worth. Yet the view that the mother's life is of greater importance is also put forward.

A particular stance is usually supported with some scriptural and theological arguments. The Bible is cited as an authority for a number of positions. For instance, the Pentecostal Assemblies of Canada interpret Scripture in the following way:

> God is the Creator and source of first human life: Genesis 2:7;
> God participates in the development of the individual before birth: Job 18:8.9; Psalm 139:16;
> God's love for the child begins in the mother's womb: Jeremiah 1:5; Luke 1:5-7; and Galatians 1:15;
> We have been given the privilege of being co-creators with God: Genesis 1: 27, 28; 46:26; Hebrews 7:10;
> The process of ensoulment begins with all the potential of emotions, intellect and will at the highest level, as well as the capacity to know and worship God, from the earliest stages of development within the womb. There is also, as an intrinsic part of the process, the capacity for and bent towards sin: Romans 5:12; 1 Corinthians 15:22; Ephesians 2:3.
> The sense of continuity and personal identity endures throughout the states of life from conception to adulthood: Psalm 51; Psalm 139.

The Missouri Synod of the Lutheran Church calls Christians to oppose abortion based on the following use of Scripture:

To hold firmly to the clear Biblical truths that
(a) the living but unborn are persons in the sight of God from the times of conception: Job 10:9-11; Psalm 51:5; 129: 13-17; Jeremiah 1:5; Luke 1:41-44;
(b) as persons the unborn stand under the full protection of God's own prohibition against murder: Genesis 9:6; Exodus 20: 13; Numbers 35:33: Acts 7:19: 1 John 3:15...

A brief look at the statements from the denominations reveals that Scripture is employed in various ways in order to provide a basis for and support of a particular position. Some statements have no Scriptural references at all.

The theological themes which appear in the statements are: God as Creator of life, sanctity of life, stewardship, personal and social conscience, responsible and conscientious decision-making, covenant demands, compassion and forgiveness. These themes are stated in the documents, but are not normally developed in depth.

It is usual for the statements on abortion to include a number of recommendations for social action and to name those who should carry out this action. These recommendations may call upon the members of the denomination, the wider community and the government to take every measure necessary to lessen the need for abortion, to lobby governments to pass laws either for easier access or for more restrictive access or the total prohibition of abortion. Other directives look to provide pregnancy counselling, to help place newborns in adoptive homes, to create accessible housing and employment and to find more effective means of contraception, to name a few.

2. STATEMENTS FROM RELIGIOUS DENOMINATIONS: UNITED STATES AND CANADA

UNITED STATES

American Baptist Churches[3]

RESOLUTION CONCERNING ABORTION AND MINISTRY IN THE LOCAL CHURCH

The General Board of American Baptist Churches in the U.S.A. has solicited and received significant response through hearings, letters, and questionnaires from individuals and congregations across the country. The response indicates that American Baptists believe that ministry to persons in situations of crisis pregnancy and abortion is a concern that primarily affects the local churches and therefore the topic needs to be addressed at that level. The General Board concurs with this and calls upon local churches to continue studying these issues, prayerfully seeking, under the guidance of the Holy Spirit, to come to a position that will direct them in ministry. The role of the General Board in this matter is not to speak for churches but to assist them in carrying out ministry and advocacy according to their convictions. Therefore, as a reflection of American Baptist thought, this resolution is offered to assist our churches.

As American Baptists, members of a covenant community of believers in Jesus Christ, we acknowledge life as a sacred and gracious gift of God. We affirm that God is the Creator of all life, that human beings are created in the image of God, and that Christ is Lord of life. Recognizing this gift of life, we find ourselves struggling with the painful and difficult issue of abortion. Genuine diversity of opinion threatens the unity of our fellowship, but the nature of covenant demands mutual love and respect. Together we must seek the mind of Christ.

As American Baptists we oppose abortion,
>   as a means of avoiding responsibility for conception,
>   as a primary means of birth control,
>   without regard for the far-reaching consequences of the act.

We denounce irresponsible sexual behavior and acts of sexual violence that contribute to the large number of abortions each year.

We grieve with all who struggle with the difficult circumstances that lead them to consider abortion. Recognizing that each person is ultimately responsible to God, we encourage women and men in these circumstances to seek spiritual counsel as they prayerfully and conscientiously consider their decision.

We condemn violence and harassment directed against abortion clinics, their staff and clients, as well as sanctions and discrimination against medical professionals whose consciences prevent them from being involved in abortions.

We acknowledge the diversity of deeply held convictions within our fellowship even as we seek to interpret the Scriptures under the guidance of the Holy Spirit. Many American Baptists believe that, biblically, human life begins at conception, that abortion is immoral and a destruction of a human being created in God's image (Job 31:15; Psalm 139:13-16; Jeremiah 1:5; Luke 1:44; Proverbs 31:8-9; Galatians 1:15). Many others believe that while abortion is a regrettable reality, it can be a morally acceptable action and they choose to act on the biblical principles of compassion and justice (John 8:1-11; Exodus 21:22-25; Matthew 7:1-5; James 2:2-13) and freedom of will (John 16:13; Romans 14:4-5, 10-13). Many gradations of opinion between these basic positions have been expressed within our fellowship.

We also recognize that we are divided as to the proper witness of the church to the state regarding abortion. Many of our membership seek legal safeguards to protect unborn life. Many others advocate for and support family planning legislation, including legalized abortion as in the best interest of women in particular and society in general. Again, we have many points of view between these two positions. Consequently, we acknowledge the freedom of each individual to advocate for a public policy on abortion that reflects his or her beliefs.

Respecting our varied perspectives, let us affirm our unity in the ministry of Christ (Colossians 3:12-17):

Praying for openness and sensitivity to the leading of the Holy Spirit within our family,

Covenanting to address both the causes and effects of abortion at the personal and social levels.

WE CALL UPON

American Baptist Congregations

To challenge members to live in a way that models responsible sexuality in accordance with biblical teaching,

To expend efforts and funds for teaching responsible sexuality,

To provide opportunities for intergenerational dialogue on responsible sexuality and Christian life,

To provide relevant ministries to adolescents and parents of adolescents in and outside the church.

Pastors and Leaders

To prepare themselves to minister compassionately and skilfully to women and men facing problem pregnancies, whatever their final decisions.

American Baptist Regions

To provide leadership and support for appropriate programs and ministries to aid the local churches in these tasks.

Seminaries and Institutions of Higher Education

To provide courses that will enrich the theological understanding and counselling skills of American Baptist leaders so that they will be able to assist persons facing decisions regarding responsible sexuality and abortion.

National Program Boards

To assist churches by production of a new study packet on abortion which could be helpful to any church's ministry regardless of its position on this subject.

To prepare, identify and make available other appropriate materials relating to responsible sexuality at all age levels.

WE ENCOURAGE CONGREGATIONS AND INDIVIDUAL MEMBERS

To engage in meaningful dialogue on abortion with openness and Christian compassion,

To initiate and/or become involved in creative community ministries in their communities that provide alternatives to. abortion for women with problem pregnancies and for their loved ones,

To provide appropriate financial and emotional support for those women who carry their pregnancies to term and further to maintain contact and provide loving community for them after birth,

To acknowledge that men are equally responsible for the creation of problem pregnancies and to help them recognize their responsibility for the social, medical, moral and financial consequences of their behavior,

To minister with love and spiritual counsel to those who choose to terminate their pregnancies,

To be actively involved in caring for children who are potentially available for adoption, including those with special needs, and to assist agencies in order to facilitate placement for them, and

To participate in organizations addressing abortion issues in ways that are consistent with their beliefs, and witness to the reconciling love of God.

BEYOND OUR OWN HOUSEHOLD OF FAITH, WE CALL UPON:

Government, industries and foundations to support the research and development of safe, reliable, affordable and culturally appropriate methods of contraception for both men and women worldwide.

Our government institutions to continue to pursue the goals of economic justice, social equality, and political empowerment without which the painful human dilemmas now being faced will continue without relief. We are concerned that many women receiving abortions are themselves adolescents who are often economically disadvantaged.

Public media (television, cinema, audio and print) to stop the depiction of sex outside of marriage as normal and desirable, the portrayal of women, men and children as sex objects and the elevation of sex as the source of all happiness. We particularly oppose print and cinematic pornography.

We acknowledge that we often lack compassion, insight and the necessary commitment needed to serve our Christian community and the wider society adequately. We affirm our commitment to continue to counsel and uphold one another, to maintain fellowship with those whose opinions differ from ours and to extend the compassion of Christ to all.

Adopted by the General Board of the American Baptist Churches - June 1988

    161 For, 9 Against, 2 Abstentions.

(General Board Reference #800.5:12/87)

The General Council of the Assemblies of God[4]

(Resolution 9)
ABORTION -- PRO-LIFE CONDUCT OF MINISTERS
(As Adopted by the General Council in session, August 12, 1989)

WHEREAS, The 1984 General Council adopted a Sanctity of Human Life resolution committing the Assemblies of God to a strong pro-life scriptural stance on the question of abortion; and

WHEREAS, The General Presbytery has issued an excellent position paper, "A Biblical Perspective on Abortion"; and

WHEREAS, Since these documents were approved a new development has taken place in the pro-life movement against abortion in the form of nonviolent and peaceful acts to prevent the killing of the unborn; and

WHEREAS, Ministers of our Fellowship are looking to the General Council for counsel regarding their participation in these nonviolent and peaceful acts; therefore be it

RESOLVED, That the General Council reaffirms its strong, pro-life biblical stance on the subject of abortion, and approves participation in the pro-life movement by all scriptural means and disapproves all unscriptural acts by its ministers; and leaves to the discretion of individual ministers the extent to which they may participate in non-violent and peaceful acts of intervention to prevent the killing of the unborn.

1985 General Council

SANCTITY OF HUMAN LIFE

WHEREAS, Abortion is in the forefront of spiritual and ethical problems confronting the church and American society today; and

WHEREAS, the Scriptures must provide the basis for an answer to this issue which is being nurtured in a general climate of moral relativism and sexual permissiveness; and

WHEREAS, The Bible recognizes that a woman is with child even in the first stages of pregnancy (Luke 1:31, 36); and

WHEREAS, The Bible recognizes that God is active in the creative process of forming new life (Job 31:15, Isaiah 44:24, Jeremiah 1:5, Psalm 139:13-16); and

WHEREAS, the Bible recognizes that God has plans for the unborn child (Jeremiah 1:15, Luke 11:17); and

WHEREAS, The Bible recognizes that God is sovereign in all things, including the quality of life of the unborn child (Exodus 4:11); therefore, be it

RESOLVED, That the Assemblies of God affirms its opposition to abortion; and be it further

RESOLVED, That we pray earnestly for a spiritual awakening to the end that our nation shall be delivered from the degrading national moral standards and consequently of laws that permit evils such as abortion; and be it further

RESOLVED, That we shall help provide for Biblical moral resolution in all possible forums in opposition to the standards of the church being influenced by an atheistic, humanist philosophy; and be it further

RESOLVED, That we shall oppose legislation which is designed to destroy the moral fibre of society; and encourage and support legislation designed to strengthen the sanctity of human life; and be it further

RESOLVED, That we counsel those with unwanted pregnancies concerning the alternative of adoption; and be it further

RESOLVED, That we compassionately minister to those who suffer overwhelming remorse and guilt from having had abortions or those who have participated in producing abortions.

A BIBLICAL PERSPECTIVE ON ABORTION
Adopted by General Council, August 6, 1985

Just a few years ago the term "abortion" in law implied criminality in producing miscarriage. An abortionist was one who practiced producing criminal abortions.

Today when the word "abortion" is used, it almost immediately brings to mind the legal practice of destroying unborn children. Even though abortion on demand has been legalized, it is still immoral and sinful.

Change of Medical Definitions

Proabortionists have done everything in their power to promote abortion on demand. They have adopted expressions by which they describe the unborn child and the abortion process to try to make the practice respectable.

Dr. C. Everett Koop is surgeon-general of the United States. When he was surgeon-in-chief of the Children's Hospital of Pennsylvania and professor of pediatrics and pediatric surgery at the School of Medicine, the University of Pennsylvania, he wrote: "We who as a people always knew that abortion was the killing of an unborn baby were brainwashed to believe that the destruction of the ‹products of conception› or the destruction of a ‹fetus› is not the same thing as killing an unborn baby. Traditional medical definitions were deliberately changed in order to do away with our moral repugnance toward abortion."[5]

Proabortionists refer to the abortion process as "interrupting" rather than terminating a pregnancy. They talk of "evacuating the contents of the uterus" or of removing "postconceptive fertility content." They refer to the unborn baby as "potential human life" when it is obvious the organism is human and alive before birth. Human life is potential only before the male sperm and female ovum join to form a new living human being.

Christians must not be deceived by inaccurate, deceptive medical terminology. They must be guided by the principles and precepts of Scripture.

What the Bible Says About the Unborn Child

While some have tried to justify abortions before the unborn child can sustain life outside the womb, the Bible does not make such a distinction in the life process. The term viable fetus may properly indicate, as a scientific fact, the time when life can be sustained outside the womb; but it does not indicate that life as a person fails to exist prior to that. Those who may be tempted to accept abortion as some early stage just because it is declared legal would find it helpful to consider several Biblical truths.

1.   The Bible recognizes that a woman is "with child" even in the first stages of pregnancy.

When the virgin Mary was chosen to be the mother of Jesus, this announcement was made to her: "Thou shalt conceive in thy womb, and bring forth a son" (Luke 1:31). The angel then informed Mary that her cousin Elizabeth was pregnant. The words used were: "She hath also conceived a son in her old age" (Luke 1:36). Scripture makes it clear that in the prenatal phase John the Baptist was recognized as a son even though it was 3 months before the time of delivery.

In Luke 1:41, 44 John before birth is recognized as a "babe." This translates a Greek word used of children both before and after birth (Acts 7:19). The words "she hath also conceived a son" indicate Jesus was recognized as a son though Mary's pregnancy was in the earliest stages.

The Bible always recognizes the prenatal phase of life as that of a child and not as a meaningless product of conception. There is no distinction made in the value of life between the born and unborn child.

Even when pregnancy in Bible times was due to an illicit relationship, the quality of that life was not questioned. The daughters of Lot were pregnant by incest (Genesis 19:36), but this was not considered a condition that called for abortion. Bathsheba recognized she was pregnant by adultery (2 Samuel 11:5), but this was not viewed as being encumbered with a mere appendage of matter to be removed from the mother's womb.

John Calvin made a very significant observation concerning abortion in commenting on Exodus 21:22, 23: "The fetus, though enclosed in the womb of his mother, is already a human being, and it is a monstrous crime to rob it of life which it has not yet begun to enjoy. If it seems more horrible to kill a man in his own house than in a field, because a man's house is his place of most secure refuge, it ought surely to be deemed more atrocious to destroy a fetus in the womb before it has come to light."[6]

2.   The Bible recognizes that God is active in the creative process of forming new life. To abort a pregnancy is to abort the work God is doing.

Concerning Leah, the wife of Jacob, Scripture indicates, "When the Lord saw that Leah was unloved, He opened her womb. ... So Leah conceived and bore a son" (Genesis 29:31, 32 NKJV).

When Job compared himself to his servants, he asked, "Did not He who made me in the womb make them? Did not the same One fashion us in the womb?" (Job 31:15, NKJV).

In pointing out God's impartiality Job said: "Yet He is not partial to princes, nor does He regard the rich more than the poor, for they are all the work of His hands" (Job 34:19, NKJV).

Isaiah speaking for God wrote: "Thus says the Lord who made you and formed you from the womb, who will help you: ‹Fear not, O Jacob My servant›" (Isaiah 44:2, NKJV). And again, "Thus says the Lord, your Redeemer, and He who formed you from the womb: ‹I am the Lord, who makes all things›" (V.24).

David summed it up well when he wrote: "For you created my inmost being; you knit me together in my mother's womb. I praise you because I am fearfully and wonderfully made; your works are wonderful, I know that full well. My frame was not hidden from you when I was made in the secret place. When I was woven together in the depths of the earth, your eyes saw my unformed body. All the days ordained for me were written in your book before one of them came to be" (Psalm 139:13-16, NIV).

Concerning Psalm 139:13-16, Donald Shoemaker wrote: "This passage can only evoke holy caution and respect for unborn life. God is at work, and as we observe we must worship, for the place where we stand is holy ground. Such respect for the divine origin of life is not to be found among the proabortionists. Theirs is an unholy intrusion into the divine laboratory to interrupt and to destroy the handiwork of the blessed Creator! God loves the unborn. This psalm will never let us forget it."[7]

The omniscient God who knows what happens to persons after their birth also knows what happens to these persons before birth. He is creatively active in the birth process, and to terminate a pregnancy is to destroy the work of God. Abortion is evil man's defiance of the Almighty. It is an indication of the depths to which a consenting society has fallen.

3.   The Bible recognizes that God has plans for the unborn child. Only He knows the potential of this new life.

When God called Jeremiah to his prophetic ministry He indicated the origination was prenatal when He said: "Before I formed you in the womb I knew you; before you were born I sanctified you; and I ordained you a prophet to the nations" (Jeremiah 1:5, NKJV).

When Zachariah the priest was ministering at the altar of incense, an angel announced that his wife Elizabeth would give birth to a son who should be called John. Then it was revealed that God had definite plans for this child. He was to be a forerunner of Jesus (Luke 1:11-17).

To destroy the life of an unborn child is flagrantly to disregard the plans God has for that life. It robs the unborn person of the privilege of choosing to be an instrument of God's design.

4.   The Bible recognizes that God is sovereign in all things, including the quality of life of the unborn child.

When people reject God, eventually they make human life relative. Some are considered worthy of life; others are considered expendable.

A study by Dr. Leo Alexander of Harvard University, a psychiatrist at the Nuremburg trials for Nazi war criminals, showed the beginnings of the holocaust were found in the belief that some human life did not deserve to exist.

As a result of this belief they killed the unwanted, the lame, the crippled, the retarded, and eventually even disabled veterans who served Germany in World War I. From there it was just a small step to the holocaust.[8]

When people set themselves up as God to determine if a life is worth living - whether before or after birth - they are rejecting the sovereignty of the Creator of all things.

There are things finite humans cannot understand. God's ways are above man's ways. While today's medical technology makes it possible to know that less than desirable conditions sometimes exist in unborn children, it is important to remember they are still God's creations.

When Moses complained of his lack of eloquence, God said, "Who has made man's mouth? Or who makes the mute, the deaf, the seeing, or the blind? Have not I, the Lord?" (Exodus 4:11, NKJV).

When man establishes criteria for what constitutes unworthy lives, he is invariably wrong because he fails to recognize the plan and purpose of God. Who but God knows whether someone destroyed in the holocaust might not have discovered a cure for cancer. Who but God knows what blessing millions of children killed before birth might bring to improve the quality of life.

In the course of an impressive address before the House of Representatives, the following quotation was included from a person who was born as a result of a rape: "Some people disclaim their natural habitat. I always name my origin. It didn't hold me back, and neither has my color. I was born in poverty. My father raped my mother when she was 12. Now they've named a park for me in Chester, Pennsylvania."[9]

The quotation was from Ethel Waters who ministered to millions through the medium of gospel song. Had abortion been legal at that time, quite possibly someone would have suggested it. If this had happened, the world would have been much poorer. The work of evangelism would have been deprived of a great gospel singer.

When Pregnancy Threatens the Life of the Mother

In earlier years mothers sometimes died as a result of pregnancy. Today because of advances in medical science, this condition rarely occurs. Should such an isolated situation develop, and if after prayer for healing God in His wisdom does not miraculously intervene, the individuals involved would need to look to God for further guidance. The diagnosis of attending prolife physicians will be helpful in arriving at the proper conclusion.

God's Attitude Toward Killing Innocent Persons

God's Word is very explicit concerning the taking of innocent human life. "You shall not murder" (Exodus 20:13, NKJV) is not only one of the Ten Commandments, but also a dictate which reoccurs throughout Scripture.

God instructed Moses to set a law before the children of Israel which brings the sanctity of life of unborn children into focus. "If men strive, and hurt a woman with child, so that her fruit depart from her, and yet no mischief follow: he shall be surely punished, according as the woman's husband will lay upon him; and he shall pay as the judges determine. And if any mischief follow, then thou shalt give life for life, eye for eye, tooth for tooth, hand for hand, foot for foot" (Exodus 21:22-24).

Dr. Stanley M. Horton, professor of Old Testament and Hebrew at the Assemblies of God Theological Seminary, stated the opinion of many when he wrote the following concerning Exodus 21:22-24: "The situation here is of two men who are fighting as a result of a quarrel. The same Hebrew verb is used in Exodus 2:13 of the two men Moses saw fighting. Somehow as they are fighting, they hit a pregnant woman, and her child ‹comes out,› that is, is born prematurely. If there is no ‹mischief,› no ‹mortal accident,› to the child or the mother, then the man who struck the woman must pay a fine as determined by her husband and ratified by the judges. But if there is ‹mortal accident› causing death of the child or the mother, then the law of a ‹life for a life› takes over.

"‹Her fruit› is the Hebrew *yeladeha*, translated ‹her children› in this same chapter (v. 4), as well as everywhere else it occurs in the Old Testament. The plural is used here because it would not be known in advance whether more than one child was in the womb.

"‹Mischief,› Hebrew *ason*, is used in Genesis 42:4 where Jacob is afraid something might happen to Benjamin (as he thought had happened to Joseph), that is, death. (See also 42:38; 44:29)

"It is clear from this that the fetus is recognized as a child and has the same rights as older children."

God's attitude toward the killing of innocents is clear. Except in capital punishment decreed through the judicial process (Numbers 35:12) or protection of property at night probably involving self-defense (Exodus 22:2), no one is guiltless who takes the life of another.

Concerned Christians and the Abortion Issue

When the evil of abortion on demand for convenience is considered, it is obvious concerned Christians must act as they would in the case of other evils of commensurate magnitude. There are steps Christians can take to restrain and hopefully reverse immoral trends.

1.   Christians should pray earnestly for divine intervention in the affairs of men. This would eliminate degrading national moral standards and consequently the laws that permit evils such as abortion on demand for convenience.

The power of a spiritual awakening can be seen in history. France and England both had revolutions in the 18th century. France had a political revolution which resulted in untold suffering and bloodshed. England had an industrial revolution. The difference between the two is that England enjoyed a spiritual awakening. It elevated the quality of life in the land, possibly averting a violent revolution such as France experienced.

A spiritual awakening in our country could have a salutary influence on today's moral climate. Not only would the sanctity of human life be honored, but moral standards in general would be lifted.

2.   Concerned Christians should help provide for Biblical moral instruction in all possible forums. Instead of the standards of the church being influenced by humanistic and even atheistic philosophies, a church thoroughly rooted in the eternal truths of God's Word can lift the standards of society. When people accept the absolutes of

Scripture rather than the relative values arising from speculative human reasoning, all levels of living will be greatly improved.

When disregard of Biblical standards of righteousness is recognized as sin, when refusal to acknowledge the sovereignty of God is recognized as sin, when rejection of Jesus' salvation and lordship is recognized as sin, the condition of society will be vastly improved. Then problems such as abortion will be greatly reduced.

Biblical instruction must be given its proper emphasis both in the church and the home. Believers must be so thoroughly rooted in Scripture that they can give a reason for convictions based on God's Word.

3.   Concerned Christians should counsel those with unwanted pregnancies about the alternative of adoption. They should support Christian agencies. They should lovingly assist in every way possible those wishing to give their children up for adoption. Such parents find themselves in a very confusing role.

4.   Concerned Christians should actively support prolife legislation and oppose any legislation designed to destroy the moral fibre of society. As citizens of our country they should express their opinions to governmental representatives. They should become influential in determining the kind of people who will be placed in public office. They should encourage committed Christians to seek positions of influence.

5.   Concerned Christians should compassionately minister to those who suffer overwhelming remorse and guilt from having had, or having participated in producing, abortions. These people need to be reminded that when they confess their sin to God, He forgives and cleanses. They need to be reminded that Jesus said, "Him that cometh to me I will in no wise cast out" (John 6:37). They need the prayerful, moral support of those who are strong in the Lord.

The Church of Jesus Christ of Latter-Day Saints[10]

ABORTION

Abortion is one of the most revolting and sinful practices of this day. Members must not submit to, be party to, or perform an abortion.

The only exceptions are when --

1. Pregnancy has resulted from incest or rape;

2. The life or health of the woman is in jeopardy in the opinion of competent medical authority; or

3. The fetus is known, by competent medical authority, to have severe defects that will not allow the baby to survive beyond birth.

Even in these cases the couple should consider an abortion only after consulting with each other and their bishop and receiving divine confirmation through prayer.

Church members who encourage, perform, or submit to an abortion are subject to Church discipline as appropriate. Priesthood leaders dealing with abortions should remember the word of the Lord, "Thou shalt not steal: neither commit adultery, nor kill, nor do anything like unto it" (D & C 59:6).

As far as has been revealed, a person may repent and be forgiven for the sin of abortion.

The Episcopal Church Center[11]

FINAL TEXT OF RESOLUTION:
(C047a)

Resolved, the House of Deputies concurring, That the 69th General Convention adopt the following statement on childbirth and abortion:

All human life is sacred. Hence, it is sacred from its inception until death. The Church takes seriously its obligation to help form the consciences of its members concerning this sacredness. Human life, therefore, should be initiated only advisedly and in full accord with this understanding of the power to conceive and give birth which is bestowed by God.

It is the responsibility of our congregations to assist their members in becoming informed concerning the spiritual, physiological and psychological aspects of sex and sexuality.

The Book of Common Prayer affirms that "the birth of a child is a joyous and solemn occasion in the life of a family. It is also an occasion for rejoicing in the Christian community" (440). As Christians we also affirm responsible family planning.

We regard all abortion as having a tragic dimension, calling for the concern and compassion of all the Christian community.

While we acknowledge that in this country it is the legal right to every woman to have a medically safe abortion, as Christians we believe strongly that if this right is exercised, it should be used only in extreme situations. We emphatically oppose abortion as a means of birth control, family planning, sex selection, or any reason of mere convenience.

In those cases where an abortion is being considered, members of this Church are urged to seek the dictates of their consciences in prayer, to seek the advice and counsel of members of the Christian community and where appropriate the sacramental life of this Church.

Whenever members of this Church are consulted with regard to a problem pregnancy, they are to explore, with grave seriousness, with the person or persons seeking advice and counsel, as alternatives to abortion, other positive courses of action, including, but not limited to, the following possibilities: the parents raising the child; another family member raising the child; making the child available for adoption.

It is the responsibility of members of this Church, especially the clergy, to become aware of local agencies and resources which will assist those faced with problem pregnancies.

We believe that legislation concerning abortions will not address the root of the problem. We therefore express our deep conviction that any proposed legislation on the part of national or state governments regarding abortions must take special care to see that individual conscience is respected, and that the responsibility of individuals to reach informed decisions in this matter is acknowledged and honored.

FINAL TEXT OF RESOLUTION:
(D124)

Resolved, the House of Deputies concurring, That this 69th General Convention of the Episcopal Church condemn all actions of violence against abortion clinics; and be it further

Resolved, That this Convention deplore any acts of violence against those persons seeking the services available at such clinics.

Greek Orthodox Archdiocese of North and South America[12]

A STATEMENT ON ABORTION

The most divine gift bestowed by God upon mankind is the gift of life itself, and throughout the centuries the sacredness of human life has been undisputed by responsible men and women of all persuasions.

We are currently confronted with a controversy surrounding the liberalization of abortion statutes stemming from the initiative of various groups and individuals whose actions, although predicated upon sincere and humanitarian motives, are nevertheless in conflict with divine law. Their position evolves from the general contention that the termination of unborn human life is justifiable when medical opinion believes there is substantial risk that continuance of the pregnancy would impair the physical or mental health of the mother, or that the child would be born with grave physical or mental defects, or if the pregnancy resulted from rape or incest.

It has been the position of the Orthodox Church over the centuries that the taking of unborn life is morally wrong. This is based upon divine law which is the most difficult law for man to comprehend for it transcends the boundaries of human frailty due to its source of divine authority. No law is perfect, and man in his diverse interpretations of the law is continually reminded of his human limitations. Even in such basic law as "Thou Shalt Not Kill": we can take no pride in its exceptions which justify war and self-defense, for they serve only to becloud our unceasing efforts toward shaping man in the image of God. This same principle of exception also extends to the unborn child. When the unborn child places the life of its mother in jeopardy, then and only then can this life be sacrificed for the welfare of its mother. To move beyond this exception would be transgressing man's duty in the protection of human life as understood and interpreted by the Orthodox Church.

We are profoundly aware that the discipline of divine law sometimes creates inequities that are difficult for human comprehension to accept, but the eternal values of divine law were not created for a man, but for mankind.

The solution to our vexing problem of an increasing need for abortion does not lie in reinterpreting the law to meet the needs of our present-day morality, but rather challenges us to find a more effective eternal protector of human life.

The Lutheran Church[13]

1979 CONVENTION PROCEEDINGS

To State Position on Abortion
Resolution 3-02A

Overtures 3-20A - 3-23 (CW, 97-99)

WHEREAS, The Lutheran Church - Missouri Synod throughout its history has opposed abortion and since 1971 has spoken in convention to condemn "wilful abortion as contrary to the will of God"; and

WHEREAS, We as members of Christian congregations have the obligation to protest this heinous crime against the will of God legally sanctioned in the United States and other lands; and

WHEREAS, The practice of abortion, its promotion, and legal acceptance are destructive of the moral consciousness and character of the people of any nation; therefore be it

RESOLVED, That The Lutheran Church - Missouri Synod in convention urgently call upon Christians -

1. To hold firmly to the clear Biblical truths that (a) the living but unborn are persons in the sight of God from the time of conception (Job 10:9-11); Ps. 51:5; 129:13-17; Jer. 1:5; Luke 1:41-44); (b) as persons the unborn stand under the full protection of God's own prohibition against murder (Gen. 9:6; Ex. 20:13; Num. 35:33; Acts 7:19, 1 John 3:15); and (c) since abortion takes a human life, abortion is not a moral option, except as a tragically unavoidable byproduct of medical procedures necessary to prevent the death of another human being, viz., the mother; and

2. To speak and act as responsible citizens on behalf of the living but unborn in the civic and political arena to secure for these defenseless persons due protection under the law; and

3.   To offer as an alternative to abortion supportive understanding, compassion, and help to the expectant parent(s) and family, and to foster concern for unwanted babies, encouraging Lutheran agencies and families to open hearts and homes to their need for life in a family; and be it further

RESOLVED, That the Synod earnestly encourage its pastors, teachers, officers, and boards -

1.   To warn publicly and privately (Prov. 31:8-9) against the sin of abortion;

2.   To instruct the community of God that abortion is not in the realm of Christian liberty, private choice, personal opinion, or political preference;

3.   To nurture a deep reverence and gratitude for God's gracious gift of human life;

4.   To oppose in a responsible way attitudes and policies in congregations, schools, hospitals, Lutheran social service agencies, and other institutions within their sphere of influence and work which suggest that abortion is a matter of personal choice;

5.   To support the efforts of responsible pro-life groups in their communities, e.g., "Lutherans for Life" (CTCR Report, CW, 74);

6.   To promote clear instruction of Christian morality in homes, schools, and churches of the Synod, showing the blessings and safeguards inherent in God's will for sexual chastity before marriage and faithfulness in marriage;

7.   To teach within our Lutheran schools and churches the biological, social, and parental functions of childbearing; and

8.   To support the efforts to secure the human life amendment to the United States Constitution.

ACTION: Adopted as amended (3).

(Three amendments were approved: the addition of the reference to Proverbs in Point 1 of the second resolve, and Points 7 and 8. The word "Lutheran" was inserted in Point

7 by common consent. In Session 7 the convention changed the order of words as given above in Point 7. An amendment referring to rape at the end of Point 1 of the first resolve was declined.)

9th All American Council of the Orthodox Church in America[14]

GENERAL STATEMENT

WHEREAS the Orthodox Church in America has consistently spoken out in defence of the sanctity of life, and has done so in connection with contemporary threats to the life of the unborn, the handicapped, the infirm, and the elderly; and

WHEREAS abortion in all cases has been condemned by the Orthodox Church in America unequivocally on the basis of Orthodox theology, which faithfully reflects for today nearly two thousand years of Christian doctrine and ethical teaching; and

WHEREAS, before the end of this century, "do-it-yourself" abortion will more than likely be commonplace (the RU 486 pill), and legislation will have little effect on whether or not a woman brings her child to term;

BE IT THEREFORE RESOLVED THAT the 9th All-American Council of the Orthodox Church in America strongly reaffirms the Orthodox Church's opposition to abortion in all cases, and that it does so on theological and moral grounds; commends the efforts of Orthodox bishops, clergy, and laity to bear witness to the sanctity of life in the public arena, especially noting in this connection the work and witness of Orthodox Christians for Life; and commits the Orthodox Church in America to continued witness on behalf of the God-given sanctity of life;

BE IT FURTHER RESOLVED THAT the Orthodox Church in America recognizes that opposition to and condemnation of abortion in all cases, except to save the life of the mother, is not enough, and that the Orthodox Church and Orthodox Christians have a moral obligation to work for the creation and maintenance of Orthodox adoption agencies and for the facilitation of adoption procedures for families to consider adopting a homeless or unwanted or disabled infant, regardless of the child's racial or ethnic background in the realization that the Church as a whole and the parish community in particular is called to give active material and spiritual support to those who accept the responsibility of adoption;

BE IT FURTHER RESOLVED THAT this Council affirms and supports the work of the Orthodox Christian Adoption Referral Service and encourages parishes and members of the Orthodox Church in America to give their material and moral support to this organization;

FINALLY, BE IT FURTHER RESOLVED THAT this Council recognizes and affirms spiritual, pastoral and educational efforts towards moral persuasion, directed to the father as much as to the mother, to help stem the present hemorrhaging of unborn and unwanted human persons and lives.

Resolution on Sanctity of Life Sunday:

WHEREAS the Orthodox Church in America has always respected the right to life of all men and women from conception to the time of natural death, and

WHEREAS the Supreme Court of the United States of America has allowed legalized abortion since January 22, 1973, leading to the deaths of 1,500,000 unborn children each year,

WE HEREBY PROCLAIM the Sunday in January falling on or before January 22 each year to be called Sanctity of Life Sunday in all churches of the Orthodox Church in America, and that on this Sunday a letter from our primate be read in all churches, and special petitions be taken at Liturgy, proclaiming our respect as a Church, for all human life.

Presbyterian Church (USA)

From
COVENANT AND CREATION:
THEOLOGICAL REFLECTIONS ON CONTRACEPTION AND ABORTION (1983).
The PC (USA)'s most recent policy statement.[15]

"Biblical faith depicts persons as stewards of life, heirs who are responsible for the care of God's world. This responsibility leads persons of faith not only to an exploration of all of creation but also to efforts that maintain order, secure justice, and improve the quality of human life. Because human life, in the biblical sense, is much more than the perpetuation of physical existence, people of faith should commit themselves to improving its quality spiritually, educationally, and culturally as well as medically. This commitment will often necessitate difficult moral choices in the midst of conflicting values." (58)

"...Bearing children is a process of covenant-initiation that calls for courage, love, patience, and strength. In addition to these gifts of the Spirit, parent-child covenants also require the economic as well as the spiritual resources appropriate to the nurture of a human life. The magnitude of the commitment to be a human parent cannot be overestimated and should not be understated...

Abortion can therefore be considered a responsible choice within a Christian ethical framework when serious genetic problems arise or when the resources are not adequate to care for a child appropriately. Elective abortion, when responsibly used, is intervention in the process of pregnancy precisely because of the seriousness with which one regards the covenantal responsibility of parenting.

Biblical faith emphasizes the need for personal moral choice and holds that persons stand ultimately accountable to God for their moral choices. The freedom to do what one judges most appropriate in an abortion decision is qualified by the fact that the purpose of such decision is the responsible exercise of stewardship. Even in the face of the most difficult decisions, of which abortion is surely one, the gospel assures us that we can trust in God's spirit to guide us to our decision."(59)

United Church of Christ[16]

FREEDOM OF CHOICE CONCERNING ABORTION

We, the delegates of the 13th General Synod, reaffirm the theological statements of the 8th, 9th and 11th and 12th General Synods on the matter of freedom of choice on abortion, and support the following statements:

1. The question of when life (personhood) begins is basic to the abortion debate. It is primarily a theological question, on which

denominations or religious groups must be permitted to establish and follow their own teachings;

2. Every woman must have the freedom of choice to follow her personal religious and moral convictions concerning the completion or termination of her pregnancy. The church as a caring community should provide counselling services and support for those women with both wanted and unwanted pregnancies to assist them in exploring all alternatives;

3. Abortion should not be considered a primary method of birth control. To reduce the need for abortion, the church is concerned that counselling, family planning information, and assistance be made available to all;

4. Freedom of Choice legislation must be passed at both the federal and state levels to provide the funds necessary to insure that all women, including the poor, have access to family planning assistance and safe, legal abortions performed by licensed physicians;

THEREFORE, BE IT RESOLVED that the Thirteenth General Synod of the United Church of Christ urges individual members of the local churches and the appropriate Instrumentalities of the United Church of Christ to continue efforts to guarantee a woman's freedom of choice as outlined above;

BE IT FURTHER RESOLVED, that the Thirteenth General Synod of the United Church of Christ urges individual members of the local churches, Associations, Conferences, and the appropriate Instrumentalities and agencies of the United Church of Christ to oppose actively the passage of constitutional amendments or legislation revoking this freedom of choice.

CONSERVATIVE JUDAISM[17]

The United Synagogue of America

WHEREAS, Jewish tradition cherishes the sanctity of life, even the potential of life which a pregnant woman carries within her. Under certain unfortunate circumstances, such as when the life or health of the mother are in jeopardy, Judaism sanctions, even mandates, abortion. Judaism does not, however, condone or permit abortion for contraceptive purposes; and

WHEREAS, Judaism does not believe that personhood and human rights begin with conception. The premise that personhood begins with conception is founded on a religious position which is not identical with Jewish tradition. Therefore, under special circumstances, Judaism chooses and requires abortion as an act which affirms and protects the life, well being and health of the mother. To deny a Jewish woman and her family the ability to obtain a safe, legal abortion when so mandated by Jewish tradition, is to deprive Jews of their fundamental right of religious freedom;

NOW, THEREFORE, BE IT RESOLVED that the UNITED SYNAGOGUE OF AMERICA continues to affirm its strong support for the 1973 Supreme Court decision of *Roe v. Wade.* Any weakening, limitation, or withdrawal of the *Roe v. Wade* decision is sure to produce tragic consequences. In light of the recent Supreme Court decision, we must be diligent in our efforts to safeguard and preserve the full personal and religious freedom given to the American people.

NOW, THEREFORE, BE IT FURTHER RESOLVED that the UNITED SYNAGOGUE OF AMERICA opposes any legislative attempt through constitutional amendments, the deprivation of medicaid, family services and/or other current welfare services, to weaken the force of the United States Supreme Court's decision permitting abortions. (1989 Biennial Convention)

Rabbinical Assembly

WHEREAS Jewish law recognizes a qualitative difference between the life of a fetus and established human life; and

WHEREAS abortion, though never condoned as elective birth control, is mandated by Jewish law when the pregnancy threatens the life or well-being of the mother; and

WHEREAS legislation outlawing abortion would compromise our obligation to preserve the established life, that is the life and well-being of pregnant women;

THEREFORE, BE IT RESOLVED that the Rabbinical Assembly oppose any legislation, including Constitutional amendment, aimed at outlawing abortion. (Convention Resolutions, 1985)

Women's League for Conservative Judaism

Reverence for life is the cornerstone of our Jewish heritage. Since abortion in Jewish law is primarily for the mother's physical or mental welfare, we deplore the burgeoning casual use of abortion. Abortion should be "legally available, but ethically restricted. Though the abortion of a fetus is not equivalent to taking an actual life, it does represent the destruction of potential life and must not be undertaken lightly ..."*

However, Women's League also believes that the practice of the principle of the separation of Church and State guaranteed by our Constitution has kept our nation strong and preserved full freedom for the individual. Women's League believes that transmitting religious values is the responsibility of the religious sector.

Women's League for Conservative Judaism urges its Sisterhoods to oppose any legislative attempts through Constitutional amendments, the deprivation of Medicaid, family services and/or other current welfare services, to weaken the force of the Supreme Court's decision permitting abortions.   Amended Resolution on Abortion (1982)
*from *Love and Sex: A Modern Jewish Perspective*, Dr. Robert Gordis

CANADA

Anglican Church of Canada

ABORTION IN A NEW PERSPECTIVE:
REPORT OF THE TASK FORCE ON ABORTION[18]

MORAL EDUCATION

We recommend:
1) that the church at all levels tackle with renewed commitment its own task of helping people to develop awareness of personal and social conscience; to understand what Christian faith is calling us to in the matter of abortion; to reflect more deeply on biblical understandings of human life as the gift of God, on the dignity of all persons made in the divine image for relationship with God, and on our calling to cooperate with God in the creation of a loving and just

society; and to learn how better to make ethical decisions that take seriously the insights of faith and the values in issue, so that we all are enabled to make choices we can live with in good conscience;

2) that in undertaking this task the church use the educational resources on abortion and sexuality which it has already developed within its own community;

3) and that parishes, dioceses, and national groups make available family life education programs, which can gather together the generations, and marriage programs, which can reach couples. These can provide educational events that help parents understand their children's development and improve their relationships with them. They can help young people both to understand their own maturing sexuality and to develop responsible and high ideals of human relationships, marriage, and their family. Such programs could encourage both men and women to take responsibility for their own sexuality and their God-given gift of the power to procreate, and should foster responsible attitudes towards contraception and abortion.

SOCIAL ACTION

We further recommend:

that a program of action on concrete and urgent needs which are related to the resort to abortion be undertaken by the church corporately and Anglicans individually, and that it focus on:

1) the need for adequate, rent-geared-to-income housing. Adequate, secure and affordable housing must be recognized as both a need and a right: the provision of housing is, ultimately, a public responsibility, since it is essential for survival in our northern climate. We should join others in the community in pressing for government assistance for non-profit, municipal, and co-operative housing that is affordable. Church people could support the initiatives of groups seeking to improve the housing situation, recognizing that in major cities it is now desperate.

2) ongoing lobbying in the workplace for just wages and pay equity (since women still on average earn only 66 cents to the man's dollar), as well as for expanded and adequate maternity and family benefits, and for longer parental leave when children are born or become ill. New models of work such as job sharing and flex time, which would support family life, are also needed.

3) the establishment of a guaranteed adequate annual income; in the meantime, a thorough upgrading of welfare benefits for single mothers who choose to stay at home working to raise their children; full cost of living increases to the now partially de-indexed family allowances; much higher children's benefits to low-income families; and tax reform to reduce the burden that has recently been increased for those earning lower incomes--disproportionately women. A nation which is already in the top 10 per cent of military spenders, in a world obscenely overarmed, and which has steadily rising defence budgets projected to spend $200 billion over the next 15 years, must be challenged on the feminization of poverty. Money to secure the dignity of mothers and children--indeed their survival--can and must be found by our governments.

4) the need for well-staffed, adequately paid, creatively-structured, and locally situated child care centres. Universally accessible, publicly funded child care is a necessary social service, not a welfare measure, and should provide both group care and licensed family home care.

5) the need for emotional support for single parent families. Such services as men becoming Big Brothers, or older people becoming "Adopted Grandparents" to single-parent families in their congregation or neighbourhood can be a real help.

6) the need for educational and retraining programs to keep pregnant women and new mothers in the mainstream of society.

7) an intensified national program to collect child support from fathers defaulting on court orders, so as to enforce the responsibility of fathers to contribute to meeting their children's economic needs.

8) increased programs and legislation to protect children and women from sexual abuse, domestic violence, sexual harassment, pornography, rape, and other forms of violence used against them.

9) training programs through schools, as well as churches, in non-violent conflict resolution; also the teaching of problem-solving skills to young people and to couples preparing for marriage.

10) the need, both in the church and in the school system, for better educational programs on sexuality that cover contraception. It is important for curricula to be developed and for school boards to mandate sex education specifically including the topic of birth control at the time in the early years of high school when health courses are

compulsory. According to a recent survey only half our schools offered any sexuality education and most of the curricula were optional. Therefore, church people should take responsibility for finding out what their school-boards provide and for exploring available community resources (such as Planned Parenthood, and SIECCAN, the Sex Information and Education Council of Canada). We should insist that such programs be established so that every young person is challenged to think about his or her own sexuality and to take responsibility for his or her own fertility.

11) greater development of birth planning services, through public health units and voluntary organizations such as Planned Parenthood, so that safe birth control is made more available for women, through clinics with easy access; to meet this need, pressure on governments to provide funding will be necessary.

12) comprehensive women's health centres, where the following services are provided: pre-abortion counselling, covering practical alternatives and providing assistance in obtaining housing accommodation, welfare benefits, child care and so forth, as well as access to adoption services; post-abortion counselling; support groups; contraceptive information; health care services; employment, education and retraining programs; and child care facilities.

13) the need for more funding by government of research into better methods of contraception, as well as for environmental protection from hazardous chemical wastes, pollution, and low level radiation, all known causes of fetal abnormalities.

14) Lastly, we commend to the church and community, as a matter of spiritual necessity, first, a renewed discussion of the meaning of sexuality, for all of us, as embodied persons made in the image of God, who by our natures are called to closeness, caring, and mutuality, and who should honour these longings, not reducing our sexuality to genital sex; and secondly, a renewed reflection on the wonder and awe of being alive, on the goodness and preciousness of life, on children as a blessing entrusted to our care, and on our deep need, under God, to celebrate life as good, as gift.

While addressing urgent needs for social and economic reforms, the church must not forget her primary calling to be a reconciled people, ministering the love and grace of Jesus Christ to those caught in the pain and brokenness of abortion. From one perspective, poverty and sexism are vying for the death of an unborn generation--abortion is a tragic arena in which the war between classes and sexes is being waged. In this war, how do we turn our weapons of destruction into instruments for peace? Through a genuine commitment to partnership and mutuality modelled in communities transformed by hope. Let us not lose heart as we seek together to respond with the love of Christ to the challenge of "restructuring our society" through justice, so that no woman feels she has to "restructure her womb" through emptying it.

Canadian Conference of Catholic Bishops[19]

FAITHFUL TO THE FUTURE
PASTORAL STATEMENT ON ABORTION
from the
PRESIDENT OF THE CCCB
Addressed to
CANADIAN CATHOLICS

Dear Sisters and Brothers in Christ:

The recent Supreme Court of Canada's decision, striking down the law regulating abortions, has left the unborn with no legal protection whatsoever. This lawless interval presents us with a crisis and an opportunity. It is now both necessary and possible to create new legislation which will recognize the right to life of the most voiceless and vulnerable in our society.

Since the Court's decision on January 28, there have been many public statements by individuals and groups within the church, and there will be more. My purpose in writing to you, the people of God, is to call forth the faith and hope that we all need at this time.

Our best energies are required for this challenging task which we face together. Let us draw on those energies which arise from the deep reservoir of our faith. This is a moment to recall not only what we are against but also what we are for, who we are for.

Our rejection of abortion flows from our affirmation of faith in God who is the Creator of all life. We believe in a God who is a God of beginnings--the mysterious Beginning of the world and of each human person. The first words of scripture sound out this mystery: "In the beginning God created...."

Each human is a whole new creation struggling to be born and to grow into the fullness of life. Because each one of us begins in

God from the moment of conception, every life assumes an infinite value at every other point along the way. What has begun in God is not ours to end. What has been created by God is not ours to destroy.

In the coming months, there will be those in our country who will dare to debate at what point human life begins in order to decide at what point the life of an unborn can be ended. There are those who will presume to discuss which of the unborn are fit to live and which ones fail to measure up to some arbitrary standard of performance. We will not join this debate: we will not play God. Human life begins in God at conception and struggles to bear forth the promise of this beginning from that point on.

We cannot play God but we can live our humanity more fully. We can participate with others in the creative process of transforming the world into a place where the promise of life can be more realized for all. We can play our part in helping to liberate human beings from whatever denies or diminishes the mystery of creation which has begun in each person.

This vision of our vocation as Christians reveals how shortsighted is the view that the Supreme Court decision is a step forward for women, for anyone. It is, in fact, a step backwards for all of us because it reasserts a social situation which women have so justly been struggling against--a situation in which persons are treated as objects, in which the rights of the weaker are defined by the stronger, a win-lose situation through practices such as adapting to such a social situation through practices such as abortion. We must commit ourselves to working towards a more inclusive and interdependent society, the kind of society longed for by so many women for generations. It would be a tragedy if the longings of so many were stopped short of including the right of the unborn, female and male, to belong to the human community.

For us to accept abortion would be to deny our belief in the value of human life. That life has a right to continue to the end of its natural course. Neither individuals nor governments may make an arbitrary decision to end that life at any point.

For us to accept abortion would be to deny our hope in the future and to despair of our God-given capacity to transform those mentalities and social conditions which perpetuate injustice against women, against all persons.

We dare to hold out such a hope, not because we ourselves are always a sign of its realization but because we believe in Jesus Christ in whom the power of redeeming love is stronger than the forces of discrimination and destruction.

We desire to hold out such a hope in Canada, particularly at this time. There are signs that our country is consumed by the present and is losing faith in its future. How we treat our youngest and the beginners in our midst is a significant measure of our commitment to the future.

The issue of abortion is often narrowly construed as a question of the rights of a woman versus the rights of the unborn. Yet, it would be more appropriate to say that it is an issue of whether the wants and needs of the women and men of the present will be allowed to predominate over the basic needs of the women and men of future generations. The society which accepts abortion as a solution to present problems (whether personal or social) is also a society which abuses its children, lays waste the environment, risks nuclear war and implements economic policies in which the immediate benefits to some now will be dearly paid for by many in the future.

All of us are tempted to live as if there were no tomorrow. Persons who are still in the process of being born are a real reminder to us of the fact that, for some, the future is just beginning. These beginners are holdouts for humanity, our humanity.

We hold out hope for a future in which the relationships between men and women, adults and children, can be transformed. We have reason to hope that we can move beyond the individualism of this culture to become a more inclusive human community in which each person is treated with ultimate respect. Changes in male attitudes and behaviour are central to this hope. Irresponsibility, neglect and violence towards women will not end if men do not grow in respect, solidarity and concern.

We hold out this hope, not because we have arrived but because we believe in the Holy Spirit present among us, moving us beyond where we ourselves could go.

We should all take heart in the many signs of fidelity to the future which are so obviously present in our country. Since the Supreme Court decision on January 28, there has been a surge of concern on the part of Catholics, other Christians and many people of goodwill. Many Canadians feel that their basic sense of decency has been deeply offended by the present situation of abortion on request.

We are encouraged by the on-going witness of those married couples whose sexual fidelity to each other bears the promise of new life, a promise which is received with joy. We are equally encouraged by those couples and single parents who bear the burden of difficult pregnancies or who commit themselves to raising children in difficult economic and social circumstances. The courage and care of parents who commit themselves to raising a child with disabilities is deeply inspiring for all of us. In joy or in suffering, parents call all of us to become more coresponsible in providing a community of real support for parents and children.

We are inspired by those who have worked long and hard to make pregnancy and child care more possible and desirable than abortion. Their efforts sometimes take the shape of simple personal support of involvement in various social projects and programs, such as providing prenatal counselling, accessible child care, economic assistance for parents who wish to be at home with their children, shelters for battered women, affordable housing, pay equity, affirmative action, medical research into the causes and treatment of disabilities, etc. Of course, such services are far from adequate. Our commitment to build up a society hospitable to all life must include increased efforts to expand and improve aid and care for all family members.

We are urged on by those who are educating and acting in order to transform the world into a place where life is respected at every stage. We stand with those who work for more economic and political equality, who work against capital punishment, war, poverty and euthanasia.

All of these signs of fidelity to the future give us energy to begin the task of effecting the kind of legislation which recognizes the right to life of the unborn from the moment of conception.

There is something for each one of us to do at this creative moment. In order to encourage informed and effective action, the Canadian Conference of Catholic Bishops has prepared an animation leaflet called "The Gift of Life--The Right to Life." It is to be used by study groups and individuals. It draws on the experiences of ordinary people, the wisdom of the tradition of the church, current theological thinking, the findings of modern science and the legal tradition of our country which has always enshrined principles of public morality in laws that value and protect human life at every stage. The leaflet suggests practical responses which can be effected by each Catholic.

We must share our faith in the future and our commitment to the unborn with the politicians of Canada and with all Canadians. We must be signs of that redeeming love and hope which come to us through Jesus Christ, who calls us to respect and love all our neighbours especially the least among us.

James M. Hayes
Archbishop of Halifax
President of the CCCB

April, 1988

Baptist Convention of Ontario and Quebec[20]

1984 RESOLUTIONS FOR THE CONSIDERATION OF THE ASSEMBLY.

I.   On Abortions
     Unwanted pregnancies present churches and society with a complex set of problems often demanding immediate answers. They challenge our theological convictions and demand deep moral probing into the meaning and purpose of life, the status and rights of the unborn, the rights of women and the roles of government in human affairs. As Christians, we need to affirm the sanctity of human life, born and unborn. We recognize that Christians concerned about women in crisis pregnancies sometimes find themselves on differing sides of the abortion issue. The concern of this resolution is not to polarize persons struggling with this important issue, but to provide an environment whereby a compassionate and loving ministry that cares for both mother and child can be developed and sustained.

     Therefore, WHEREAS we believe in the inherent value of human life, as expressed in the lives of both the unborn child and the mother; that human life is precious to God, our Creator; that human life begins at fertilization and that any interruption of its continuation involves destroying a unique, unrepeatable human life;

BE IT RESOLVED that this Assembly go on record as affirming:

(a) that the concept of "Abortion on demand" be repudiated;
(b) that abortion be repudiated as a vehicle for resolving socioeconomic difficulties;
(c) that abortion be repudiated, both in principle and in practice, as a population control measure;
(d) that the intentional use of abortion as a form of birth control is morally wrong and that we support the promoting of responsible planning toward the conception of new life;
(e) that the right to life is the paramount and most fundamental right of a person, the only instance where an unborn person should be deprived of life is in the rare case where an abortion would prevent the death of the mother.
(f) that our homes, churches and communities engage in an intensive and integrated program aimed at developing moral and responsible attitudes toward human sexuality and respect for the value of human life;
(g) that we urge the federal and provincial governments to enforce penalties for people who, without the required medical qualifications, perform or attempt to perform abortions, or who perform or attempt to perform abortions in places other than those approved for that purpose;
(h) that we support conscience clauses in hospital policy whereby health personnel who in conscience object to participating in abortion procedures have the option of non-participation without risk of demotion, job loss or loss of advancement opportunities; and that the policies of health and educational institutions expressly prohibit the non-acceptance of a student or the refusal to graduate a student for non-participation in abortion procedures;
(i) that in order to protect the unborn child and the woman from an ill-advised abortion and to help the woman make a responsible decision, our churches determine to take an active role in educating, counselling and offering practical assistance to women facing this dilemma and that we urge the churches to develop and to cooperate with counselling services that include--

> (1) early pregnancy counselling to help the woman understand her own feelings, to explore all the options

for coping with the pregnancy, carrying the pregnancy to term and giving up or keeping the baby;
(2) information about available supportive community services, should she choose to have and to keep the baby, or have and give up the baby;
(3) adoption possibilities and procedures;
(4) a complete description of abortion procedures and the possible mental, spiritual and social ramifications;
(5) contraceptive counselling, aimed at developing moral and responsible attitudes toward human sexuality and respect for the value of human life;
(6) follow-up counselling and practical supportive assistance;
(j) that we urge the Department of Christian Education to develop further provisions which will encourage and enable pastors and lay people to prepare themselves to counsel individuals and families involved in a crisis pregnancy.

The Lutheran Church Canada[21]

K88-3-04   TO STATE THE POSITION OF THE LUTHERAN CHURCH--CANADA

ON ABORTION

WHEREAS   The Supreme Court of Canada has struck down the Criminal Code provisions dealing with abortions, resulting in a state of "abortion on demand" in this country; and

WHEREAS   The practice of abortion, its promotion, and legal acceptance are destructive of the moral consciousness and character of the people of any nation; and

     A) the living but unborn are persons in the sight of God from the time of conception (Job 10, 9-11; Psalm 51, 5; Psalm 139, 13-17; Jeremiah 1, 5; Luke 1, 41-44); and

     B) as persons the unborn stand under the full protection of God's own prohibition against murder (Genesis 9, 6; Exodus 20, 13; Numbers 35, 33; Acts 7, 19; 1 John 3, 15); and

WHEREAS Since abortion takes a human life, abortion is not a moral option, except as a tragically unavoidable by-product of medical procedures necessary to prevent the death of another human being, that is, the mother; therefore be it

RESOLVED That we of The Lutheran Church--Canada

1. Provide education to all our members about these truths, and encourage both men and women to live responsible sexual lives in accordance with the standards of God's word; and

2. Encourage all of our members to speak out and to oppose in a responsible way, attitudes and policies in congregations, schools, hospitals, social service agencies, and other institutions within their sphere of influence and work, which promulgate, encourage, promote or endorse the view that abortion is a matter of personal choice; and

3. Encourage all of our members to make clear to our representatives and leaders in government our support for the living but unborn, and to urge upon those leaders our demand that they provide for those defenceless persons due protection under the law; and

4. To appoint the President of The Lutheran Church-- Canada to be our official representative to convey to the Government of Canada our stand on abortion and our continuing desire for legislation that will protect the life of the unborn; and

5. Offer as an alternative to abortion, supportive understanding, compassion, and help to the expectant parent(s) and family, and foster concern among Lutheran agencies and families to open their hearts and homes to children who need homes.

ACTION ADOPTED as amended, Session 7

Resolution adopted by The Lutheran Church--Canada at its Constituting Convention, May 18-21, 1988.

Lutheran Council in Canada[22]

RESOLUTIONS ADOPTED BY THE EVANGELICAL LUTHERAN CHURCH IN CANADA

BIENNIAL CONVENTION
July 12-16, 1989, Saskatoon, Saskatchewan.

Abortion

To adopt the following Statement on Abortion as the interim statement of this convention and that the statement be referred to the Division for Church and Society and to the congregations of the Church for further study over the next biennium, with report back to the next convention.

OUR THEOLOGICAL BASIS

The Evangelical Lutheran Church in Canada holds firmly to the biblical truths that:
1) all human beings are created in the image of God (Genesis 1:27);
"So God created man in His own image, in the image of God He created him; male and female He created them."

2) we are human beings from the time of conception, known and deeply valued by God;
"For Thou didst form my inward parts, Thou didst knit me together in my mother's womb. I praise Thee, for Thou art fearful and wonderful. Wonderful are thy works! Thou knowest me right well; my frame was not hidden from Thee, when I was not being made in secret, intricately wrought in the depths of the earth. Thy eyes beheld my unformed substance; in Thy book were written every one of them, the days that were formed for me, when as yet there were none of them" (Ps. 139:13-16)
"Before I formed you in the womb, I knew you, and before you were born, I consecrated you; I appointed you a prophet to the nations." (Jer. 1:5)

"And when Elizabeth heard the greeting of Mary, the babe leaped in her womb; and Elizabeth was filled with the Holy Spirit and she exclaimed with a loud cry, ‹Blessed are you among women, and blessed is the fruit of your womb! And why is this granted to me, that the mother of my Lord should come to me? For behold, when the voice of your greeting came to my ears, the babe in my womb leaped for joy.›" (Lk. 1:41-44)

3) God stands with all people in times of distress. (Peter 5:7)
"Cast all your anxieties on Him, for he cares about you."
In light of the biblical witness, we affirm that:

1) all life is precious to God, including the life of the woman and her unborn child;
2) such life is a gracious gift of God, and both the man and the woman as co-creators of this new life, as well as the community, hold responsibility for it as a sacred trust;
3) abortion is the taking of a human life and as such is a reflection of our sinful nature;
4) that bondage is evident when we fail to value, care for and support pregnant women;
5) all human beings at all stages of development have the right to life, love, support, security, and all that they need for their growth and nurture.

OUR MINISTRY

We affirm the sanctity of life and protest those who would diminish God's intention for that gift. The reality that we are both saints and sinners calls us to acknowledge that there are many couples who have conceived life but find the conception difficult to deal with. We, as members of the Evangelical Lutheran Church in Canada, have a responsibility to minister to those persons who, faced with the reality of an unwanted pregnancy, come to us for help. As families, pastors, care-givers, and members, our ministry is to listen with compassion to those wrestling with the continuation of an unborn life. In the light of their personal histories, we are called to explore redemptive alternatives that would first and foremost seek to provide for the continuation of the pregnancy.

In the event that a decision is made to abort, this same community of faith is called to show love and compassion and to offer to those seeking forgiveness, the assurance of God's gracious pardon.

Recognizing that this healing is a continuing process, we affirm that all who have suffered can experience healing and renewal in the context of God's grace and in the family of God. We would extend this same ministry to those who have facilitated the process of abortion.

OUR APPLICATION

In seeking ways to reduce the felt need for abortion, the Evangelical Lutheran Church in Canada, as a loving community of faith, calls upon its congregational, synodical, and national leadership, and to all its members to:

1) speak and act as responsible citizens on behalf of the living but unborn;

2) produce and promote resources which can help all its members grow towards developing health and life-giving relationships wherein the responsibility for birth control and parenting is shared by the partners;

3) encourage the school system and work places to support women who are pregnant, so that pregnancy is not seen as a reason for expulsion, but acknowledged with dignity and support;

4) support the efforts being made to deal with the causes and the elimination of all forms of family violence so that children may be raised in safety;

5) affirm and communicate to all levels of our government:

    a) the need to develop consistent and fair legislation regarding abortion,

    b) the need for quality child care, affordable housing, access health care, recreational opportunities, and a healthy environment,

    c) the need to extend pubic funding on an equitable basis to all community agencies which offer preventative or crisis counselling in the area of sexuality, pregnancy, and family planning;

6) encourage adoption as an alternative to abortion, fostering concern for unwanted babies and encouraging open hearts and homes to these children in their need for life in a family.

AS A COMMUNITY OF FAITH, WE COMMIT OURSELVES TO:

1) PRAY for wisdom, guidance, understanding, and love as we seek to support those struggling with unwanted pregnancies;

2) PRAISE God by celebrating and demonstrating in our worship, education, service, and outreach the sanctity of human life;
3) PROCLAIM in word and deed God's compassion for those who, because of circumstances, believe that abortion is their only alternative.

The Pentecostal Assemblies of Canada (Position Paper)[23]

THE CHRISTIAN ALTERNATIVE TO ABORTION

PART I

Introduction

The Pentecostal Assemblies of Canada believes the unborn child is a human person. Human life, possessing a special sanctity in that it is created in the image of God, begins at conception. We believe this view is in conformity with the teachings and principles of the Word of God.

Resolutions

The Pentecostal Assemblies of Canada initially declared its official position on abortion in resolutions of the General Conferences of 1968 and 1976. (See appendix.)

Purpose

The purpose of this position paper is to state in brief and simple terms the views of The Pentecostal Assemblies of Canada on certain fundamental issues concerning the unborn child including the following:

1.   Human life begins at conception.

2.   Human life is a continuum from the moment of conception to the moment of death. The only possible justification for the interruption of a pregnancy would be in the extremely rare situation in which an abortion is performed in order to save the life of the mother. Abortion performed for any other reason is the deliberate taking of human life and is equivalent to murder.

3. It is the clear duty of Christians to provide the means of counsel, care, and love for those who are faced with an unwanted pregnancy until and subsequent to the birth of the child. A request for an abortion is a cry for help.

4. It is the clear duty of Christians to declare that abortion is never an acceptable alternative as a form of birth control.

5. It is the clear duty of Christians to provide the means of protection, care, and love for the newborn child and the mother.

6. It is the clear duty of Christians to provide the means of counsel, forgiveness, and care for those who have already experienced an abortion.

7. It is incumbent upon Christians to protest, by lawful means, against the practice of abortion-on-demand and the laws that permit the same.

8. It is our obligation, as Christians, to expose the true ramifications of an abortion on the mother, with an emphasis on the spiritual, physical, and psychological after effects.

It is not the purpose of this paper to give detailed Biblical and theological, moral and ethical, legal or medical explanations for the position taken. More detailed information is available from the Office of Information.

Biblical and Theological Considerations

It is important to consider the many passages and principles of Scripture which give us a firm foundation for a Christian and humane perspective on the issue of abortion and the right to life.

The Scriptures state that God is the creator and source of first human life (Genesis 2:7), that He participates in the development of the individual before birth (Job 10:8, 9; Psalm 139:16), and that, on occasion, He quickens the mortal body to enable conception (Genesis 17:19, 30:22). God's love, purpose, and concern for the child in the mother's womb are shown in such Scriptures as Jeremiah 1:5, Luke 1:5-17, and Galatians 1:15.

We have been given the privilege of being co-creators with God (Genesis 1:27, 28; 46:26; Hebrews 7:10). At the very earliest stages of development within the womb, the process of ensoulment begins with all of the potential of emotions, intellect, and will at the highest level, as well as the capacity to know and worship God. There is also, as an intrinsic part of this process, the capacity for and bent towards sin (Romans 5:12; 1 Corinthians 15:22; Ephesians 2:3).

Such Scriptures as Psalm 51 and Psalm 139, with their abundant use of personal and possessive pronouns, indicate a sense of continuity and personal identity throughout the states of life from conception to adulthood. There is a significance found in the literal translation of the Hebrew word translated "substance" in verse 16 of Psalm 139. The word used signifies a wrapping or folding together, perhaps pointing to the embryo at the stage of its being folded together (gastrulation). It would seem, in God's sight, even this is a very important stage, and it is here the psalmist declares in verses 13-16 "For thou hast possessed my reins: thou hast covered me in my mother's womb. I will praise thee; for I am fearfully and wonderfully made: marvellous are they works; and that my soul knoweth right well. My substance was not hid from thee, when I was made in secret, and curiously wrought in the lowest parts of the earth. Thine eyes did see my substance, yet being unperfect; and in thy book all my members were written, which in continuance were fashioned, when as yet there was none of them."

The most significant Scripture supporting the view that the unborn child is a human person is found in Exodus 21:22-25:

"If men who are fighting hit a pregnant woman and she gives birth prematurely but there is no serious injury, the offender must be fined whatever the woman's husband demands and the court allows. But if there is serious injury, you are to take life for life, eye for eye, tooth for tooth, hand for hand, foot for foot, burn for burn, wound for wound, bruise for bruise" (NIV).

A number of evangelical writers have taken the position, based on Hebrew text, that verse 22 refers not to a miscarriage, as indicated by some translators, but to the premature birth of an otherwise healthy child. Any further harm (e.g. death) to either woman or child would demand the application of *lex talionis* - life for life.

It is noted, in the phrase found in the Authorized Version, "so that her fruit depart," the common Hebrew word for child, *yeled*, is used. The verb in this phrase is *yatza*, which simply means to "go out" or "come forth" and is so translated in such Scriptures as Genesis 15:4, 46:26, 1 Kings 8:19, Isaiah 39:7, Ecclesiastes 5:15, Jeremiah 1:5, 20:18, when reference is made to the ordinary birth of a child. Also, if the resulting harm had been a miscarriage rather than a premature birth, one would wonder why the specific word for miscarriage, *shachol*, had not been used. It would seem, from the most natural interpretation of the text, that the unborn child is considered to be a separate human being having the same intrinsic value as the mother and offered equal protection, and therefore, equal right to live.

The Bible makes it clear that God has a special interest in, and attaches special importance to, the individual from the earliest stage of development. We conclude, therefore, that human life, with all of its potential and sanctity, as we understand it, begins at conception.

Moral and Ethical Considerations

From the Biblical and theological considerations, we know that it is morally and ethically wrong to take the life of an innocent and defenceless unborn child, except in a desperate effort to save the life of the mother. Some would rationalize that abortion is justified because it is felt that the woman has the right to privacy or the right to control her own body, and also it is justified in the case of pregnancy resulting from rape, incest, an unwanted pregnancy or an abnormality. In our view, these rationalizations are not acceptable for the following reasons:

1. **The Woman's Right**

    The argument that the woman has the sole right to control what happens to her body assumes that the unborn child is only an extension of her body. The medical facts are that the unborn child is genetically unique and separate from the body of the mother, although sustained by her until birth.

    In addition, the Scriptures teach that no one has the sole right to control his or her own body. The Apostle Paul, writing to the Ephesians, instructs a wife to submit herself to her own husband in everything as the husband submits himself to Christ (Ephesians 5:22-28). Husband and wife are one flesh (Ephesians 5:31), not merely two independent individuals. According to the Word of God, the husband does not have the sole right to his own body; likewise, the wife does not have the sole power over her own body, but rather it is shared with her husband (1 Corinthians 7:3-4).

Furthermore, our bodies belong to God and are to be the temples, or dwelling places, of the Holy Spirit (1 Corinthians 6:19, 20).

2. **Rape: The Unborn Child's Right to Life**

We recognize that the consequences of a rape are very traumatic and devastating for the victim, and that she must be given special care and support. However, we maintain that the unborn child resulting from such a crime is entitled to life. We do not believe that the innocent unborn child should be killed for the crime of his or her father. It should be noted that pregnancy resulting from rape is extremely rare.

3. **Incest: The Unborn Child's Right to Life**

Again, we believe in the unborn child's right to life even if that life is the result of an incestuous relationship. We believe that the mother, in these circumstances, requires special care, guidance, and compassion. We do not believe that society should kill an innocent unborn child because his or her father is a close relative.

4. **The Unwanted Child's Right to Life**

We believe the unborn child, because of the sanctity of life, has the right to life whether the child is wanted or unwanted by his or her mother. If the child remains unwanted by the mother following birth, it is our view that an adoption, in these circumstances, is an understandable and acceptable alternative.

5. **The Abnormal Unborn Child's Right to Life**

We believe the abnormal child has the right to life. Discrimination on the basis of abnormality is no more acceptable before birth than after birth. The Scriptures give examples of persons born with abnormalities which turned out to be to the glory of God. In some cases, these persons were later healed. History records that many who were born with abnormalities have contributed greatly to society. It should be noted, as well, that tests for abnormalities may indeed prove to have been inaccurate.

LEGAL CONSIDERATIONS

1. Criminal Code

The Criminal Code of Canada clearly provides that the performance of an abortion is a crime unless exceptional circumstances exist and prescribed procedure is complied with (Section 251). The foundation of this section of the Criminal Code is a recognition of the value and sanctity of the life of the unborn, even if that unborn life is only a few days old.

In 1969, Section 251 of the Criminal Code was amended for the purpose of defining the exceptional circumstances in which an abortion could be performed.

Since 1969, a more liberal interpretation of the amendments significantly altered the perception of the abortion crime. The effect was to legalize the procurement of an abortion provided that it is performed by a qualified medical practitioner in an accredited or approved hospital, and that such medical intervention has been approved by a majority of the members of the abortion committee of the approved hospital. Furthermore, the Criminal Code specifies that a certificate in writing must be given by the committee to the medical practitioner. That certificate must state that the continuation of the pregnancy of the female person concerned would, or would be likely to, endanger the woman's health or life.

The tragedy is that, once the application for abortion is received from the mother, the therapeutic abortion committees have been allowed to have absolute power over the life of the unborn child. These committees are composed of medical volunteers and are functioning without supervision or adequate controls. It should be noted that, under our law, no one on the therapeutic abortion committees is specifically assigned to represent the rights of the unborn child. Since the condition of the woman's health is not defined for the abortion committees, abortions are often granted for socioeconomic reasons; i.e., for the purpose of relieving the woman of anxiety. Abortion is frequently chosen not because it is necessary, but simply because it is convenient.

The 1969 amendment to the Criminal Code, in effect, undermined the most basic right of all - the right to life. The net result of this has been an undermining of the value that society places on life, and accordingly, a loss of protection for unborn children.

2. Charter of Rights

The Charter of Rights and Freedoms in the Constitution of Canada states: "Everyone has the right to life, liberty, and security of the person and the right not to be deprived thereof except in accordance with the principles of fundamental justice."

3. Human Rights

The United Nations Universal Declaration of Human Rights (1948), Article #3, reads: "Everyone has the right to life, liberty, and security of person." Canada is a signatory to this declaration. The World Health Organization in 1948 further defined the word "life" when it stated: "Utmost respect for human life was to be from the moment of conception on."

PART II

Recommendations

We believe the Scriptural view of life includes compassion not only for the unborn, but for the mother as well. It addresses the sins of permissiveness and provides redemptive alternatives. There are better methods of dealing with family planning than abortion. We are prepared to provide loving alternatives to abortion in the following ways:

1. Sex Education

We recommend churches and Christian schools provide Scripturally-based sex education and family planning programs in order to instill Biblical values. These should be designed for parents as well as for children and young people.

2. **Counselling Centres**

    We recommend churches provide or give direction to counselling centres which recognize and uphold the sanctity of life and which provide available information and loving care to pregnant mothers who face serious questions on matters of human life. These centres should supply information regarding homes for unwed mothers, adoption agencies, and day-care facilities.

3. **Resource Centre**

    The Pentecostal Assemblies of Canada is developing a Christian Resource Centre to service churches and Christian schools which request direction and materials on matters of social concern. Books, films, audiovisuals, and curriculum materials are available. Write to The Christian Resource Centre, Office of Information.

How to Take Action

We believe the majority of Canadians, when educated to the facts relating to abortion, will act in favour of maintaining the sanctity of life for the unborn. We believe they will insist that the present laws limiting the performing of abortions to accredited hospitals be enforced. We believe they will act further to request legislation that will amend the Criminal Code to restrict the circumstances under which an abortion may be performed. These amendments should also provide for strict supervision of therapeutic abortion committees and include provisions for a change in the composition of the committees to furnish representation for the unborn child.

Therefore, we urge Christians to:

1. Form social concerns committees within their churches and communities.

2. Expose the spiritual, physical, and psychological damage done to the mother who has undergone an abortion.

3. Provide books, tapes, audiovisuals, bulletins, and guest speakers to educate themselves and others on the subject of abortion.

4.   Encourage parents to take an active role in their local school boards and parent-teacher associations.

5.   Urge pastors and Christian leaders to teach about abortion.

6.   Write letters to the premiers, the ministers of justice, the attorneys general, and the members of the provincial parliament of Canada in order to make their views known.

7.   Write letters to the premiers, the ministers of justice, the attorneys general, and the members of the provincial parliaments to request that the therapeutic abortion committees and accredited hospitals be held accountable not to exceed the strict intent of the abortion laws.

8.   Write letters to the federal minister of justice to request amendments to the abortion laws in order to ensure the representation of the unborn on the therapeutic abortion committees.

9.   We urge Christians to seek to become elected to public office or employed in influential positions ("Ye are the salt of the earth" - Matthew 5:13).

The Presbyterian Church in Canada[24]

ABORTION

1967 The following resolution was adopted by the 93rd General Assembly and forwarded to the Government of Canada. A brief was then prepared on the basis of the resolution and presented to the House of Commons Committee on Health & Welfare in November 1967.

WHEREAS, an abortion involves a decision fraught with serious moral and spiritual implications,
WHEREAS, it is morally indefensible to legalize abortion in order to reduce the number of illegal abortions, or as a method of population control, and
WHEREAS, notwithstanding the foregoing we believe that the mother's life is a matter of even greater importance than the life of the foetus, and indeed that the physical and mental health of

the mother, when these are most seriously threatened may be adjudged to be of such importance as not to preclude an abortion, and
WHEREAS, the Criminal Code Section 209(1), (2) provides for the preserving of "the life of the mother of a child that has not become a human being", but is ambiguous with regard to the legality of such an abortion, leaving medical doctors liable to prosecution even in such cases,
THEREFORE, be it resolved that the General Assembly ask Parliament to amend the law with regard to abortion to make therapeutic abortion lawful, when the continuance of a pregnancy endangers the mother's life or is likely seriously to impair her physical or mental health, when authorized by a panel of qualified medical authorities.

1972 Recommendations Adopted by the 98th General Assembly

(a) that the position taken by the 93rd General Assembly on this matter be reaffirmed, namely,
"an abortion involves a decision fraught with serious moral and spiritual implications:
it is morally indefensible to legalize abortion in order to reduce the number of illegal abortions, or as a method of population control:
notwithstanding the foregoing we believe that the mother's life is a matter of even greater importance than the life of the foetus, and indeed that the physical and mental health of the mother, when these are most seriously threatened may be adjudged to be of such importance as not to preclude an abortion."

(b) That the General Assembly out of deep concern over the sharp increase in the number of legal abortions being performed each year in Canada call on provincial governments to maintain a close supervision of all therapeutic abortion committees within their jurisdiction to assure adequate consultation with the mother and, if possible, with the father and the family physician before permission for abortion is granted and that such permission be granted only for the reasons of danger to the mother's life or serious impairment of physical or mental health.

(c) That the church urge all concerned actively to minister to those who find themselves faced with the question of having an abortion, pointing out the alternatives that are open to them, and supporting and counselling them both before and after abortion or birth.

(d) That the General Assembly express its disapproval of such advertisement as "Abortion on Demand", "Undesirable Pregnancy - Safe Abortion" and the like and such disapproval be directed to the governments and the media.

(e) That this General Assembly strongly request our ministers, sessions and presbyteries to take urgent measures to engage all our young people, parents and people working in the helping professions in forthright study and discussion on the above resolutions on abortion in the context of sex education, education in family life and education in the problem of world overpopulation.

1975 The 101st General Assembly granted an overture from the Presbytery of Westminster requesting the Assembly "to urge the Government of Canada to take the necessary steps to ensure that the laws of the land respecting abortion are not abused." Noting that these matters fall within provincial jurisdiction, the Assembly notified the Minister of Justice of Canada and the Attorneys General of the Provinces of this concern.

The 101st General Assembly also adopted a recommendation of The Board of Congregational Life regarding a conscience clause for medical practitioners and staff. The Minister of Justice of Canada, the Law Reform Commission and, subsequently, the provincial governments were notified of this action. The resolution read:

> That the General Assembly recommend to the Minister of Justice of Canada and the Law Reform Commission of Canada that a law be enacted to protect medical workers from demotion, suspension or discharge from employment who refuse on grounds of conscience to take part in abortions.

1976 The 102nd General Assembly received the following statement from The Board of Congregational Life and referred it for study and report to presbyteries and congregations, in order that a final statement could be submitted to the 103rd General Assembly. The statement is in response to an instruction of the 99th General Assembly "to study the term ‹mental health› with respect to the matter of therapeutic abortion."

ABORTION: THE LIFE AND HEALTH OF THE MOTHER AS THE CRITERION (1976 334)

"(1) Everyone who, with intent to procure the miscarriage of a female person is guilty of an indictable offence;

(2) Every female person who, being pregnant, with intent to procure her own miscarriage, uses any means is guilty of an indictable offence;

Subsections (1) and (2) do not apply if, before the use of those means, the therapeutic abortion committee stated that in its opinion the continuation of the pregnancy of such female person would or would be likely to endanger her life or health" (The Criminal Code of Canada, Section 237)

In the present state of gynecology and obstetrics, the danger of a woman's death through complications arising from pregnancy is rare indeed, nor are there many occasions when it is indicated that the continuation of pregnancy might result in the mother's permanent physical impairment. Nevertheless many abortions occur - abortions authorized by legally constituted therapeutic abortion committees.

The issue is in what is meant by "life" and "health". In this debate the question is whether "life" ought to mean more than simply being alive, with consideration being given to the threat of an unwanted pregnancy to a woman's total life; in relation to her family, her work or her environment. On this side of the argument, it is pointed out that there are circumstances that may not be "life-threatening" but can be "life-devastating".

In the same way, "health" may be seen to include questions of social or economic well-being. Further, the question is whether the health of the foetus ought not to be taken into consideration. If it is indicated that there is a 50% chance that a child will be born deformed, deficient or with a lethal disease, what then? Of if there is the likelihood of being neglected, abandoned or deprived, should this not be taken into account?

Far from being academic questions, these factors are at work in the emotion-charged struggle of any woman who considers having an abortion. It is a struggle to decide what is right, what is best, and whether the right and the best are in conflict. The question of rights involves the question of quality of life. An unwanted pregnancy may be seen as a threat to a woman's right to a certain quality of life that she possesses or is attempting to acquire. If a foetus seems to be unhealthy, has it not a right to be healthily born or not to be born at all?

The 93rd General Assembly (1967) stated, in a resolution reaffirmed in 1972 by the 98th General Assembly, that "an abortion involves a decision fraught with serious moral and spiritual implications." Among these implications must be affirmed the fundamental right to live. This principle must be seen to obtain also for the unborn. There is no point in time when it can be asserted that the foetus does not qualify as human life. It is unseen, unconscious, dependent and perhaps unwanted, but these are not grounds for its termination.

In view of this fundamental right, it is proper to conclude that the interpretations of "life" and "health" must be strict. In the case of the word "life", it ought to have the plain meaning of life as distinct from death, and that danger to life means the danger that the person might die. The claim of danger to "health" is more complex; in fact there is no way to produce a catalogue of "disease states" or conditions that constitute medical indications for abortion. The law provides that therapeutic abortion committees which are accountable to the Minister of Health in the Province, have the responsibility of making the decisions in these difficult cases.

1977 That the General Assembly request Provincial Ministers of Health that therapeutic abortion committees be instructed to give priority to the principle that the unborn has the right to life and that only a danger to the mother's health indicating the likelihood of permanent or prolonged mental or physical impairment be regarded as grounds for abortion.

1988 Recommendations Adopted by the 114th General Assembly:

1. That the basic principles as presently held on the question of abortion be reaffirmed and communicated to the Ministers of Health and Justice of the Federal Government; that the Board of

Congregational Life be requested to continue to study the implications of whatever legislation may emerge dealing with this subject and take appropriate action that is consonant with our Church's stated position; and that Overtures 10 and 19 be answered in terms of this recommendation.

The United Church of Canada[25]

CONTRACEPTION AND ABORTION

RECOMMENDATIONS of the 1980 Report as amended and approved by the Twenty-Eighth General Council of The United Church of Canada

Preamble

As Christians we wish to affirm:
The sanctity of human life, born or unborn. That life is much more than physical existence.

We also affirm that:
The taking of human life is evil.

Our concern must not be limited to a concern for the unborn but it must also include a concern for the quality of life as a whole.

Life in this imperfect world often places us in complex circumstances of moral dilemma and ambiguity where values ultimate in themselves seem at times to be in conflict with other values and rights.

We are called as a people of God to take responsibility for our lives and the world in which we live. This may involve making grave decisions relating even to life itself.

Each of us is called upon in a freedom that is given by God and within the context of the community of faith to make responsible personal decisions, even when choosing between two wrongs.

As a forgiven people in Christ, it is possible for us to live in the midst of moral dilemmas.

Within our community strong differences of opinion on moral issues are our strength and not our weakness.

1. Massive Contraception Program

(a) A child has a right to be wanted, so that it may have some assurance of this essential element in human development. Bringing unwanted children into the world is irresponsible.

(b) Thus, family planning, including vasectomy and tubal ligation is a Christian duty. Our Canadian society has to make every effort to ensure that contraception is the only completely acceptable form of birth control. Some practice of abortion is inevitable for the next few years while contraceptive techniques are imperfect and contraceptive ignorance is widespread, but the aim of all education, research and social pressure must be always to reduce the incidence of abortion and to promote effective contraception.

(c) To anticipate the use of abortion as a form of birth control and therefore neglect to practise contraception is medically and morally deplorable and socially expensive. Such intentional use of abortion, by individuals or governments, is morally wrong.

THEREFORE

(i) We call on all persons to appreciate their own sexuality primarily in terms of personal relationships and only secondarily in terms of physiology, programs, techniques and services; and charge parents, educators and churches to represent adequately sexuality as intimate, awesome and holy.

(ii) We call on all parents to accept the responsibility to discuss sexual attitudes and information with their children as frankly and as fully as necessary, from the time children begin to ask such questions or need such enlightenment.

(iii) We call on all educators, in provincial departments, regional boards and local schools, to arrange for comprehensive programs, appropriate to the developmental stages of the children and young people, in family life, sex education, contraception information, personality development, relationships and the development of their own values as responsible sexual persons.

(iv) We recommend that sexually mature young people should be informed, by parents, congregations, schools, Health Departments, etc., as to where contraception information and prescriptions are available, and should be instructed in the dangers of venereal disease.

(v) We commend the federal Government for making available funds for education in family planning and birth control, ask it to continue to do so, and urge our people to take action to ensure that the fullest possible use is made of these funds by provincial and local departments of health.

(vi) We call on all United Church people, congregations and presbyteries to urge provincial and local governments to make use of funds available to establish family-planning clinics in hospitals and Public Health units, and to support the efforts of public or voluntary agencies to develop or expand such facilities.

(vii) We urge congregations to accept their responsibility to carry out programs on family life education, contraception information, personality development, relationships and the development of sexual values, appropriate to the needs of their members or constituencies.

2. Abortion

(a) We affirm the inherent value of human life, both as immature in the foetus and as expressed in the life of the mother and related persons. The foetus is a unique though immature form of human life and, as such, has inherent value. Christians should witness to that value by stressing that abortion is always a moral issue and can only be accepted as the lesser of two evils and should be the most responsible alternative available in each particular situation. Therefore, abortion is acceptable only in certain medical, social and economic situations.

(b) The previous law, which required a hospital therapeutic abortion committee to authorize an abortion was unjust in principle and unworkable in practice.

(c) We do not support "abortion on demand". We believe that abortion should be a personal matter between a woman and her doctor, who should earnestly consider their understanding of the particular situation permitting the woman to bring to bear her moral and religious insights into human life in reaching a decision through a free and responsive exercise of her conscience.

Because we see theological significance in the process of growing biological development and in the developing human relationships of the foetus, each of which become factors in ethical decision-making, and because the possibility of physical and emotional harm will be reduced, we consider that any interruption in the pregnancy is less objectionable in the early stages.

We will further believe that her male partner and/or other supportive people should have a responsibility to both the woman and the foetus and should be involved in the decision wherever possible.

THEREFORE

1. We Urge the Government of Canada:
(a) Not to use the provisions in the Criminal Code to regulate abortion.

(b) To enact and enforce penalties for people who perform or attempt to perform abortions without the required medical qualifications or who perform or attempt to perform abortions in places other than those approved for that purpose.

(c) To use shared funding under the Canada Health Act to require all provincial governments to provide adequate contraceptive education and services to effectively reduce the incidence of unwanted pregnancies; and to provide early access to diagnosis and, if necessary, termination of pregnancy so that any such abortion could be performed as early as possible.

2. We Urge Provincial Governments to:
(a) Provide adequate contraceptive education and services.

(b) Provide facilities and personnel necessary to meet the need for abortions, and to make known the availability of such facilities, and require all hospitals to declare publicly their policy on abortion.

3. In order to protect the foetus and the woman from an ill-advised abortion, and to help the woman make a responsible decision, we urge the federal and provincial governments to co-operate with churches and other helping agencies in the funding and further development of counselling services in all centres where abortions are performed, and in geographic areas where such hospital and medical services are not available.

This counselling should include:
(a) Early Pregnancy Counselling
To help the woman to:

- understand her own feelings about being pregnant,
- explore all the options for coping with the pregnancy,
     - carrying the pregnancy to term,
     - giving up or keeping the baby,
     - abortion,
- articulate her reasons for choosing an abortion or carrying the pregnancy to term,
- relate to family members or friends to whom she can look for support in her situation.

To inform the woman about:

- available community services, should she choose to have and to keep the baby, or have and give up the baby
- adoption possibilities and procedures
- abortion procedures and possible mental, spiritual and social ramifications.

(b) Contraceptive Counselling
Ensure that the client and, if possible, her male partner understand the facts of fertility, are informed about contraceptive methods and have access to devices and prescriptions.

(c) Follow-up Counselling
To deal with personal problems that may arise from the operation and to encourage the continued use of contraceptives.

4. Further, as an expression of our Christian concern, we urge churches, governments, and all helping agencies to work through all possible avenues to ensure adequate community support for mothers choosing to give birth, both those giving up and those keeping their babies.

5. We commend members of the medical and nursing profession for their responsible and compassionate involvement in the matter of abortion, while reiterating their right to refuse to participate on grounds of conscience.

We repeat our request to all hospital boards to grant nurses and other medical personnel the option of non-participation and at the same time refer medical personnel to the Canadian Medical Association Code of Ethics in this matter.

We draw attention to the action of the Society of Obstetricians and Gynaecologists of Canada at their meeting in June, 1971:
"That for the time being the fees for the performance of termination of pregnancy should not exceed that set in the local and provincial fee schedules."

6. We instruct the Division of Mission in Canada and the Division of Ministry Personnel and Education to develop further the provisions which encourage and enable ministers and lay people to prepare themselves for the counselling of women faced with an abortion dilemma and, where appropriate, their partners or parents.

7. We instruct the Division of Mission in Canada to continue to study the church's position on both birth control and abortion, and to make available to the congregations current statements that will enable the church to maintain a responsive involvement in these important concerns.

3. BIBLIOGRAPHY

See also Philosophy Bibliography and Advocacy Bibliography for related material.

Christian

Alton, Bruce, ed. *The Abortion Question.* Toronto: Anglican Book Centre, 1983.

Andrusko, Dave. "Echoes of Nuremberg" [research use of tissues from aborted fetuses]. *Fundamentalist Journal* 8 (April 1989): 30-33.

Baertschi, Bernard. "Qu'est-ce qu'une personne humaine? Reflexions sur les fondements philosophiques de la bioethique." *Revue de Théologie et de Philosophie* 121 (1989): 173-193.

Barry, O. "Personhood: The Conditions of Identification and Description." *Linacre Quarterly* 45 (1978): 64-81.

Baum, Gregory. "Abortion: An Ecumenical Dilemma." *Commonweal* 99 (November 30, 1973): 231-235.

Bernardin, Cardinal Joseph. "The Consistent Ethic: What Sort of Framework?" *Origins* 16 (October 30, 1986): 347-350. This article also appears in Patricia Beattie Jung and Thomas Shannon. *Abortion and Catholicism: The American Debate.* New York: Crossroad, 1988.

_____. "The Consistent Ethic After *Webster*: Opportunities and Dangers." *Commonweal* 127 (April 20, 1990): 242-248.

Brody, Baruch. "Religious, Moral and Sociological Issues: Some Basic Distinctions." *Hastings Center Report* 8 (August 1978): 13.

Burtchaell, James. "Continuing the Discussion: How to Argue About Abortion: II." *Christianity and Crisis* 37: (December 26, 1977): 313-316.

Byrne, Harry. "Thou Shalt Not Speak." *America* 155 (December 6, 1986): 356-359. This article also appears in Patricia Beattie Jung and Thomas Shannon. *Abortion and Catholicism: The American Debate.* New York: Crossroad, 1988.

Callahan, Daniel. "Abortion: Thinking and Experiencing." *Christianity and Crisis* 32 (January 8, 1973): 295-298.

Callahan, Joan. "The Fetus and Fundamental Rights." *Commonweal* 123 (April 11, 1986): 203-209. This article also appears in Patricia Beattie Jung and Thomas Shannon. *Abortion and Catholicism: The American Debate.* New York: Crossroad, 1988.

Callahan, Sidney. "Abortion and the Sexual Agenda: A Case for Pro-Life Feminism." *Commonweal* 123 (April 25, 1986): 232-238. This article also appears in Patricia Beattie Jung and Thomas Shannon. *Abortion and Catholicism: The American Debate.* New York: Crossroad, 1988.

Canadian Conference of Catholic Bishops. *Contraception, Divorce, Abortion.* Ottawa: CCCB, 1968.

Churchill, Larry R. and Jose Jorge Siman. "Abortion and the Rhetoric of Individual Rights." *Hastings Center Report* 12 (February 1982): 9-12.

Congdon, Robert. "Exodus 21:22-25 and the Abortion Debate." *Biblioteca Sacra* 146 (April-June 1989): 132-147.

Connery, John. *Abortion: The Development of the Roman Catholic Perspective.* Chicago: Loyola University Press, 1977.

_____. "A Seamless Garment in a Sinful World." America 153 (July 14, 1984): 5-8. This article also appears in Patricia Beattie Jung and Thomas Shannon. *Abortion and Catholicism: The American Debate.* New York: Crossroad, 1988.

Coughlin, Ellen K. "Research on Emotional Consequences of Abortion Fails to Bolster Cause of Procedure's Opponents [Surgeon General Koop calls evidence inconclusive]." *Chronicle of Higher Education* 35 (March 1, 1989): 4-6.

Creighton, Phyllis, ed. *Abortion, An Issue for Conscience.* Toronto: The Anglican Church of Canada, 1974.

Culliton, Joseph. "Rahner on the Origin of the Soul: Some Implications Regarding Abortion." *Thought* 53 (1978): 203-214.

Curran, Charles. "Abortion, Law and Morality in Contemporary Catholic Theology." *The Jurist* 33 (1973): 162-182.

_____. "Abortion: Ethical Aspects." *Encyclopedia of Bioethics.* Ed. Warren T. Reich. New York: Free Press, 1978: Vol. 1, 17-25.

_____. "Civil Law and Christian Morality," *Clergy Review* 62 (June 1977): 227-242.

_____. *Contemporary Problems in Moral Theology.* Notre Dame, IN: Fides, 1970.

_____. "*In Vitro* Fertilization and Embryo Transfer." No. 4 in *Appendix: HEW Support of Research Involving Human In Vitro Fertilization and Embryo Transfer.* Washington, DC: U.S. Government Printing Office, 1979.

_____. *Issues in Sexual and Medical Ethics.* Notre Dame, IN: University of Notre Dame Press, 1978.

_____. *New Perspectives in Moral Theology.* Notre Dame, IN: Fides, 1974. 163-193.

_____. "Public Dissent in the Church." *Origins* 16 (July 31, 1986): 178-184. This article also appears in Patricia Beattie Jung and Thomas Shannon. *Abortion and Catholicism: The American Debate.* New York: Crossroad, 1988.

_____. *Tradition and Transition in Moral Theology.* Notre Dame, IN: University of Notre Dame Press, 1979.

Dedek, John. "Abortion: A Theological Judgment." *Chicago Studies* 101 (Fall 1971): 313-333.

Degnan, Daniel. "Laws, Morals and Abortion." *Commonweal* 100 (May 31, 1974): 305-308.

_____. "Prudence, Politics, and the Abortion Issue." *America* 155 (December 6, 1986): 121-124. This article also appears in Patricia Beattie Jung and Thomas Shannon. *Abortion and Catholicism: The American Debate.* New York: Crossroad, 1988.

Diamond, J. "Abortion, Animation, and Biological Hominization." *Theological Studies* 36 (1975): 305-324.

Di Ianni, Albert. "Is the Fetus a Person?" *American Ecclesiastical Review* 168 (1974): 323-324.

Dobson, Edward G. Ed. "Abortion." *Fundamentalist Journal* 7 (January 1988): 26-61.

Dombrowski, Daniel A. "St Augustine, Abortion and *libido crudelis.*" *Journal of Historical Ideas* 49 (January-March 1988): 151-156.

Donceel, Joseph. "Abortion: Mediate vs. Immediate Animation." *Conti nuum* 5 (Spring 1967): 167-171.

_____. "Immediate Animation and Delayed Hominization." *Theological Studies* 31 (March 1970): 76-105.

_____. "Why Is Abortion Wrong?" *America* 133 (August 16, 1975): 65-67.

Drinan, Robert. "Abortions on Medicaid." *Commonweal* 97 (February 16, 1973): 438-440.

_____. "Catholic Moral Teaching and Abortion Laws in America." *Catholic Theological Society of America Proceedings* 23 (1968): 118-130.

_____. "Contemporary Protestant Thinking." *America* 117 (December 9, 1967): 713.

_____. "Jurisprudential Options." *Theological Studies* 31 (March 1970): 149-169.

_____. "The Right of the Fetus to Be Born." *Dublin Review* 514 (Winter 1967-1968): 365-381.

Dupre, Louis. "New Approach to the Abortion Question." *Theological Studies* 38 (September 1973): 481-488.

Evans, Ruth. Ed. *Abortion: A Study.* Toronto: United Church of Canada, 1971.

Fletcher, Joseph. "Abortion and the True Believer." *Christian Century* 91 (November 27, 1974): 1126-1127.

_____. *Humanhood: Essays in Biomedical Ethics.* Buffalo: Prometheus Books, 1979.

_____. *Situation Ethics.* Philadelphia: Westminster Press, 1966.

Fortin, Renee. "A Comparison of Church Statements on Abortion, Pt 2: A Working Tool." *Ecumenism* 84 (December 1986): 23-36.

Frame, Randall L. "Abortion Takes Center Stage for Presbyterians" [1988 General Assembly, St Louis]. *Christianity Today* 32 (August 12, 1988): 64-65.

_____. "Rescue Theology." *Christianity Today* 33 (November 17, 1989): 46-48.

Glaeser, Linda L. et al. "What Had I Done?" *Fundamentalist Journal* 8 (January 1989): 16-20, 22-24.

Green, Ronald, "Conferred Rights and the Fetus." *Journal of Religious Ethics* 2 (Spring 1974): 55-73.

Grisez, Germain, C. *Abortion: The Myth, the Realities and the Arguments.* Washington, D.C.: Corpus Books, 1969.

Gudorf, Christine. "To Make a Seamless Garment, Use a Single Piece of Cloth." *Cross Currents* 34 (Winter 1984): 473-491. This article also appears in Patricia Beattie Jung and Thomas Shannon. *Abortion and Catholicism: The American Debate.* New York: Crossroad, 1988.

Gustafson, James. "A Christian Approach to the Ethics of Abortion." *Dublin Review* 514 (Winter 1967-68): 346-364.

_____. "A Protestant Ethical Approach." *The Morality of Abortion.* Ed. John T. Noonan Jr. Cambridge, MA: Harvard University Press, 1970. 101-122.

Häring, Bernard. *Faithful and Free in Christ.* Vols I, II. New York: Seabury Press, 1978, 1979.

_____. *Medical Ethics.* Ed. Gabrielle Jean. Notre Dame, IN: Fides, 1973. 94-119.

_____. "New Dimensions of Responsible Parenthood." *Theological Studies* 37 (1976): 120-132.

_____. "A Theological Evaluation." *The Morality of Abortion.* Ed. John T. Noonan, Jr. Cambridge, MA: Harvard University Press, 1970. 123-145.

Harris, Michael P. "Second Thoughts About Abortion: Many Protestant Groups Are Edging to the Right." *Time* 132 (July 4, 1988): 44.

Harrison, Beverly Wildung. "Theology of Pro-Choice: A Feminist Perspective." *The Witness* 64 (July, September 1981): 7,8.

Hauerwas, Stanley. "Abortion and Normative Ethics." *Cross Currents* 21 (Fall 1971): 399-414.

_____. "Abortion: The Agent's Perspective." *American Ecclesiastical Review* 167 (February 1973): 102-120.

_____. *Vision and Virtue.* Notre Dame, IN: University of Notre Dame Press, 1981.

Heim, David. "American Baptists Maximize the Middle" [Abortion and the National Council of Churches]. *Christian Century* 105 (July 20-27, 1988): 660-662.

Hellegers, A. "Fetal Development." *Theological Studies* 31 (1970): 3-9.

Higgins, George C., "The Pro-Life and the New Right." *America* 143 (September 13, 1980): 107-110.

Jaffe, Frederick. "Enacting Religious Beliefs in a Pluralistic Society." *Hastings Center Report* 8 (August 1978): 14-16.

Jung, Patricia Beattie. "Abortion and Organ Donation: Christian Reflections on Bodily Life Support." *Journal of Religious Ethics* 16 (Fall 1988): 273-305.

Jung, Patricia Beattie, and Thomas Shannon. *Abortion and Catholicism: The American Debate.* New York: Crossroad, 1988.

Kelly, James. "Ecumenism and Abortion: a Case Study of Pluralism, Privatization and the Public Conscience." *Review of Religious Research* 30 (March 1989): 225-235.

Kolbenschlag, Madonna. "Abortion and Moral Consensus: Beyond Solomon's Choice." *Christian Century* 102 (February 20, 1985): 179-183. This article also appears in Patricia Beattie Jung and

Thomas Shannon. *Abortion and Catholicism: The American Debate.* New York: Crossroad, 1988.

Kraus, James. "Is Abortion Absolutely Prohibited?" *Continuum* 6 (Fall 1968): 436-440.

Lake, Randall. "The Metaethical Framework of Anti-Abortion Rhetoric." *Signs* 11 (Spring 1986): 478-499.

Lancaster, Kathy. Ed. "National Dialogue on Abortion Perspectives." *Church and Society* 80 (January-February 1990): 1-124.

Leddy, Mary Jo, and James H. Olthuis. "Thoughtful Perspective on Abortion." *Catalyst* 6 (November 1983): 4-5.

Maguire, Marjorie Riley. "Personhood, Covenant and Abortion." *Annual of the Society of Christian Ethics* (1983). This article also appears in Patricia Beattie Jung and Thomas Shannon. *Abortion and Catholicism: The American Debate.* New York: Crossroad, 1988; and *American Journal of Theology and Philosophy* 6 (1985): 28-46.

Maloney, Susan. "Religious Orders and Sisters in Dissent" [1984 statement on abortion]. *Christian Century* 105 (March 9, 1988): 238-240.

Mavrodes, George I. "Abortion and Imagination: Reflections on Mollenkott's ‹Reproductive Choice.›" *Christian Scholar's Review* 17 (1988): 286-293; 18 (1988): 168-170; rejoinder, 171-172.

McCormick, Richard. "Aspects of the Moral Question." *America* 117 (December 9, 1967): 716-719.

_____. "A Changing Morality and Policy." *Hospital Progress* 60 (February 1969): 36-44.

_____. *How Brave a New World? Dilemmas in Bioethics.* Garden City, NY: Doubleday, 1981.

_____. "Notes on Moral Theology: The Abortion Dossier." *Theological Studies* 35 (1974): 312-359.

_____. "Past Church Teaching on Abortion." *Catholic Theological Society of America Proceedings* 23 (1968): 131-151.

_____. "Rules For Debate." *America* 139 (July 15-22, 1978): 26-30.

McDonagh, Enda. "Ethical Problems of Abortion." *Irish Theological Quarterly* 35 (July 1968): 268-297.

Milhaven, John G. "The Abortion Debate: An Epistemological Interpretation." *Theological Studies* 31 (March 1970): 106-124.

Mollenkott, Virginia Ramey. "Reproductive Choice: Basic to Justice for Women." *Christian Scholar's Review* 17 (1988): 286-293.

Mollenkot, Virginia and Frances Beckwith. "Abortion and Public Policy: A Response to Some Arguments." *Journal of the Evangelical Theological Society* 32 (December 1989): 503-518.

National Council of Churches in the U.S.A., Faith and Order Commission. *Guidelines for Ecumenical Debate on*

Homosexuality and Abortion. New York: National Council of Churches, 1979.

Nelson, J. Robert. "What Does Theology Say About Abortion?" *Christian Century* 90 (January 31, 1973): 124-128.

Nelson, James. "Abortion: Protestant Perspectives." *Encyclopedia of Bioethics.* Ed. Warren T. Reich. New York: Free Press, 1978: Vol. 1, 13-17.

Newton, Lisa. "The Irrelevance of Religion in the Abortion Debate." *Hastings Center Report* 8 (August 1978): 16-17.

Nicholson, Susan T. *Abortion and the Roman Catholic Church.* Knoxville, Tenn.: Religious, Inc., 1978.

Noonan, John T., Jr. "Abortion and the Catholic Church: A Summary History." *Natural Law Forum* 12 (1967): 85-131.

Noonan, John T., Jr. et al. *Abortion.* Cambridge, MA: Harvard University Press, 1968.

O'Connor, June. "The Debate Continues: Recent Works on Abortion." *Religious Studies Review* 11 (1985): 105-114.

Pastrana, G. "Personhood at the Beginning of Human Life." *Thomist* 41 (1977): 247-294.

Petchesky, Rosalind Pollack. "Antiabortion, Antifeminism, and the Rise of the New Right." *Feminist Studies* 7 (Summer 1981): 206-246.

Ramsey, Paul. "Abortion: A Review Article." Thomist 37 (1973): 174-226. Later views.

_____. "The Morality of Abortion." *Life or Death: Ethics and Options.* Eds. Edward Shils et al. Seattle: University of Washington Press, 1968. Early views.

Ranck, Lee. Ed. A special issue on abortion. *Christian Social Action* 3 (April 1990): 1-16, 25-40.

Rankin, John C. "The Corporeal Reality of *Nepes* and the Status of the Unborn. *Journal of the Evangelical Theological Society* 31 (June 1988): 153-160.

Ratzinger, Cardinal Joseph. "Bishops, Theologians, and Morality." *Origins* 13 (March 15, 1984): 665-666. This article also appears in Patricia Beattie Jung and Thomas Shannon. *Abortion and Catholicism: The American Debate.* New York: Crossroad, 1988.

Roach, Archbishop John R. and Cardinal Terence Cooke. "Testimony in Support of the Hatch Amendment." *Origins* 11 (November 19, 1981): 357-372. This article also appears in Patricia Beattie Jung and Thomas Shannon. *Abortion and Catholicism: The American Debate.* New York: Crossroad, 1988.

Robertson, John A. Rights. "Symbolism, and Public Policy in Fetal Tissue Transplants." *Hastings Center Report* 18 (December 1988): 5-12.

Rossi, Philip. "Abortion and the Pursuit of Happiness." *Logos* 3 (1982): 61-77.

Ruether, Rosemary Radford. "Catholics and Abortion: Authority vs. Dissent." *Christian Century* 102 (October 2, 1985): 859-862. This article also appears in Patricia Beattie Jung and Thomas Shannon. *Abortion and Catholicism: The American Debate.* New York: Crossroad, 1988.

Ryan, Thomas. Ed. "The Churches on Abortion." *Ecumenism* 83 (1986): 1-285.

Sacred Congregation for the Doctrine of the Faith. "Declaration on Procured Abortion." *Linacre Quarterly* 2 (1975): 132-147.

Sacred Congregation for the Doctrine of the Faith. "Declaration on Abortion." Washington, DC: U.S. Catholic Conference, 1975.

Shannon, Thomas. "Abortion: A Challenge for Ethics and Public Policy." *Annual of the Society of Christian Ethics* (1982). This article also appears in Patricia Beattie Jung and Thomas Shannon. *Abortion and Catholicism: The American Debate.* New York: Crossroad, 1988.

_____. "Abortion: Ethical Review of Ethical Aspects of Public Policy." *The Annual Selected Papers* (Society of Christian Ethics, 1983).

Simmons, Paul. "A Theological Response to Fundamentalism on the Abortion Issue." *Church and Society* 71 (March-April 1981): 22-35.

------. "Dogma and Discord: Religious Liberty and the Abortion Debate." *Church and State* 43 (January 1990): 17-21.

Sinclair-Faulkner, Tom. "Canadian Catholics: At Odds on Abortion." *The Christian Century* 107 (September 9, 1981): 870-871.

Soley, Genny Earnest. "To Preserve and Protect Life: A Christian Feminist Perspective on Abortion." *Sojourners* 15 (October 1986): 34-37.

Steinfels, Margaret O'Brien. "Consider the Seamless Garment." *Christianity and Crisis* 43 (May 14, 1984): 172-174. This article also appears in Patricia Beattie Jung and Thomas Shannon. *Abortion and Catholicism: The American Debate.* New York: Crossroad, 1988.

Suhor, Mary Lou. Ed. "Procreative Freedom." *Witness* 72 (June 1989): 5-23.

Synder, Graydon F. "Covenant Theology and Medical Decision Making." *Brethren Life and Thought* 33 (Winter 1988): 27-35.

"Taking the Middle Road" [News: American Baptist Churches' abortion position]. *Christian Century* 105 (March 16, 1988): 273.

Tauer, Carol A. "The Tradition of Probabilism and the Moral Stance of the Early Embryo." *Theological Studies* 45 (March 1984): 3-33. This article also appears in Patricia Beattie Jung and Thomas Shannon. *Abortion and Catholicism: The American Debate.* New York: Crossroad, 1988.

Tickle, Phyllis. Ed. *Confessing Conscience: Churched Women on Abortion.* Nashville: Abingdon, 1990)

Tilley, Terrence W. "The Principle of Innocents' Immunity." *Horizons* 15 (Spring 1988): 43-63.

Wall, James. Ed. "Abortion: Is There a Middle Ground?" *Christian Century* 107 (February 21, 1990): 180-186.

Wassner, Thomas. "Contemporary Attitudes of the Roman Catholic Church Toward Abortion." *Journal of Religion and Health* 7 (October 1968): 311-323.

Weakland, Archbishop Rembert. "Abortion Issue Far from Black-and-White." *National Catholic Reporter* 26 (June 1, 1990): 24,4.

Weddington, Sarah Raggle. "The Woman's Right of Privacy." *Perkins Journal* 27 (Fall 1973): 35-41.

Williams, George H. "Religious Residues and Presuppositions in the American Debate on Abortion." *Theological Studies* 31 (March 1970): 10-75.

_____. "The Sacred Condominium." *The Morality of Abortion.* Ed. John T. Noonan, Jr. Cambridge, MA: Harvard University Press, 1970. 146-171.

Wind, James, ed. "Abortion: A Middle Ground." *Second Opinion* 10 (1989): 38-79.

Jewish

Biale, Rachel. "Abortion in Jewish Law." *Tikkun* 4 (July-August 1989): 26-28.

Bleich, David. "Abortion in Halakhic Literature." *Tradition* 10 (1968): 70-120.

Daum, Annette. "Assault on the Bill of Rights: The Jewish Stake." New York: Union of American Hebrew Congregations, 1982. 112-139.

_____. "The Jewish Stake in Abortion Rights." *Lilith* 8 (1982).

Feldman, David M. *Birth Control and Jewish Law.* New York: New York University Press, 1968.

_____. *Marital Relations, Birth Control, and Abortion in Jewish Law.* New York: Schocken, 1975.

Jakobiwitz, Isaac. *Jewish Medical Ethics*, Second Edition. New York: Block Publishing Company, 1975. 170-191.

Klein, Isaav. "Abortion: A Jewish View." *Dublin Review* 514 (Winter 1967-68): 382-390.
Letich, Larry. "Bad Choices" [abortion]. *Tikkun* 4 (July-August 1989): 22-26.
Rosen, Ruth. "Historically Compromised: the Abortion Struggle; Summer 1989. *Tikkun* 4 (July-August 1989): 20-21.

Islamic

Fazlur, Rahman. "Contraception and Abortion." In *Health and Medicine in the Islamic Tradition*. New York: Crossroads, 1984. 113-118.

Buddhist

Phillip, A. "A Buddhist View of Abortion." *Journal of Religion and Health* 26 (Fall 1987): 214-218.

Notes

1. The following official statements were collected by writing to the various religious groups to ask for their positions as well as to request permission to include them in the collection. Approximately 40 groups were contacted, representing a wide range of religious views within and among particular denominations. 18 responses were received.

2. Even though other views were sought, all the responses came from Christian denominations, except one conservative Jewish response. The author acknowledges that other religious traditions have important views on abortion, but these are not included.

3. National Ministries, American Baptist Churches USA, P.O. Box 851, Valley Forge, Pennsylvania 19482-0851.

4. The General Council of the Assemblies of God, Office of the General Secretary, 1445 Boonville Avenue, Springfield, Missouri 65802.

5. C. Everett Koop, "A Physician Looks at Abortion," in *Thou Shalt Not Kill*, ed. Richard L. Ganz (New York: Crown Publishers Inc., 1978), 8.

6. John Calvin, *Commentaries on the Four Last Books of Moses*, trans. Charles William Bingham, 4 vols. (Grand Rapids: Wm. B. Eerdmans Publishing Co., 1950), 3:41-42.

7. Donald Shoemaker, *Abortion, the Bible and the Christian* (Grand Rapids: Baker Book House, 1976).

8. Francis Shaeffer and C. Everett Koop, *Whatever Happened to the Human Race?* (Old Tappan, N.J.: Fleming H. Revell Co., 1979), 106.

9. Thomas J. Bliley, Jr., of Virginia, *Congressional Records, Extension of Remarks* (Washington, D.C., House of Representatives, July 25, 1983).

10. The Church of Jesus Christ of Latter-Day Saints, Office of the First Presidency, Salt Lake City, Utah 84150.

11. The Episcopal Church Center, 815 Second Avenue, New York, New York 10017.

12. Greek Orthodox Archdiocese of North and South America, 10 East 79th Street, New York, New York 10021.

13. The Lutheran Church--Missouri Synod, International Center, 1333 South Kirkwood Road, Saint Louis, Missouri 63122-7295. (314)965-9000 Telex 43-4452 Lutheran STL.

14. 9th All American Council of the Orthodox Church in America, St. Louis, Missouri, Sept. 19-24, 1989. Orthodox Church in America, P.O. Box 675, Route 25A, Syosset N.Y. (516) 922-

0550. Orthodox Christians for Life, P.O. Box 805, Melville, N.Y. (516) 271-4408.

15. Presbyterian Church (USA), 100 Witherspoon Street, Louisville, Kentucky 40202-1396.

16. United Church of Christ, Office for Church in Society, 110 Maryland Avenue N.E., Washington, D.C. 20002. (202)543-1517 (1990 address).

17. The United Synagogue of America, 155 Fifth Avenue, New York, New York 10010-6802; Rabbinical Assembly, 3080 Broadway Avenue, New York, New York 10027; Women's League for Conservative Judaism, 48 East 74th Street, New York, New York 10021.

18. *Abortion in a New Perspective: Report of the Task Force on Abortion,* April 1989. The Anglican Church of Canada, 600 Jarvis Street, Toronto, M4Y 2J6.

19. Canadian Conference of Catholic Bishops, 90 Parent Avenue, Ottawa, Canada K1N 7B1.

20. Baptist Convention of Ontario and Quebec, 217 George Street, Toronto, Ontario M5R 2M2.

21. The Lutheran Church--Canada, 59 Academy Road, Winnipeg, Manitoba R3M 0E2.

22. Lutheran Council in Canada, 25 Old York Mills Road, Willowdale (Toronto), Ontario M2P 1B5.

23. The Pentecostal Assemblies of Canada, Social Concerns, 10 Overlea Blvd., Toronto, Ontario M4H 1A5.

24. The Presbyterian Church in Canada, 50 Wynford Drive, Don Mills, Ontario M3C 1J7.

25. The United Church of Canada, 85 St. Clair Ave. East, Toronto, Ontario M4T 1M8.

Chapter Four

The Advocates and Advocacy Groups

1. ABORTION ADVOCACY

Advocates, either pro-life or pro-choice, actively campaign to bring about their vision of a morally appropriate societal response to the practice of abortion. This involvement includes participation in organizations, writing letters, lobbying, demonstrating and protesting. The advocate simply does not express his or her attitude on the abortion controversy, but actively attempts to direct its outcome.

On the issue of abortion, different moral positions are held, based on different world views. A world view is the larger context within which facts, reasons and arguments make sense. The way of life, belief, story, sense of reality, religious, political and economic traditions--each contributes to what a person holds as true and valuable. A person's world view is so fundamental as to the way he or she understands reality that it is often taken for granted. The response given to a particular ethical issue is based on deeply held world view assumptions. World views are modified or reinforced by experience.

It is because of seemingly irreconcilable world views that abortion is an ethical issue. Beliefs about the beginning of personhood, the roles and responsibilities of men and women in parenthood, the freedom and control of pregnant women, are all central to the abortion controversy. Because they involve such basic beliefs about human life, convictions are held strongly. Those on one side of the debate find it difficult to empathize with the position held by those on the other side. Sometimes, the people who are holding different positions are seen to be irrational or morally wrong.[1]

Kristen Luker conducted interviews with activists involved in the abortion debate. She was able to identify "an internally coherent and mutually shared view of the world" for the pro-choice and anti-abortion advocates, respectively. Furthermore, she points out that these world views are at odds with each other.[2] It is recognized that these proposed world views do not necessary hold for each and every advocate in the abortion debate. Each person's world view is distinctive to a certain degree. These characterizations may be helpful in a general way.

Luker characterizes the pro-life views of the world as based on the assumption that men and women are intrinsically different. As a result, men and women have different roles. Men belong in the public sphere of business and industry while the proper sphere for women is in the home with their children and families.

Based on these views, abortion is wrong for a number of reasons. Luker explains:

> First, it is intrinsically wrong because it takes a human life and what makes women special is their ability to nourish life. Second, it is wrong because *by giving women control over their fertility*, it breaks up an intricate set of social relationships between men and women that has traditionally surrounded (and, in ideal cases, protected) women and children. Third and finally, abortion is wrong because it fosters and supports a world view that deemphasizes (and therefore, downgrades) the traditional roles of men and women.[3]

Pro-choice people assume that men and women are substantially equal. Motherhood and family roles pose a threat to this equality. Involuntary motherhood is considered as low status within this organization of society. Control over reproduction gives women the opportunity to live up to their potential. Family life is important for women but it does not have to be their only meaningful role within society. This group holds a "gradualist" view of personhood. The personhood of the embryo develops over time. Potential rights are recognized for the embryo/fetus. At times, these potential rights may have to be sacrificed for the actual rights of the mother. Repeat abortions are troubling for this group because, with the aid of contraceptive counselling, possibly missing before the first abortion, the need for subsequent abortions should be eliminated. The conflict between the potential rights of the embryo/fetus and the mother should be minimized as much as possible. The normative view of parenthood is based on the assumption that the child will be given the best set of emotional, psychological, social and financial resources that the parents can provide. Control over the birth of the children is important so that these conditions can be met.[4]

Michael Cuneo takes issue with Luker's depiction of American anti-abortionists as a unitary group with a common set of demographic and ideological characteristics. In Canada, he has been able to identify three different types of activists within the anti-abortion movement.[5] Each type is directed by a different *emergent norm*, which serves as a kind of ideological charter.[6] These types can be briefly summarized as followed:

1. Civil rights activists. In their view, the case against abortion should be made by appealing exclusively to scientific evidence and to the civil rights of the fetus. Awareness of the humanity of the fetus can be achieved by educational, legislative and institutional reform.
2. Family heritage activists. This type of activist holds that the movement toward liberalized abortion is a strategy on the part of cultural elites (feminists, humanists) to subvert the traditional family and religious values.
3. Revivalist Catholic activists. This group of activists is distinguished by their belief that what is at stake in the abortion issue is the survival of Catholicism as the authentic source of transcendence and salvation, as well the killing of human life and the threat to traditional religious and family values.

Cuneo explains that changes which have taken place in the movement's history have been caused by an on-going contest between these norms.[7] Developments are generated as a result of challenges to existing practices of abortion, the court decisions on abortion, and the responses of the Church hierarchy, to name a few.

Luker and Cuneo are helpful in offering a framework in which to identify some of the different sorts of assumptions about human life and society. However, the usefulness of these categorizations is limited. As the statements below indicate, it is possible to find Catholics who advocate for free choice and feminists who take a strong anti-abortion position.

Advocacy on the abortion issue cannot be accurately categorized if it is done without considering the time and context in which it is carried out. The work by Luker and Cuneo is only an example of the kind of on-going research which needs to be conducted on this subject.

Jacqueline Scott and Howard Schuman, sociologists, have been interested in the views of the majority of the American public, who do not take "hard core" pro-choice or anti-abortion stances.[8] Even though the majority is pro-abortion, many support this position not because they feel passionately about the woman's right to choose, but rather that they hold mixed views and do not want to prohibit legal abortion entirely.[9] As a result, they may feel less intensely about the abortion issue than those at either extreme. Research carried out on attitude strength and social action in the abortion debate indicates that opponents of abortion are far more likely than proponents to regard the issues as important.

Advocates and Advocacy Groups

Many well-known activists and advocacy groups have emerged to fight the abortion cause. A few well known examples of advocates and groups are mentioned below.

United States

Bernard Nathanson

Bernard Nathanson has been a figure of major importance for the anti-abortion movement in both the United States and Canada, even though he did not start out in support of the cause. In fact in 1969, Dr. Nathanson, an obstetrician-gynecologist in New York City, was one of the founders of the National Association for the Repeal of the Abortion Laws (NARAL) in New York. Beginning in 1971, he also served as the director of the world's largest abortion clinic, known as the Center for Reproductive and Sexual Health. However, by 1974, he changed his position regarding the status of the fetus. He became an articulate campaigner for the pro-life cause. In terms of the types of activists which Cuneo has identified, Nathanson can be described as a civil rights activist, arguing for the humanity of the fetus based on the scientific testimony of fetology.[10]

Operation Rescue

The founder and director of Operation Rescue is Randell A. Terry. The supporters of Operation Rescue follow the admonition of Proverbs 24:11: "Rescue those who are unjustly sentenced to death; don't stand back and let them die."[11]

The main purpose of Operation Rescue is to prevent abortions from taking place. Efforts are made to shut down abortion clinics for short periods of time. Other purposes include repentance for the existing lethargy towards current abortion practices and for consciousness-raising. The strategy employed is civil disobedience.

Participants are mainly from the Evangelical and Roman Catholic traditions.[12]

Canada

Joseph Borowski

In 1971 Joe Borowski, a cabinet minister in the Manitoba government of Ed Schreyer, clashed with the New Democratic Party policy on abortion and left formal politics to promote his pro-life convictions. He established an organization called Alliance Against Abortion. In 1981, he began a fast to protest the proposed *Canadian Charter of Rights and Freedoms*, because explicit protection for the unborn had not been included. In 1983, in the Saskatchewan Provincial Court, Borowski challenged the constitutionality of Canada's 1969 abortion law. He was unsuccessful. He asked the Supreme Court to find that the fetus is a person with the right to life, liberty and security of the person and the right to equal protection of the law. In 1989, the Supreme Court refused to rule on the matter of fetal rights without an abortion law.[13] At this time, there was no law regulating the practice of abortion.

Henry Morgentaler

The most significant and successful advocate for the pro-choice movement has been Dr. Henry Morgentaler.[14] In 1968, he opened his first free-standing abortion clinic in Montreal. Later, he opened several others as well. He was charged with conspiracy to commit an abortion and the procuring of an abortion on three occasions. Three different juries acquitted him. Free-standing abortion clinics were at issue with the law because they did not comply with the requirements set out in Section 251 of the *Criminal Code*. The *Code* specified that abortions were to take place in an accredited or approved hospital, with the approval from the therapeutic abortion committee.

In June 1983, Morgentaler opened the Toronto abortion clinic on Harbord St. Later that month, Dr. Morgentaler and two colleagues were charged with abortion related offences. In December 1984, the three doctors were acquitted by a Supreme Court of Ontario jury on charges of conspiring to procure a miscarriage. The clinic was reopened. However, a few days later, the Ontario government launched an appeal of the acquittals and the clinic was closed again. New charges were laid against Morgentaler. In January 1985, the clinic was reopened. On April 25, 1985, the Ontario Court of Appeals overturned the jury acquittal. A retrial was ordered on Morgentaler's first charges. In 1986, Morgentaler appealed this decision to the Supreme Court of Canada. In 1988, Morgentaler's 1984 acquittal was upheld, ruling that the 1969 abortion law is unconstitutional because it violates the *Canadian Charter of Rights and Freedoms*.

Morgentaler has opened clinics in Montreal, Toronto, Winnipeg and Vancouver. In the Fall of 1990, he successfully challenged a provincial law in Nova Scotia, allowing him to operate a clinic in Halifax.

2. OFFICIAL STATEMENTS

UNITED STATES

Catholics For A Free Choice[15]

"I am here to say that the Catholic position [on abortion] is not so cohesive, not so monolithic as is often presented. It is my conviction that the church will come to a more nuanced position in this area....

Sister Mary Theresa Glynn, S.M.
Testimony before the Florida State Legislature, May 1978

Established in 1973, Catholics for a Free Choice (CFFC) is a national educational organization that supports the right to legal reproductive health care, especially to family planning and abortion. CFFC also works to reduce the incidence of abortion and to increase women's choices in childbearing and child-rearing through advocacy of social and economic programs for women, families, and children. **We believe in:**

- The Moral Agency of Women
Women are to be respected as moral agents. They can be trusted to make decisions that support the well being of their families, children and society and enhance their own integrity and health.

- The Primacy of Informed Conscience

A Catholic who is convinced that her conscience is correct, in spite of a conflict with magisterial Church teaching, not only may, but must follow the dictates of conscience rather than the teaching of the magisterium.

- The Right to Dissent

The teaching of the hierarchical magisterium on moral issues related to human reproduction, while serious, is not infallible. Catholics have the right to dissent from such non-infallible teachings without fear of reprisal from the institutional Church.

- Religious Freedom

Faith groups in the United States hold a number of different beliefs on both the morality and legality of abortion. Catholics need to respect this diversity of legitimate views. We must not seek legislation that would limit the groups in the practice of their religion.

- Social Justice

Catholic principles of social justice speak to a preferential option for the poor. Poor women are entitled to public funding for abortion and family planning as well as for childbearing and child-rearing. Denial of such funding is discriminatory and unjust.

CFFC is a visible alternative to religious antichoice groups, particularly those identified with the Roman Catholic Church.

We provide:

- A forum for dialogue on ethical questions related to human reproduction.
- An active public education and media program, including publications, a speaker's bureau, seminars, and conferences.
- A bimonthly newsjournal, *Conscience.*
- A national public affairs program that provides policymakers with the data necessary to make informed public policy decisions, as well as to articulate an ethically sound prochoice position.
- Grassroots advocacy through the Key Activist program, which assists local groups with educational and legislative projects.
- Partnership with both prochoice and Catholic organizations to increase the level of concern and responsiveness to the moral and ethical dimensions of the prochoice issue.
- An international network focused on education and information exchange.

Feminists For Life Of America[16]

ABORTION DOES NOT LIBERATE WOMEN

Most modern feminists have made easy access to abortion the very symbol of the liberation of women. The literature of the National Organization for Women repeatedly refers to abortion as "the most fundamental right of women"--more important even than the right to vote and the right to free speech. NOW has designated the protection of abortion rights as its top priority.

This is ironic, because abortion does not liberate women. On the contrary, abortion--and the perceived need for it--validate the patriarchal world view which holds that women, encumbered as they are by their reproductive capacity, are inferior to men.

Abortion liberates men, not women. There are three reasons for this:

> "Feminism is part of a larger philosophy
> that values all life."

Truly liberated women reject abortion because they reject the male world view that accepts violence as a legitimate solution to conflict. Rather than settling for mere equality--the right to contribute equally to the evil of the world--prolife feminists seek to transform society to create a world that reflects true feminist ideals.

Feminism is, properly, part of a larger philosophy that values all life. Feminists believe that all human beings have inherent worth and that this worth cannot be conferred or denied by another. True feminist thinking recognizes the interdependence of all living things and the new responsibility we all have for one another. This feminism rejects the male view that sees individuals as functioning separately from their fellows, in mutual competition.

Abortion is incompatible with this feminist vision. Abortion atomizes women. It pits them against their own children as competitors for the favors of the patriarchy. Abortion is of great benefit to employers who do not have to make concessions to pregnant women and mothers, to schools which do not have to commit themselves to their mates or their children. Women who accept abortion have agreed to sacrifice their children for the convenience of a man's world.

Women who have been liberated from male thought patterns refuse to participate in their own oppression and in the oppression of their children. They refuse to accept abortion, which denigrates the life-giving capacity of women. They strive instead to create a world that recognizes the moral superiority of maternal thinking and is, therefore, gentle, living, nurturing, and pro-life. Every abortion frustrates this goal and perpetuates the patriarchy. Liberated women will not cooperate. They refuse abortion and all it represents.

Efforts to establish abortion as a legitimate solution to the problems of being a woman in a male-dominated society surrender women to pregnancy discrimination. Those feminists who demand the right to abortion concede the notion that a pregnant woman is inferior to a non-pregnant one. They admit that pregnancy and motherhood are incompatible to being a fully functioning adult, and that an unencumbered, unattached male is the model for success. By settling for abortion instead of working for the social changes that would make it possible to combine children and career, pro-abortion feminists have agreed to participate in a man's world under a man's terms. They have betrayed the majority of working women--who want to have children.

Abortion allows men to escape responsibility for their own sexual behavior. A man whose child is aborted is relieved of the requirement that he support his children. It is not surprising that the Playboy Foundation is a major supporter of abortion rights, because abortion is a natural consequence of the Playboy's ideal of uncommitted, anonymous sex without consequences. Women can be reduced to the status of a consumer item, which if "broken" by pregnancy can be "fixed" by abortion.

Proabortion feminists have corrupted feminism by embracing male standards, which hold that it is permissible to treat "unequals" unequally, and for the powerful to oppress the weak. By accepting this patriarchal world view, these feminists have capitulated to male dominance. Women who agree to conform to the ideals of a world made by and for men are not liberated; they have merely altered their roles within the patriarchy.

National Abortion Federation[17]

KEEPING ABORTION SERVICES LEGAL, ACCESSIBLE AND SAFE

Clinics and physicians who display the symbol of the National Abortion Federation have joined with their colleagues in the only national, professional organization committed to making abortion services accessible and safe for all women.

Founded in 1977, four years after the Supreme Court decision in *Roe v. Wade* legalized abortion throughout the United States, the National Abortion Federation has several functions:

1. To unite the providers of abortion services into a professional community dedicated to quality care.

2. To offer providers the standards, guidelines, training and education that will help them upgrade their services.

3. To serve as a clearinghouse on the variety and quality of services offered in abortion facilities. This information is needed by legislative bodies, public policy organizations, medical groups, concerned citizens and women with unwanted pregnancies.

4. To keep abreast of public policy developments affecting reproductive health care and to find effective ways in which to participate in these developments.

5. To provide public information that will allow women to obtain quality abortion services.

National Organization for Women

National NOW Times "Resolutions Passed In Cincinnati"[18]

FREEDOM CAMPAIGN FOR WOMEN'S LIVES

WHEREAS, from July 3, 1989, the women of America no longer can entrust their fundamental constitutional right to abortion to the U.S. Supreme Court, and

WHEREAS, the executive branch of the federal government, under President George Bush, has demonstrated unequivocally its hostility to abortion rights and has called for both the overturn of *Roe v. Wade* and the enactment of a "Human Life Amendment" which would give a fertilized egg superior rights to a living woman or girl, and

WHEREAS, the Congress of the United States has regularly abdicated its responsibility to protect women's rights to abortion, led by an anti-abortion majority in the House of Representatives, by adopting amendments injurious to women, such as the anti-abortion amendment on the 1988 Civil Rights Restoration Act and an amendment that barred the District of Columbia from using its locally-raised revenues to fund abortions for poor women, and

WHEREAS, Congress has the responsibility to enforce and protect the constitutional rights of all Americans and will be considering legislation to reverse the impact of the Webster decision this fall, and

WHEREAS, the reality of the composition of state legislatures is that only a handful of legislatures can be counted upon to protect abortion rights in 1989, and

WHEREAS, public opinion polls, the 1989 March for Women's Lives, and continuing expressions of outrage by the abortion rights majority in America clearly demonstrate that people support, and are willing to fight for, the fundamental right to abortion for women and girls,

THEREFORE, BE IT RESOLVED that the National Organization for Women launch the Freedom Campaign for Women's Lives by going directly to the people in a mass organizing effort with a multi-faceted strategy:

1) To bring hundreds of thousands of Americans to the nation's capital on November 12, 1989 to demonstrate their outrage at the erosion of abortion rights by the Supreme Court and to demand Congressional protection of those rights;

2) To pass federal legislation that will restore the fundamental right to abortion for women and girls throughout our nation;

3) To analyze and target key states for ballot initiatives that will protect the fundamental right to abortion;

4) To formulate strategies and legislation to stop anti-abortion legislation in the states;

5) To initiate or join litigation efforts to protect abortion rights in states with right to privacy provisions in their constitutions;

6) To pressure pharmaceutical companies and the Food and Drug Administration to allow research on, and testing of, RU-486, the abortion pill, in our nation;

7) To research, examine, analyze and build support for a constitutional amendment that would protect abortion rights for women and girls for all time;

BE IT FURTHER RESOLVED that the Freedom Caravan for Women's Lives be used as the major organizing vehicle at the state level to activate and train the "political army" mobilized by the April 9, 1989, March for Women's Equality/Women's Lives, the November 12, 1989, mass demonstration, and the overwhelming public reaction to the Webster decision.

BE IT FURTHER RESOLVED that National NOW assist in coordinating actions in the states to mark the anniversary of *Roe v. Wade* in 1990.

Planned Parenthood Federation of America[19]

1988 ANNUAL REPORT

NATIONAL OFFICE ACTIVITIES
Serving the Field of Family Planning

Planned Parenthood enjoys worldwide recognition as an authority on all aspects of family planning and reproductive health care. PPFA's national office provides comprehensive, up-to-date information to other national agencies, health care professionals, the media, and individuals.

AFFILIATE ACTIVITIES

Planned Parenthood has built its outstanding reputation on a record of high-quality, low-cost, easily accessible medical services, meeting the reproductive health needs of an extremely diverse range of communities in every region of the U.S.

In addition to more than 330,000 referrals for prenatal care, abortion, sterilization, infertility treatment, social services, and other care, affiliates provided the following (figures approximated):

- Contraceptive services for 1.7 million people.
- Pregnancy diagnosis for 261,000 women; of those who were pregnant, 2,400 received prenatal care from Planned Parenthood.
- Infertility diagnosis and treatment for 540 men and women.
- Screening for cervical and breast cancer, including more than 1.4 million Pap smears, of which more than 36,000 or 2.6 percent, revealed evidence of cervical disease. Planned Parenthood screens

more women for cervical cancer than does any other single health provider in the U.S.
- Testing and counselling services for sexually transmitted diseases for more than one million people.
- Voluntary sterilization services for 3,800 men and 700 women.
- Abortions for 104,000 women.
- Diagnosis and treatment for a broad range of other reproductive and general health care conditions, including nutrition and genetic counselling, premarital examinations, and testicular cancer screening and self-examination instruction, for 178,000 women and men.

Amid international controversy, the French government last year approved the use of RU 486, the new drug developed in France that safely ends an early pregnancy without surgery. Anti-abortion pressure and threats, however, caused Roussel-Uclaf, the pill's manufacturer, to pull the drug from the market. But in response to a resounding outcry from Planned Parenthood, the international medical community, and others, the French government ordered Roussel-Uclaf to proceed with marketing and distribution, calling RU 486 "the moral property of women."

Family planning experts around the world regard the new drug as a significant therapeutic advance. RU 486 can revolutionize the experience of abortion for all women--making the procedure safer, less invasive, and truly private. But RU 486 holds the greatest promise for women in the developing world, where unsafe, often self-induced abortions kill an estimated 200,000 each year and brutally maim millions more.

In addition to its abortifacient properties, RU 486 also shows great potential for the treatment of glaucoma, breast cancer, tubal pregnancies, infertility, and difficult or prolonged labor.

In 1988, to encourage further exploration and marketing of this important new drug, the national office and affiliates worked in coalition with several health and public policy organizations to: build popular support for RU 486 in the U.S.; clear the way for further research into the actions and effects of the drug; counter the efforts of the anti-family planning minority to block women's access to this and all other means of controlling their reproduction; and, ultimately, make RU 486 available to American women.

CANADA

Canadian Abortion Rights Action League (CARAL)[20]

The purpose of CARAL is to ensure that no woman in Canada is denied access to safe, legal abortion. Our aim is to keep abortion out of the Criminal Code. We want to see the establishment of comprehensive contraception and abortion services, including appropriate counselling, across the country. We regard the right to safe, legal abortion as a fundamental human right.

Right To Life Association (Toronto and Area)[21]

RIGHT TO LIFE is an educational association. We are a charitable, volunteer, non-sectarian, human rights organization which holds these principles:

- The right to life is the basic human right on which all other rights depend.

- All human beings share this right both before and after birth.

- Society has a duty to protect this right.

3. BIBLIOGRAPHY

For related material, see Demographics, Sociological Research and Opinion Polls and Law and Politics Bibliography.

Amyotte, Earl. "Charter No Help to Unborn." *The Interim* 1 (March 1983): 4.

Andrusko, Dave. Ed. *To Rescue the Future: The Pro-Life Movement in the 1980s.* Toronto: Life Cycle Books, 1983.

Bader, Elenor J. "Operation Rescue: The Name's A Lie." [Also Pro-choice Forces Fight Back by Suzanne Messing, 1] *New Directions for Women* 18 (March-April 1989).

Bernardin, Cardinal Joseph. *The Seamless Garment.* Kansas City: National Catholic Reporter Publishing, 1984.

Bottcher, Rosemary. "Pro-Abortionists Poison Feminism." *Pro-Life Feminism*. Ed. Gail Grenier Sweet. Toronto: Life Cycle Books, 1985. 45-47.

Brennan, William. *The Abortion Holocaust: Today's Final Solution*. St. Louis: Landmark Press, 1983.

Brockhouse, Gordon. "Giant Rally a 'Success.'" *The Interim* 3 (November 1985): 1, 2.

Burtchaell, James T. *Rachel Weeping: The Case against Abortion*. Kansas City: Andrews and McMeel, 1982.

Cavanaugh-O'Keefe, John. *No Cheap Solutions*. Gaithersburg, Md.: Prolife Nonviolent Action Project, 1984.

------. *Nonviolence Is an Adverb*. Gaithersburg, Md.: Prolife Nonviolent Action Project, 1985.

Connors, Joseph M. "Operation Rescue." *America* (April 29, 1989): 400-406.

Corelli, Rae. "An Inflamed Debate: Judgments on Abortion Trigger New Protests." *Maclean's* (July 17, 1989): 36-37.

Cryderman, Lyn. Ed. "‹Prolife›: What Does It Really Mean?" *Christianity Today* 33 (July 14, 1989): 27-38.

Davis, Susan. "Pro-Choice: A New Militancy." *Hastings Center Report* 19 (November-December 1989): 32-33.

De Valk, Alphonse. *Morality and Law in Canadian Politics: The Abortion Controversy*. Montreal: Palm Publishers, 1974.

------. *The Worst Law Ever*. Edmonton: Life Ethics Centre, 1979.

------. *Abortion: Christianity, Reason and Human Rights*. Edmonton: Life Ethics Centre, 1982.

------. *Abortion Politics: Canadian Style*. Edmonton: Life Ethics Centre, 1982.

------. "Open Letter to Catholic Bishops: Let's Put Our House in Order." *The Interim* 2:9 (December 1984): 8-9.

------. "Our Bishops on *Humanae Vitae*." *The Interim* 4:6 (September 1986): 12.

------. "The Sexual Revolution, Feminism and the Churches (Part X): Catholic Bishops of Canada." *The Interim* 5:9 (December, 1987): 17.

De Veber, L.L., and Jessica Pegis. *Heroin vs Morphine: The Current Debate*. Toronto: Human Life Research Institute, 1985.

English, Deirdre. "The War Against Choice: Inside the Antiabortion Movement." *Mother Jones* (February-March 1981).

Fairweather, Eugene R., and Ian Gentles, Eds. *The Right to Birth*. Toronto: Anglican Book Centre, 1976.

Falik, Marilyn M. "Ideology and Abortion Policy Politics." Unpublished Ph.D. dissertation, New York University, 1975.

Fried, Marlene Gerber. *From Abortion to Reproductive Freedom: Transforming a Movement*. Boston: South End Press, 1990.

Gallagher, John. *Is the Human Embryo a Person?* Toronto: Human Life Research Institute, 1985.

Gentles, Ian. *The Law and Abortion*. Toronto: Human Life Research Institute, 1985.

Granberg, Donald. "The Abortion Activists." *Family Planning Perspectives* 13 (1981): 158-161.

Hayes, Kathleen. "Fully Prolife." *Sojourners* 18 (November 22, 1989): 27-38.

Hierlihy, Sue. "Ottawa Inquest Exposes Rubber-Stamp Abortions." *The Interim* 4 (June 1986): 3.

"I Support You But I Can't Sign My Name": Pro-Choice Catholics Testify. Catholics for a Free Choice, Washington, DC. 1982.

Jones, E. Michael, "Abortion Mill Rescue: Are Sit-ins the Answer?" *Fidelity* 6 (July-August 1987): 28-37.

Koop, C. Everett, and Francis A. Schaeffer. *Whatever Happened to the Human Race?* Westchester, Ill: Crossway Books, 1983.

Kremer, E.J., and E.A. Synan, eds. *Death before Birth: Canada and the Abortion Question*. Toronto: Griffin House, 1974.

Landolt, C. Gwendolyn. "The Borowski Case (What's It All About)." *The Interim* 1 (May 1983): 1, 3.

Little, David. "Announcing the Catholic Foundation for Human Life." *The Interim* 2 (April 1984): 13.

Loesch, Juli. *Acts of Aggression*. Chapel Hill, NC: Prolifers for Survival, 1985.

------. *Imagining the Real*. Chapel Hill, NC: Prolifers for Survival, 1985.

Marx, Paul. *The Death Peddlers: War on the Unborn*. Collegeville, Minn.: Saint John's University Press, 1971.

------. "Explaining the Contraceptive Mentality." *The Interim* 6 (April 1987): 27.

McLuhan, Sabina. "All in the Family." *The Interim* 4 (June 1986): 27.

Meehan, Francis X. *Abortion and Nuclear War: Two Issues, One Moral Cause*. Liguori, MO: Liguori Publications, 1984.

Meehan, Mary. "On the Road with the Rescue Movement." *The Human Life Review* 15 (Summer 1989): 7-23.

Migliorino, Monica M. "Report from Rats' Alley: Down and Out with the Unborn in Chicago and Milwaukee." *Fidelity* 6 (July-August 1987): 38-45.

Morris, Heather, and Lorraine Williams. *Physical Complications of Abortion*. Toronto: Human Life Research Institute, 1985.

National Abortion Rights Action League. "Post-*Webster* Anti-Choice Legislative Activity." Washington, DC. memorandum. March 29, 1990.

National Family Planning and Reproductive Health Association. "The 1980s: Decade of Disaster for Family Planning." Washington, DC: April, 1990.

Nathanson, Bernard N. (with R.N. Ostling). *Aborting America.* Garden City, NY: Doubleday, 1979.

------. *The Abortion Papers.* New York: Frederick Fell, 1983.

Paige, Connie. *The Right to Lifers: Who They Are, How They Operate, Where They Get Their Money.* New York: Summit Books, 1983.

Parthun, Mary. *The Psychological Effects of Induced Abortion.* Toronto: Human Life Research Institute, 1985.

Pegis, Jessica, L.L. de Verber, and Ian Gentles. *Sex Education: A Review of the Literature from Canada, the United States, Britain and Sweden.* Toronto: Human Life Research Institute, 1986.

Pelrine, Eleanor. *Abortion in Canada.* Toronto: New Press, 1972.

Petrasek, Grace. "REAL Women and Election '84." *The Interim* 2 (September 1984): 17.

Powell, John, *Abortion: The Silent Holocaust.* Allen, Texas: Argus Communications, 1981.

Rice, Charles. *Fifty Questions on Abortion, Euthanasia, and Related Issues.* Notre Dame, Ind.: Cashel Institute, 1986.

Scheidler, Joseph M. *Closed: 99 Ways to Stop Abortion.* Toronto: Life Cycle Books, 1985.

Summerhill, Louise. *The Story of Birthright: The Alternative to Abortion.* Libertyville, Ill.: Prow Books, 1973.

Sweet, Gail Grenier. Ed. *Pro-Life Feminism.* Toronto: Life Cycle Books, 1985.

Tabisz, Ellen. "A Farewell Work." *Pro-Life News* (May 1983): 10.

Thimmesch, Nick. *When Abortion Fails: The Unborn's Uncertain Destiny.* Toronto: Life Cycle Books n.d.

Toth, Kathleen. "A Message from the President." *The Interim* 1 (March 1983): 5.

Verny, Thomas and John Kelly. *The Secret Life of the Unborn Child.* Toronto: Collins, 1981.

Watters, Wendell W. *Compulsory Parenthood: The Truth About Abortion.* Toronto: McClelland and Stewart, 1976.

Willke, J.C. "From the President's Desk: A Place for Public Witness?" *National Right to Life News* (May 15, 1986): 3, 8.

Wills, Garry. "'Save the Babies' Operation Rescue: A Case Study in Galvanizing the Antiabortion Movement." *Time* (May 1, 1989): 23-25.

Notes

1. For a discussion of how members of social movements are depicted, see R. H. Turner and L.M. Killam, *Collective Behavior* (3rd ed., Englewood Cliffs, NJ: Prentice-Hall, Inc. 1987).

2. Kristen Luker, *Abortion and the Politics of Motherhood* (Berkeley: University of California Press, 1984), 159. For scholarly reviews of her book, see Carole Joffe, "The Meaning of the Abortion Conflict," *Contemporary Sociology* 14 (1985): 26-28; and James Kelly, "Tracking the Intractable: A Survey on the Abortion Controversy," *Cross Currents* (Summer-Fall 1985): 212-218.

3. Ibid., 161-162.

4. Ibid., 175-186.

5. Michael Cuneo, *Catholics Against the Church: Anti-Abortion Protest in Toronto, 1969-1985* (Toronto: University of Toronto Press, 1989), 84-116.

6. Cuneo noted that there has not been a great deal of unbiased study on advocates with regard to the abortion issue (81).

7. Ibid., 86.

8. Jacqueline Scott and Howard Schuman, "Attitude Strength and Social Action in the Abortion Dispute," *American Sociological Review* 53 (October 1988): 785-793.

9. Jacqueline Scott, "Conflicting Values and Compromise Beliefs about Abortion" (Ph.D. dissertation. University of Michigan, University Microfilms International). As quoted in Scott and Schuman, "Attitude Strength and Social Action in the Abortion Dispute," 786.

10. B.N. Nathanson (with Richard N. Ostling), *Aborting America* (Garden City, NY: Doubleday, 1979), 187-217; and B.N. Nathanson, *The Abortion Papers* (New York: Frederick Fell, 1983), 177-209. As cited in Cuneo.

11. Joseph Connors, "Operation Rescue," *America* (April 29, 1989), 400.

12. Ibid., 401. See also Mary Meehan, "On the Road with Rescue Movement," *The Human Life Review* 15 (Summer 1989), 2-23.

13. *Borowski v. Canada* (Attorney General) [1989] 1 S.C.R. 342.

14. See Eleanor Pelrine, *Morgentaler: the Doctor Who Couldn't Turn Away* (Toronto: Gage, 1975); The National Film Board documentary, *Democracy on Trial: The Morgentaler Affair*; and "Step-by-Step History of Morgentaler Fight," *Toronto Star*, January 29, 1988, A12.

15. Catholics for a Free Choice, 1436 U Street, NW, Suite 301, Washington, DC 20009.

16. Feminists for Life of America, 811 East 47th Street, Kansas City, Missouri 64110.
17. National Abortion Federation, 1436 U Street, N.W., Suite 103, Washington, DC 20009.
18. *National NOW Times* (July/August/September 1989).
19. Planned Parenthood Federation of America, 810 Seventh Avenue, New York, New York 10019.
20. Canadian Abortion Rights Action League (CARAL), 344 Bloor Street West, Suite 306, Toronto, Ontario M5S 3A7.
21. Right to Life Association of Toronto and Area, 144A Yonge Street, Toronto, Ontario M5C 1X6.

Chapter Five

Politics and Law

Participants in the abortion debate monitor the events surrounding policy development in other countries. When legislation is changed or an important court ruling is made in one country, policy-makers in neighbouring countries examine the rationale for the change and assess any possible implications within their own jurisdictions. This on-going interaction takes place between Canada and the United States.

1. THE AMERICAN SITUATION

Before 1825, the precedents of common law governed the practice of abortion. At this time, abortion prior to "quickening" (detection of movement) was left to the women themselves. Until the woman could feel movement in the womb, it was held that the fetus was not a person, and termination prior to this point was neither a moral or civil issue.[1] The state laws enacted between 1821 and the mid-1830s had the intent of protecting women from "unscrupulous practitioners and the use of poisons, and the fetus from post-quickening abortions."[2] In the mid-1930s, a number of factors led to the passing of increasingly restrictive abortion laws. These laws developed as the result of the mobilization of bias and interest group pressure, composed primarily of physicians and ministers. The physicians were attempting to regularize and professionalize their practice. The ministers were concerned with the fact that non-Protestant immigrants had a higher birth rate than the Protestants. In fact, at this time, abortion was widely used as a means of birth control, especially among the white, Protestant, middle and upper classes.[3] By 1873, the Comstock Act was passed which made illegal the publication, selling or possession of materials which prevented conception, or induced abortion.[4]

Changes began to occur in the 1960s. The 1965 Supreme Court decision, *Griswold v. Connecticut* held that it was unconstitutional to prohibit the selling of contraceptive devices to married persons. This ruling was based on the right to privacy of marital relationships.[5] In 1969, a federal district court decision *U.S. v. Vuitch* held that: "...as a secular matter a woman's liberty and right to privacy extends to family, marriage, and sex matters and may well include the right to remove an unwanted child, at least in the early stages of pregnancy."[6] In the 1970s, the Comstock Law was amended by Congress "to eliminate references to contraception."[7]

The 1973 Supreme Court Decision, *Roe v. Wade*

In the 1960s, with the Supreme Court's recognition of the right to privacy, the abortion issue became politically significant. Activists put forward a series of legal challenges to the validity of the state abortion laws. As a result, on January 23, 1973 the Supreme Court in a 7-2 majority struck down as unconstitutional the Texas and Georgia abortion laws in *Roe v. Wade*[8] and *Doe v. Bolton*.[9] These cases have served as landmarks in the abortion controversy, with important implications in practice.[10]

Roe v. Wade

Roe v. Wade invalidated a 1857 Texas statute which prohibited abortion except for "the purpose of saving the life of the mother."[11]

The overall decision made in *Roe*, written by Justice Harry A. Blackmun, was based on the Ninth Amendment and the Fourteenth Amendment rights of the woman. The Court held that "This right of privacy...is broad enough to encompass a woman's decision whether or not to terminate her pregnancy. The detriment that the State would impose upon the pregnant woman by denying this choice altogether is apparent."

However, the right to privacy was not considered to be absolute. The state does have some interest in what happens to the pregnant woman and the fetus. Thus, the "state may properly assert important interests in safeguarding health, in maintaining medical standards, and in protecting potential life." According to the Court, "at some point in the pregnancy these respective interests [became] sufficiently compelling to sustain regulation of the factors that govern the abortion decision." The degree of this interest was categorized in terms of three trimesters.

Abortions in the first trimester are considered to be comparatively safe because the mortality for abortion is lower than for childbirth. On the basis of this fact, the Court decided that the abortion decision should be left to the pregnant woman in consultation with her attending physician.

In the second and third trimesters, restrictions were placed on abortion decisions. In the second trimester, the state may enact regulations. However, their purpose was limited to insure a safe abortion for the pregnant woman. For example, it may be required that the abortion be carried out by a qualified physician in an abortion clinic.

In the third trimester, the laws of the state may intervene to restrict the availability of abortion. The Court held that the state may regulate or even proscribe "abortion" in order to promote "its interest in the potentiality of human life, or the health of the mother" in "the stage subsequent to viability," in which the fetus "has the capacity of meaningful life outside the mother's womb." The exception is in those cases where the "preservation" of a mother's life or health is involved.

Doe v. Bolton

Doe v. Bolton is the companion case to *Roe v. Wade*. In this decision, Georgia's "reform" abortion statute was invalidated. This statute permitted abortion where the continued pregnancy would endanger the woman's life or health, including mental health, where there was the possibility that the fetus would likely be born with a serious defect, or where the pregnancy resulted from rape. Also, it required that abortion be carried out in an accredited hospital, and that two physicians confirm the judgment of the necessity of the abortion with the physician performing the abortion. The Supreme Court acknowledged that the State of Georgia did have a right to license all facilities where abortion may be performed, but the standards adopted must be legitimate. Special barriers placed upon hospitals and other facilities in the area of abortion services which did not apply in other areas of health services would not be considered legitimate.[12]

Responses to the 1973 Supreme Court Decision

Pro-choice advocates were jubilant about the *Roe v. Wade* decision. However, the anti-abortion advocates responded with strategies either to limit or to reverse the Supreme Court's decision.

Albert Pearson and Paul Kurtz have examined the political reaction to the abortion controversy and the legal cases which have followed *Roe*.[13] They present the aftermath to *Roe* in the two following aspects: 1) the post-*Roe* legislation at both the state and federal levels with the intent to regulate abortion through time, place and manner restrictions; and 2) the various proposals designed not merely to mitigate the effects of *Roe*, but to overrule it. These proposals include a variety of constitutional amendments put forward in Congress and legislative substitutes for a constitutional amendment.

The outline of the political and legal aftermath to *Roe* is presented by Pearson and Kurtz in a clear and helpful way, and so is followed here.

Indirect Regulation of Abortion

Some state legislatures implemented strategies for the indirect legislation of abortion. It was done in defiance of *Roe*, with the hope of eroding the Supreme Court's authority.[14] Two approaches were used to carry this challenge forward. These strategies are known as "power investiture" and "burden creation."

1. The power investiture means the delegation to a third party of the power to prevent an abortion. Usually, husbands or parents served as the third party who was given the power to veto the decision to abort. There were two advantages to this strategy. Without the fear of criminal liability for the pregnant woman, the third party may be more willing to report the proposed abortion to the authorities. Second, this strategy seemed to support the constitutionally protected interests of the husband and the parents.

However, in *Planned Parenthood of Central Missouri v. Danforth*,[15] the Court rejected the requirement of written spousal consent for first-term abortion. It reasoned that since the legislature could not stop abortion in the first term under *Roe*, then neither could the husband. The woman's right to abort was greater than the father's constitutionally rooted interests. In *Bellotti v. Baird*,[16] it was ruled that minor females have a constitutional right to decide for themselves on abortion, on the condition that they possess some maturity of judgment. Parental permission is not required. Even immature minors may obtain an abortion without parental approval, though approval may be necessary by a state official.[17]

2. The burden creation strategy is the enhancement of the costs or risks associated with abortion. The intent of this approach is to reduce the appeal of abortion as a choice for pregnant women. Pearson and Kurtz point out that the Supreme Court has been less hostile to this strategy.[18] It is the plaintiff who must prove that the exercise of her constitutional right is unduly burdened by the statute regulating the abortion. This can be a difficult task. Burdensome schemes have been allowed by the Supreme Court because it appears that legitimate state goals are furthered by them or that the right to an abortion is not violated by them. Four types of abortion statutes fell within the burden creation strategy. These include the following:

a. *Increasing the risks.* One type of statute increased the risks associated with undergoing or performing an abortion. For example, a special duty of care could be placed on physicians to preserve fetal life if they believed that the fetus is viable. If the physician breached this duty, then he or she could be held liable under criminal homicide statutes. Another approach to increase the risk is the forbidding of specific abortion procedures as deleterious to maternal health, supposedly in keeping with the *Roe* decision.

In the Pennsylvania statute *Collautti v. Franklin*,[19] physicians were given a special duty to care whenever they had sufficient evidence to believe that the fetus was viable after the abortion. Thus, physicians faced a risk of prosecution for erroneous judgment about viability. However, the Supreme Court struck this statute down because of an ambiguity in the wording of the statute. The result of the ambiguity would make physicians unwilling to perform abortions and thus, constricting the right to have an abortion.

In *Planned Parenthood of Central Missouri v. Danforth*, a statute was enacted which forbade saline amniocentesis after the first term of pregnancy because it was held to be deleterious to maternal health.[20] The state held that this statute was consistent with *Roe* since it was concerned for the preservation of maternal health in the second trimester of the pregnancy. The Court struck this statute down for a number of reasons. The most important reason was that in forbidding a relatively safe abortion technique of saline amniocentesis, more dangerous methods of abortion would be permitted, with the effect of increasing the risks to the mother.[21]

b. *Restricting the availability of abortion facilities.* In the attempt to decrease the number of abortions, some laws were enacted to limit the location of where abortions could be performed.

In *Akron v. Akron Center for Reproductive Health*,[22] the city of Akron required all abortions after the first trimester to be performed in hospitals rather than in the more easily accessible and less costly clinics. The intent was supposedly in keeping with the *Roe* specification of concern for maternal health. The Akron ordinance was struck down by the Supreme Court. In its view, the restriction on abortion clinics did not protect maternal health interests sufficiently to justify the increased burden on the woman in obtaining the abortion.

In *Deerfield Medical Center v. Deerfield Beach*,[23] an occupational license was denied for the operation of the abortion clinic in an area zoned for business operations. This Fifth Circuit Court found that the city did not base its rejection of the license on traditional zoning concerns. Rather, the refusal of the license served to burden a constitutional right.[24]

c. *Statutes increasing the costs of abortion.* Another way to increase the burden to the women seeking abortion is to increase the costs.

In *Planned Parenthood Association of Kansas City v. Ashcroft*[25] two separate cost-increasing provisions were included in the Missouri statute. The first required the presence of two physicians at all abortions performed after the first trimester. While the first physician was to take primary care of the mother, the second physician was to take care of the fetal life and health. Even though this requirement did increase the cost of the abortion, the Supreme Court upheld this part of the statute because it supported the state's interest in the potentiality of fetal life at that stage.

The second part of the statute specified that a qualified pathologist make a tissue sample analysis in all abortions. Even though the cost of the abortion was increased by such a requirement, the Supreme Court also upheld this part of the statute on the grounds that it served the legitimate state interest of protection of the mother's health and was not unduly burdensome.

d. *Other abortion laws with potentially coercive effects.* State laws have been enacted which can discourage the woman seeking the abortion by the administrative and procedural process.[26]

In *H.L. v. Matheson*,[27] the Court upheld a Utah provision which required that an unemancipated minor who lived with her parents must notify them. Even though earlier state attempts to establish parental consent requirements had not been successful, in this case, the Court reasoned that state interests in preserving parental authority within the family, in providing necessary health-related information and in allowing parental consultation were important enough to uphold the notification statute.

On June 25, 1990, decisions were made in two abortion cases before the court involving state requirements that the parents be notified when their minor daughters seek an abortion. These regulations were challenged as unduly burdensome to a young pregnant woman.[28]

In *Hodgson v. Minnesota*, the court, in a 5-4 vote, said that states may require a woman under 18 to tell both parents before obtaining an abortion as long as she has the alternative of seeking permission from a judge. In a separate 5-4 vote, the justices struck down a provision in the same Minnesota law that would have required two-parent notification with no judicial bypass.[29]

In *Ohio v. Akron Center for Reproductive Health*, the Court ruled 6-3 that the state can require notice be given to one parent or that a judge's permission be granted. The intention of the judicial bypass is to allow the teenager to show either that she is mature enough and well informed enough to make the abortion decision herself or that the abortion would be in her best interest.

Another approach to creating an administrative deterrence to abortion are statutes which require a third party to speak to the woman about her decision. In *Danforth*, the Court upheld a statute which required that the physician obtain written consent from the woman seeking the abortion. Even though it did not give its reasons, the Court did acknowledge that abortion was an important and stressful decision and that it was good for the woman to be aware of the nature and consequences of the abortion.[30]

The *Danforth* case also raised another possible burdensome requirement, the detailed record-keeping of abortions. The risk to the woman related to possible violations of privacy and confidentiality. However, the Court upheld the statute on the grounds that the maternal health interests asserted by the state in collecting the data outweighed the privacy interests and the risks of disclosure.[31]

Public Assistance for Pregnancy and Abortion

Roe established that states must recognize that women have the right to decide for themselves about having an abortion. However, it was not clear that there was an affirmative duty to subsidize abortions for those women who could not afford them.

In *Mather v. Roe*, the Supreme Court ruled that the withholding of Medicaid assistance by the state of Connecticut from indigent women desiring non-therapeutic abortions did not violate their equal protection rights or due process.[32]

The next question to emerge had focused on the state's obligation to indigent women who medically required an abortion. Could a state, in the interest of promoting childbirth, deny financial assistance to an indigent woman when she had a medical need for the abortion? In *Harris v. McRae*, the Supreme Court upheld the constitutionality of the "Hyde Amendment," a federal Medicaid abortion funding restriction, with terms which varied year by year. This amendment prohibited the use of federal Medicaid funds for the reimbursement of the costs of abortion except in limited circumstances.[33]

The Direct Attempts to Overrule Roe v. Wade

Another possibility of undermining *Roe* has been through a constitutional amendment. In order for an amendment to pass in Congress, it requires two-thirds approval from either the House or the Senate. A number of different approaches have been attempted without success.

The Constitutional Amendment Movement

1. Extending the Constitutional Protection to the Unborn. Some proponents of a constitutional amendment held the position that it was possible to overrule *Roe* either by a clarification of the word "person" as used in the due process and equal protection clauses of the Constitution or by a declaration of the exact time when life begins.[34] There have been many amendments of this type proposed. An example of this kind of amendment is S.J. Res. 119:

> Section 1. With respect to the right to life, the word "person," as used in this article and in the fifth and fourteenth articles of amendment to the Constitution of the United States, applies to all human beings, including their unborn offspring at every stage of their biological development, irrespective of age, health, function, or condition of dependency.
> Section 2. This article shall not apply in an emergency when a reasonable medical certainty exists that continuation of the pregnancy will cause the death of the mother.[35]

The effect of this amendment would appear to establish legislative control over abortion standards.[36] The decision to enact legislation to set substantive abortion rules would be left to the discretion of each jurisdiction.

2. Direct Constitutional Prohibition of Abortion. This type of an amendment would require the state to enact a general ban on

abortions. One such amendment, section 2 of S.J. res. 17, proposed in 1981, specified that:

> No unborn person shall be deprived of life by any person: Provided, however, that nothing in this article shall prohibit a law permitting only those medical procedures required to prevent the death of the mother.[37]

The effect of this amendment would be to mandate the legal protection of all prenatal life.

3. "Deconstitutionalizing" the Right to Abortion. The Human Life Federalism Amendment ("the Hatch Amendment") stated that "A right to abortion is not secured by the Constitution."[38] Its purpose was directly to overrule *Roe*'s claim that abortion is protected by a constitutionally based right of privacy. This amendment would allow the states the opportunity to enact legislation prohibiting abortion. It remained possible, however, for states to recognize the right to an abortion and, if they so chose, to decline to address the issue legislatively.[39]

The Human Life Federalism Amendment is the only proposed amendment to reach Congress. It was rejected by the Senate on June 28, 1983, after failing to receive the two-thirds approval.

Federalism and Abortion

The effect of a constitutional amendment enacted to overrule *Roe* would increase the role of the state legislature, or of Congress in setting abortion standards. The role of the judicial branch would be significantly reduced. Related to this issue is the question of where the primary responsibility for setting abortion standards was located: either in Congress or in the states. Almost all of the proposed constitutional amendments have contained a section authorizing the enactment of enforcement legislation.[40]

1. Non-concurrent enforcement of power. A common expression of this type of provision is: "Congress and the several States shall have the power to enforce the article by appropriate legislation within their respective jurisdiction."[41] This provision would grant Congress and the States the power to pass legislation in their respective spheres.

2. Concurrent enforcement of power. An example of this type of provision is: "Congress and the several States shall have concurrent power to enforce the article by appropriate legislation."[42] The

implication of this type of proposed amendment is to suggest that federal and state legislation would apply simultaneously.[43]

Legislative Substitutes for an Abortion Amendment

Another approach to a constitutional amendment for the purpose of limiting or prohibiting abortion is to consider alternatives which would serve the same purpose.

1. <u>Subject Matter Restriction on Lower Federal Court Jurisdiction</u>. In this approach, the jurisdiction of the Supreme Court or the lower federal courts to hear abortions cases would be restricted, entirely or partially. The reasoning of this approach is that if it is not possible to overturn *Roe*, then this decision can be rendered ineffective by denying abortion rights claimants access to the federal judicial system, which has often acted in support of them.[44]

2. <u>Subject Matter Restrictions on the Supreme Court Appellate Jurisdiction</u>. The effect of these types of bills is to eliminate Supreme Court jurisdiction in certain classes of cases, specifically abortion cases.[45]

3. <u>The Human Life Bill</u>. Senator Helms introduced the Human Life Bill in 1981. One provision restricted the jurisdiction of the lower courts in cases involving state and local abortion legislation. In the second provision, the due process analysis of section 5 of the Fourteenth Amendment is used to include a certain definition of the word "person." This definition would have the effect of neutralizing the Supreme Court's reasoning in *Roe*. A relevant section of S. 158 is as follows:

> Section 1. The Congress finds that present day scientific evidence indicates a significant likelihood that the actual human life exists from conception.
> The Congress further finds that the fourteenth amendment to the Constitution of the United States was intended to protect all human beings.
> Upon the basis of these findings, and in the exercise of the powers of Congress, including its power under section 5 of the fourteenth amendment to the Constitution of the United States, the Congress hereby declares that for the purpose of enforcing the obligation of the States under the fourteenth amendment not to deprive persons of life without due process of law, human life shall be deemed to exist from conception, without regard

to race, sex, age, health, defect, or condition of
dependence: and for this purpose 'person' shall include all
human life as defined herein.[46]

The passage of this bill would have a serious impact on the
Supreme Court's power of judicial review. This power would be
greatly diminished, if the Congress under section 5 could actually
impose an interpretive gloss on the due process and equal protection
clauses.[47]

Thornburgh v. American College of Obstetricians and Gynaecologists

In this case, the creation-burden strategy was employed by those
seeking to restrict abortions. The Supreme Court invalidated
provisions of Pennsylvania's Abortion Control Act (1982) in
Thornburgh v. American College of Obstetricians and Gynaecologists.[48]
The provisions which were ruled invalid were portions relating to
informed consent, informational reporting requirements and
performance of abortions after viability. This case is notable because
of the position taken by the justices. Five justices appeared hostile to
abortion regulation, while the four justices who dissented called for a
reexamination or reversal of *Roe.*[49] This change in the make-up of the
justices on the Supreme Court could signal a change in the direction
of rulings previously favourable to *Roe* to one which is more
restrictive as demonstrated on the following case.

**The 1989 Supreme Court Decision, *Webster v. Reproductive Health
Services***

Lawyers representing Reproductive Health Services had argued
that the provisions of Missouri's abortion law conflicted with the
constitutional right of privacy in making an abortion choice.[50] The
Court discarded the trimester framework that barred states from
interfering with a woman's decision in the early months of pregnancy
without a "compelling" reason for doing so. Chief Justice William H.
Rehnquist expressed the opinion that the trimester framework was
judged to be "unsound in principle and unworkable in practice."
On July 3, 1989 the Supreme Court ruled by a 5-4 margin that
three out of four provisions of Missouri's 1986 abortion law could
stand.[51] These provisions have the effect of indirectly regulating
abortion through the creation burden strategy of increasing the costs
and risks.[52]

The first provision concerned the preamble which contained the finding that "the life of each human being begins at conception." The constitutionality was not decided by the Court. It held that the preamble did not regulate abortion, but was simply an expression of the state's preference for childbirth over abortion.

The second provision upheld by the Court is a ban on the use of public facilities for the performance of abortions. It is considered as a logical extension of earlier rulings that the states and the federal government do not have to provide Medicaid benefits to indigent women. This ban was not considered to be an insurmountable barrier to access to abortion.

The Court accepted the state's third provision which prohibited the use of public funds to encourage or counsel a woman to have an abortion. This prohibition applies only to state employees who are responsible for spending public funds, not to doctors or other health care providers. The nine justices held that this issue was moot because none of those challenging the law is adversely affected by this interpretation.

The fourth provision upheld by the Court required physicians to perform tests on fetuses believed to be at least 20 gestational weeks to determine their viability. The physician must determine if the fetus is viable by using commonly exercised "care, skill and proficiency." In addition, the law requires that the physician will carry out medical examinations and tests that are necessary to make a finding of the fetus' gestational age, weight, and lung maturity.

In view of the three most recent Supreme Court rulings, *Webster v. Reproductive Health Services* (1989), *Hodgson v. Minnesota* (1990) and *Ohio v. Akron Center for Reproductive Health* (1990), sponsors of an abortion rights bill (S 1912, HR 3700) hope that support will be increased for legislation that would write *Roe v. Wade* into law. Rep. Don Edwards, D-Calif., forwards the view that, with a divided Supreme Court and a hodgepodge of legislation developing in each of the states, Congress should take the lead in the abortion law. The sponsors do acknowledge that such legislation would have a difficult time passing either chamber.[53]

The chart summarizes the status of the abortion laws in each state.[54]

Status of Abortion Laws
(Enacted since 1973)

	Protection of Fetus	Determination of Fetal Viability before Abortion			Public Funding Restrictions: Abortions and Related Activities				Tougher Laws	Pre-1973 Laws
	Preamble	Degree of Care Required	Tests	Viability Assumed (weeks)	Prohibits Abortion Counselling	Prohibits Involvement of Public Employees	Prohibits Use of Public Facilities	Restricts Funds for Abortions†	Make Abortion Illegal	Never Repealed
Total States	9	6	2	13	4	2	4	37	5	25
Alabama								X		A
Alaska										A
Arizona					X*			X		A
Arkansas	X††									B
California										B
Colorado								X		B
Connecticut										A
Delaware								X		B
Florida								X		
Georgia								X		
Hawaii								X		C
Idaho	X							X		
Illinois								X	X	
Indiana		X						X	X	
Iowa								X		
Kansas								X		B
Kentucky	X*						X	X	X*	
Louisiana	X	X		24*		X		X	X	A
Maine								X		
Maryland										B
Massachusetts				24						A
Michigan								X		A

State			(weeks)					
Minnesota							X	A
Mississippi			18				X	
Missouri	X*	X*	20*	X*	X*	X*	X	A
Montana	X						X	
Nebraska	X	X					X	
Nevada			24					
New Hampshire							X	A
New Jersey								
New Mexico							X	B
New York			20					C
North Carolina			20					
North Dakota††	X				X	X	X	
Ohio				X				
Oklahoma		X	24				X	A
Oregon							X	
Pennsylvania	X	X*	19*	X**	X*	X*	X	
Rhode Island							X	A
South Carolina			24*				X	
South Dakota			24			X	X	
Tennessee			22				X	
Texas							X	A
Utah			24				X	
Vermont							X	
Virginia								A
Washington							X	C
West Virginia								A
Wisconsin							X	A
Wyoming							X	A

* Voided by Court Decision
** Repealed by legislature
† Public funding not at issue in Webster case
†† Amendment to state constitution

A. Most restrictive pre-1973 laws.
B. Less restrictive pre-1973 laws.
C. Least restrictive pre-1973 laws.

SOURCE: The Alan Guttmacher Institute

2. THE CANADIAN SITUATION

In 1892, the first *Criminal Code* in the Dominion of Canada was enacted.[55] By this time, the criminal law had come under federal jurisdiction. It contained a number of provisions on birth related offenses. One section identifies as criminal those actions against the fetus undertaken later in pregnancy and another section refers to miscarriage. Sub-section 271(1) states that to cause the death of a child not yet a human being, in such a manner that it would have been murder if such a child had been born is an indictable offence subject to life imprisonment. There is a provision for a defence of acting in good faith to save the life of the mother (sub-section 271(2)). Section 272 holds that to attempt to procure a woman's miscarriage whether or not she is with child is also an offence also punishable with life imprisonment. It is not possible to appeal to the good faith defence for this crime.[56]

The Omnibus Bill, 1969

In December 1967, the federal government introduced an omnibus bill to Parliament which included changes to the abortion law among its more than one hundred items. Approval for the specific amendment to the *Criminal Code*'s section on abortion was given in May 1969. It authorized that abortions could be performed for broad therapeutic reasons in accredited Canadian hospitals with the approval from a duly constituted therapeutic abortion committee. These therapeutic abortion committees became the gatekeepers for abortions.

Section 251(1) makes it an offence to perform an abortion. According to 251(2) it is an offence to have an abortion. The exemptions allowing an abortion to be performed on pregnant women by their doctors are set out in 251(4).[57] The following conditions must be met: the abortion must be performed in an "accredited or approved" hospital; the qualifying hospital must have a therapeutic abortion committee, defined as a committee consisting of at least three doctors appointed by the hospital board; the doctor performing the abortion must not be a member of the abortion committee; a majority of the abortion committee must determine that continuing the pregnancy would endanger the life or health of the pregnant woman, and must issue a certificate to that effect to her doctor.[58]

These amendments in the abortion law were an attempt to create a compromise solution to the abortion controversy.[59] At this time, other western countries were reforming their abortion laws. Also, as a result of the thalidomide tragedy, there was a question for some people about the appropriateness of forcing the continuation of a pregnancy in those cases where severe defects in the fetus were likely.[60]

The criteria for decision-making, based on the woman's 'life or health,' provided to the therapeutic abortion committee, was understood by the government as a rejection of eugenic, sociological, or criminal offense reasons for abortion.[61] It was implied that a proportionately grave reason for allowing the abortion was necessary. There was a recognition that fetal life did hold some independent value. However, the term 'life or health' was sufficiently ambiguous to allow for a wide range of interpretations by the therapeutic abortion committee in order to allow for abortions in both medical and social circumstances.

R. v. Morgentaler, 1988

On January 28, 1988, the Supreme Court of Canada gave judgment in *R. v. Morgentaler*.[62] In a 5-2 majority, the Supreme Court found that the provisions of the law, section 251 of the *Criminal Code*, infringed on the certain rights. These rights are guaranteed to all, including pregnant women by section 7 of the *Canadian Charter of Rights and Freedoms*.[63] It states:

Everyone has the right to life, liberty and the security of the person and the right not to be deprived thereof except in accordance with the principles of fundamental justice.

Because of the violation of the *Charter*, the 1969 abortion law was struck down as being unconstitutional.[64]

The majority opinions of the judges follow a similar form. First, the meaning of the right specified in section 7 is discussed. It is then determined if the right has been violated by section 251 of the *Criminal Code*. The next part of the decision addresses the question of whether such a violation is justified by invoking the principles of fundamental justice. The final part of the decision is concerned with the application of section 1 of the *Charter* which states that the rights in section 7 are subject to:

such reasonable limits prescribed by law as can be demonstrably justified in a free and democratic society.

The general principles governing the application of section 1 to legislation, which were affirmed and used in *Morgentaler*, were elaborated in *R. v. Oakes*. The application of the principles involved asking whether the object of 251 is of sufficient importance to warrant overriding a constitutionally protected right. This step is then followed by a discussion of the objectives of the legislation. In order to meet the criteria that the limits should be reasonable and demonstrably justifiable, three requirements were necessary. The therapeutic abortion committee process, which was the means of the objective, must be found to be rational and fair, not arbitrary; to impair the section 7 as little as possible; and to impose limits on section 7 rights which are not out of proportion to the objectives sought by section 251.[65]

As a result of the Supreme Court decision, it was no longer an offence to have an abortion, nor was it an offence to perform abortion. The therapeutic abortion committee process no longer had a legislative basis.

The Government Response to the Morgentaler Decision

On May 20, 1988, the Government presented the House of Commons with a number of policy options for the regulation of abortion.[66] The options were to be subject to a vote by the Members of Parliament. The Government hoped to get some help in direction for drafting further abortion legislation. The policy options were tabled in the form of a motion with two amendments.[67] The motion would allow easy access to abortion in the early stages, but would place more restrictions in the later stages. The motion stated:

> ...Such legislation should prohibit the performance of an abortion, subject to the following exceptions:
> When, during the early stages of pregnancy: a qualified medical practitioner is of the opinion that the continuation of the pregnancy of a woman would, or would be likely to threaten her physical or mental well-being; when the woman in consultation with a qualified medical practitioner decides to terminate her pregnancy; and when the termination is performed by a qualified medical practitioner; and when, during the subsequent stages of pregnancy: the termination of the pregnancy satisfies further conditions, including a condition that after a certain point in time, the termination would only be permitted where, in the opinion of two qualified medical practitioners, the continuation of the pregnancy would, or would be likely to, endanger the woman's life or seriously endanger her health.

Amendment A was the anti-abortion option. It read:

> ...Such legislation, giving preeminence to the protection of the foetus, should prohibit the performance of an abortion except when: two independent qualified medical practitioners have, in good faith and on reasonable grounds, stated that in their opinion the continuation of the pregnancy would, or would be likely to, endanger the life of the pregnant woman or seriously endanger her health and there is no other commonly accepted medical procedure for effectively treating the health risk; but grounds for such opinion are not to include
> (1) the effects of stress or anxiety which may accompany an unexpected or unwanted pregnancy, or
> (11) social or economic consideration.

Amendment B was the pro-choice option. It read:

> ... Such legislation, giving preeminence to a woman's freedom to choose, should permit the performance of an abortion under the following conditions:
> (1) When the woman in consultation with a qualified medical practitioner decides to terminate her pregnancy, and
> (11) When the termination of the pregnancy is performed by a qualified medical practitioner.

Under criticism from the opposition parties, the Government withdrew Amendments A and B. A free vote was held on the original motion in the House of Commons. The motion was defeated (147 to 76).[68]

The Supreme Court After R. v. Morgentaler

In March 1989, the Supreme Court of Canada refused to rule on a constitutional challenge put forward by pro-life activist Joe Borowski. He asked the court to find that the fetus is a person with the constitutional right to life, liberty and the security of the person and the right to the equal protection of the law.[69] It was the decision of the court that it would not be in the public interest to rule on fetal rights without an abortion law.[70]

The Attempt to Recriminalize Abortion, 1989 and the Defeat of Bill C-43, 1991

On November 3, 1989, a bill was tabled in the House of Commons, which would place abortion back in the *Criminal Code*. Earlier in the year, there was some suggestion that new abortion legislation would be a part of the Canada Health Act. The implication of locating the legislation within this act is that abortion practice could come under provincial jurisdiction. However, by placing abortion within the *Criminal Code*, it remains within the control of the federal government and must be practiced uniformly across Canada.

The proposed changes were drafted by a caucus committee chaired by Lise Bourgault, MP, and Benno Friesen, MP. The committee considered three proposals. One of the proposals was based on a trimester system, allowing unrestricted abortions up to the 14th week of pregnancy. Restrictions would be introduced after the 14th week and abortions would be forbidden after the 20th week. The second proposal would have permitted abortion in the first five months of pregnancy. The proposal on which the committee reached a consensus did away with the gestational approach.

Sections 287 and 288 of the *Criminal Code* are to be substituted with the proposed amendment. A partial text provides the major changes:

> Every person who induces an abortion on a female person is guilty of an indictable offence and liable to imprisonment for a term not exceeding two years, unless the abortion is induced by or under direction of a medical practitioner who is of the opinion that, if the abortion were not induced, the health or the life of the female person would likely to be threatened.
>
> For the purposes of this section, "health" includes, for greater certainty, physical, mental and psychological health.
>
> "Medical practitioner," in respect of an abortion induced in a province, means a person who is entitled to practise medicine under the laws of that province.
>
> "Opinion" means an opinion formed using generally accepted standards of the medical profession.
>
> Inducing an abortion does not include using a drug, device or other means on a female person that is likely to prevent implantation of a fertilized ovum.
>
> Every one who unlawfully supplies or procures a drug or other noxious thing or an instrument or thing, knowing that

it is intended to be used or employed to induce an
abortion on a female person, is guilty of an indictable
offense and liable to imprisonment.[71]

On May 29, 1990, Bill C-43 was passed with 140-131 vote in
the House of Commons. Bill C-43 needed to pass in the Senate and
then receive royal assent. It was not clear what would have been the
effect of the new legislation. Physicians were afraid that they would
have been arrested and charged with a criminal offence. Access to
legal abortions could have been delayed, reduced or disappeared. The
federal government had indicated that the doctors' fears were
exaggerated due to a misunderstanding of the law. Physicians would
have been required by law to "form an opinion" about a woman's
state of health. A government official stated that it would have been
unlikely that any provincial Attorney-General would permit an
individual to lay a frivolous charge against a doctor. The onus would
rest on that person to prove that no such opinion had been formed.[72]
But many doctors were unconvinced. Some provincial premiers have
expressed anti-abortion positions, so it is uncertain in what circumstances physicians may have been charged.

Both pro-choice and anti-abortion groups agreed that the
legislation would face court challenges. One challenge could have
raised the argument that by criminalizing a procedure required only
by women, they are discriminated against. Or, the challenge could
have been based on the large differences in access to abortion among
regions of the country.[73]

On January 31, 1991, the Senate defeated Bill C-43, by a tied
vote of 43-43. It was a free vote for the Senators, but the
Government had lobbied for the bill. Justice Minister Kim Campbell
has stated that the federal government does not intend to introduce
new abortion legislation. She predicted that the focus of the abortion
debate will be directed to provincial measures and court challenges.[74]

Attempts at Court Injunctions to Prohibit Abortions

During the summer of 1989, ex-boyfriends in Manitoba, Ontario
and Quebec sought court injunctions to prevent their ex-girlfriends
from having abortions. In Winnipeg, Steven Diamond applied for a
court injunction to prevent his ex-girlfriend from aborting an eight
week fetus. The judge did not grant it, maintaining that there was no
medical evidence to support the claim that a fetus of eight weeks
constitutes a human being.[75]

Barbara Dodd

In Toronto on July 4 1989, Justice John O'Driscoll, an Ontario Supreme Court judge, granted Gregory Murphy an injunction preventing his ex-girlfriend Barbara Dodd from aborting a fifteen week old fetus. The judge did not give any reasons for his decision.

Mr. Justice Gibson Grey of the Ontario Supreme Court set aside the injunction on technical grounds. He stated that Dodd was not provided with sufficient notice of the court action and that Murphy had committed fraud by not telling the original judge that there was another man who could also be the father. He indicated that he was not going to address the underlying issues of fetal and paternal rights.[76]

Chantel Daigle

Jean-Guy Tremblay obtained a temporary injunction on July 7, 1989 in Quebec City to prevent his ex-girlfriend from having an abortion. On July 17, the lawyers argued their case before Superior Court judge, Jacques Viens, in the northern town of Val d'Or. He ruled that the twenty week old fetus was a human being according to the *Quebec Charter of Human Rights and Freedoms.*[77]
Viens cited:

Article 1 "Every human being has the right to life, as well as security, integrity and personal freedom."

Article 2 "Every human being whose life is in peril has the right to protection."

Viens argued that if these rights and freedoms applied only from birth, the *Charter* would have used the term "persons," instead of "human beings." He claimed that fetuses would come under protection of the *Charter.*[78] Daigle appealed this decision, but it was upheld by the Quebec Court of Appeals. The Quebec Appeal Court judges argued that it was Daigle's responsibility to bring the five month-old fetus to term. A woman does not have an absolute right to abortion which she can exercise anytime before the moment of birth. Justice Yves Bernier explained that to permit an abortion under these circumstances, despite the opposition of the father, would be a sanction to abortion on demand.[79]

At this point, the appeal was taken to the Supreme Court of Canada, which unanimously ordered that the injunction be lifted. The

Court did not give the reasons for its decision at the time, but did so on November 16, 1989.

The Court saw as its task to answer the legal question of whether the Quebec legislature has accorded personhood to the fetus. It was the Court's view that the Quebec *Charter* makes no reference to the fetus or fetal rights, nor does it include any definition of "human being."

The arguments of the respondent, Jean-Guy Tremblay, are examined. The first argument was based on a linguistic analysis. It makes the claim that the fetus is simply a human being in the meaning of the term. The term "human" refers to the human race of which the fetus is a part and "being" signifies "existing." "The fetus does exist. On this basis, the fetus is a human being." The Court suggested that this explanation was too simple. Instead, what was needed were substantive legal reasons to support the conclusion that the term "human being" in fact has such and such a meaning. The conclusion of the Court was that the Quebec *Charter*, taken as a whole, does not display any clear intention to consider the status of the fetus.

The appellant, Chantel Daigle, presented the most persuasive argument to the Court. The lack of intention to deal with the status of the fetus provides a strong reason for not finding fetal rights under the *Charter*. If the intention of the legislature were to grant fetal rights, a more effective way of ensuring those rights would likely have been created than by the discretionary request of third parties. The second argument of the respondent refers to the Civil Code.

> The respondent argues that a fetus is recognized as a human being under the Civil Code. His argument rests on two propositions: 1) that Article 18 directly recognizes that a fetus is a human being; and (2) that a variety of other articles in the Code indirectly recognize that a fetus is a "juridical person," and, since juridical persons are natural persons... a fetus is a human being...[80]

> The Court rejects these arguments. It concludes that it is recognized in law that a fetus is treated as a person only where it is necessary to do so in order to protect its interests after it is born...[81]

The third argument is based on the potential father's rights. It is proposed that the potential father's contribution to the act of conception gives him an equal say in what happens to the fetus. The Court rejected this claim by pointing out that the argument has never been accepted by any court in Quebec or elsewhere that a father's interest in a fetus could uphold a right to veto a woman's decisions in respect of the fetus she is carrying. As a result of the examination of the arguments offered by the respondent, the Court concluded that substantive reasons were lacking for an injunction, and so the appeal should succeed.

Provincial Responses

British Columbia

Shortly after the federal law was struck down in 1988, the British Columbia cabinet issued a regulation to deny health insurance coverage to women seeking abortions, unless their lives were significantly threatened. British Columbia Chief Justice Allan McEachen did not rule in favour of the regulation. He indicated that the regulation defied common sense and exceeded cabinet's authority. He also said that it might be possible to remove abortion from the *Medical Services Act* as an insured service, as long as there was no assessment made of its medical necessity. However, even this move would be subject to a *Charter* challenge.[82]

Nova Scotia

The government of Premier John Buchanan took a strong stand against the establishment of free-standing abortion clinics. In the summer of 1989, the Nova Scotia government passed the *Medical Services Act*. It prohibits a number of procedures among which are abortions. The Canadian Abortion Rights Action League (CARAL) put forward a court challenge to the law, arguing that it was unconstitutional. The suit was dismissed on October 17, 1989 by the Supreme Court of Nova Scotia on the grounds that CARAL was not directly affected.[83]

In October 1989, Dr. Henry Morgentaler defied the law by performing seven abortions in his Halifax clinic and announced this publicly. He was charged.

On October 19, 1990, a provincial court judge ruled that Dr. Morgentaler could not be convicted under the *Medical Services Act*. Judge Joseph Kennedy explained that the province had no right to enact the legislation which restricted abortions to provincially approved hospitals. The regulation of abortion is a matter for the federal government.[84]

3. IMPORTANT LEGAL DECISIONS AND PROPOSED LEGISLATION: EXCERPTS FROM AMERICAN AND CANADIAN DOCUMENTS

UNITED STATES

Roe v. Wade

Mr. Justice Blackmun delivered the opinion of the Court....

We forthwith acknowledge our awareness of the sensitive and emotional nature of the abortion controversy, of the vigorous opposing views, even among physicians, and of the deep and seemingly absolute convictions that the subject inspires. One's philosophy, one's experiences, one's exposure to the raw edges of human existence, one's religious training, one's attitudes towards life and family and their values, and the moral standards one establishes and seeks to observe, are all likely to influence and to color one's thinking and conclusions about abortion.

In addition, population growth, pollution, poverty, and racial overtones tend to complicate and not to simplify the problem.

Our task, of course, is to resolve the issue by constitutional measurement, free of emotion and of predilection....

Jane Roe, a single woman who was residing in Dallas County, Texas, instituted this federal action in March 1970 against the District Attorney of the county. She sought a declaratory judgment that the Texas criminal abortion statutes were unconstitutional on their face and an injunction restraining the defendant from enforcing the statutes.

Roe alleged that she was unmarried and pregnant; that she wished to terminate her pregnancy by an abortion "performed by a competent, licensed physician, under safe, clinical conditions"; that she was unable to get a "legal" abortion in Texas because her life did not appear to be threatened by the continuation of the pregnancy; and that she could not afford to travel to another jurisdiction in order to secure a legal abortion under safe conditions. She claimed that the Texas statutes were unconstitutionally vague and that they abridged her right of personal privacy, protected by the First, Fourth, Fifth, Ninth, and Fourteenth Amendments. By an amendment to her complaint Roe purported to sue "on behalf of herself and all other women" similarly situated....

The principal thrust of appellant's attack on the Texas statutes is that they improperly invade a right, said to be possessed by the pregnant woman, to choose to terminate her pregnancy. Appellant would discover this right in the concept of personal "liberty" embodied in the Fourteenth Amendment's Due Process Clause; or in personal, marital, familial, and sexual privacy said to be protected by the Bill of Rights....

It perhaps is not generally appreciated that the restrictive criminal abortion laws in effect in a majority of States today are of relatively recent vintage. Those laws, generally proscribing abortion or its attempt at any time during pregnancy except when necessary to preserve the pregnant woman's life are not of ancient or even of common-law origin. Instead, they derive from statutory changes effected, for the most part, in the latter half of the nineteenth century....

It is undisputed that at common law, abortion performed before "quickening"--the first recognizable movement of the fetus in utero, appearing usually from the sixteenth to the eighteenth week of pregnancy--was not an indictable offense....

Whether abortion of a quick fetus was a felony at common law, or even a lesser crime, is still disputed....A recent review of the common-law precedents argues, however, that ...even post-quickening abortion was never established as a common-law crime....

It is thus apparent that at common law, at the time of the adoption of our Constitution, and throughout the major portion of the nineteenth century, abortion was viewed with less disfavor than under most American statutes currently in effect. Phrasing it another way, a woman enjoyed a substantially broader right to terminate a pregnancy than she does in most States today. At least with respect to the early stage of pregnancy, and very possibly without such a limitation, the opportunity to make this choice was present in this country well into the nineteenth century. Even later, the law continued for some time to treat less punitively an abortion procured in early pregnancy....

Three reasons have been advanced to explain historically the enactment of criminal abortion laws in the nineteenth century and to justify their continued existence. It has been argued occasionally that these laws were the product of a Victorian social concern to discourage illicit sexual conduct. Texas, however, does not advance this justification in the present case, and it appears that no court or commentator has taken the argument seriously...

A second reason is concerned with abortion as a medical procedure. When most criminal abortion laws were first enacted, the procedure was a hazardous one for the woman. This was particularly true prior to the development of antisepsis. Antiseptic techniques, of course, were based on discoveries by Lister, Pasteur, and others first announced in 1867, but were not generally accepted and employed until about the turn of the century. Abortion mortality was high. Even after 1900, and perhaps until as late as the development of antibiotics in the 1940s, standard modern techniques such as dilatation and curettage were not nearly so safe as they are today. Thus, it has been argued that a State's real concern in enacting a criminal abortion law was to protect the pregnant woman, that is, to restrain her from submitting to a procedure that placed her life in serious jeopardy.

Modern medical techniques have altered this situation. Appellants and various amici refer to medical data indicating that abortion in early pregnancy, that is, prior to the end of the first trimester, although not without its risk, is now relatively safe. Mortality rates for women undergoing early abortions, where the procedure is legal, appear to be as low as or lower than the rates for normal childbirth. Consequently, any interest of the State in protecting the woman from an inherently hazardous procedure, except when it would be equally dangerous for her to forgo it, has largely disappeared. Of course, important state interests in the areas of health and medical standards do remain. The State has a legitimate interest in seeing to it that abortion, like any other medical procedure, is performed under circumstances that insure maximum safely for the patient. This interest obviously extends at least to the performing physician and his staff, to the facilities involved, to the availability of after-care, and to adequate provision for any complication or emergency that might arise. The prevalence of high mortality rates at illegal "abortion mills" strengthens, rather than weakens, the State's interest in regulating the conditions under which abortions are performed. Moreover, the risk to the woman increases as her pregnancy continues. Thus, the State retains a definite interest in protecting the woman's own health and safety when an abortion is proposed at a late stage of pregnancy.

The third reason is the State's interest--some phrase it in terms of duty--in protecting prenatal life. Some of the argument for this justification rests on the theory that a new human life is present from the moment of conception. The State's interest and general obligation to protect life then extends, it is argued, to prenatal life. Only when the life of the pregnant mother herself is at stake, balanced against the life she carries within her, should the interest of the embryo or fetus not prevail. Logically, of course, a legitimate state interest in this area need not stand or fall on acceptance of the belief that life begins at conception or at some other point prior to live birth. In assessing the State's interest, recognition may be given to the less rigid claim that as long as at least potential life is involved, the State may assert interests beyond the protection of the pregnant woman alone.

Parties challenging state abortion laws have sharply disputed in some courts the contention that a purpose of these laws, when enacted, was to protect prenatal life. Pointing to the absence of legislative history to support the contention, they claim that most state laws were designed solely to protect the woman. Because medical advances have lessened this concern, at least with respect to abortion in early pregnancy, they argue that with respect to such abortions the laws can no longer be justified by any state interest. There is some scholarly support for this view of original purpose. The few state courts called upon to interpret their laws in the late nineteenth and early twentieth centuries did focus on the State's interest in protecting the woman's health rather than in preserving the embryo and fetus....

The Constitution does not explicitly mention any right of privacy. In a line of decisions, however, going back perhaps as far as *Union Pacific R. Co. v. Botsford* (1891)...the Court has recognized that a right of personal privacy, or a guarantee of certain areas of zones of privacy, does exist under the Constitution. In varying contexts, the Court or individual Justices have, indeed, found at least the roots of that right in the First Amendment,...in the Fourth and Fifth Amendments,...in the Ninth Amendment,...or in the concept of liberty guaranteed by the first section of the Fourteenth Amendment....These decisions make it clear that only personal rights that can be deemed "fundamental" or "implicit in the concept of ordered liberty"...are included in this guarantee of personal privacy. They also make it clear that the right has some extension to activities relating to marriage ...procreation ... contraception ... family relationships ... and child rearing and education. ...

This right of privacy, whether it be founded in the Fourteenth Amendment's concept of personal liberty and restrictions upon state action, as we feel it is, or, as the District Court determined, in the Ninth Amendment's reservation of rights to the people, is broad enough to encompass a woman's decision whether or not to terminate her pregnancy. The detriment that the State would impose upon the pregnant woman by denying this choice altogether is apparent. Specific and direct harm medically diagnosable even in the early pregnancy may be involved. Maternity, or additional offspring, may force upon the woman a distressful life and future. Psychological harm may be imminent. Mental and physical health may be taxed by child care. There is also the distress, for all concerned, associated with the unwanted child, and there is the problem of bringing a child into a family already unable, psychologically and otherwise, to care for it. In other cases, as in this one, the additional difficulties and continuing stigma of unwed motherhood may be involved. All these are factors the woman and her responsible physician necessarily consider in consultation.

On the basis of elements such as these, appellant and some amici argue that the woman's right is absolute and that she is entitled to terminate her pregnancy at whatever time, in whatever way, and for whatever reason she alone chooses. With this we do not agree. Appellant's arguments that Texas either has no valid interest at all in regulating the abortion decision, or no interest strong enough to support any limitation upon the woman's sole determination, are unpersuasive. The Court's decisions recognizing a right of privacy also acknowledge that some state regulation in areas protected by that right is appropriate. As noted above, a State may properly assert important interests in safeguarding health, in maintaining medical standards, and in protecting potential life. At some point in pregnancy, these respective interests become sufficiently compelling to sustain regulation of the factors that govern the abortion decision. The privacy right involved, therefore, cannot be said to be absolute.

In fact, it is not clear to us that the claim asserted by some amici that one has an unlimited right to do with one's body as one pleases bears a close relationship to the right of privacy previously articulated in the Court's decisions. The Court has refused to recognize an unlimited right of this kind in the past....

We, therefore, conclude that the right of personal privacy includes the abortion decision, but that this right is not unqualified and must be considered against important state interests in regulation.

We note that those federal and state courts that have recently considered abortion law challenges have reached the same conclusion....

Although the results are divided, most of these courts have agreed that the right of privacy, however based, is broad enough to cover the abortion decision; that the right, nonetheless, is not absolute and is subject to some limitations; and that at some point the state interests as to protection of health, medical standards, and prenatal life, become dominant. We agree with this approach....

The appellee and certain amici argue that the fetus is a "person" within the language and meaning of the Fourteenth Amendment. In support of this, they outline at length and in detail the well-known facts of fetal development. If this suggestion of personhood is established, the appellant's case, of course, collapses, for the fetus's right to life would then be guaranteed specifically by the Amendment. The appellant conceded as much on reargument. On the other hand, the appellee conceded on reargument that no case could be cited that holds that a fetus is a person within the meaning of the Fourteenth Amendment.

The Constitution does not define "person" in so many words. Section 1 of the Fourteenth Amendment contains three references to "person." The first, in defining "citizens," speaks of "Persons born or naturalized in the United States." The word also appears both in the Due Process Clause and in the Equal Protection Clause. "Person" is used in other places in the Constitution: in the listing of qualifications for Representatives and Senators, Art, I, § 2, cl. 2, and § 3, cl. 3; in the Apportionment Clause, Art. I, § 2, cl. 3; in the Migration and Importation provision, Art. I, § 9, cl. 1; in the Emolument Clause, Art. I, § 9, cl. 8; in the Electors provisions, Art. II, § 1, cl. 2, and the superseded cl. 3; in the provision outlining qualifications for the office of President, Art. II, § 1, cl. 5; in the Extradition provisions, Art. IV, § 2, cl. 2, and the superseded Fugitive Slave Clause 3; and in the First, Twelfth, and Twenty-second Amendments as well as in §§ 2 and 3 of the Fourteenth Amendment. But in nearly all these instances, the use of the word is such that it has application only postnatally. None indicates, with any assurance, that it has any possible pre-natal application.

All this, together without observation, supra, that throughout the major portion of the nineteenth century prevailing legal abortion practices were far freer than they are today, persuades us that the word "person," as used in the Fourteenth Amendment, does not include the unborn....

We need not resolve the difficult question of when life begins. When those trained in the respective disciplines of medicine, philosophy, and theology are unable to arrive at any consensus, the judiciary, at this point in the development of man's knowledge, is not in a position to speculate as to the answer.

It should be sufficient to note briefly the wide divergence of thinking on this most sensitive and difficult question. There has always been strong support for the view that life does not begin until live birth. This was the belief of the Stoics. It appears to be the predominant, though not the unanimous, attitude of the Jewish faith. It may be taken to represent also the position of a large segment of the Protestant community, insofar as that can be ascertained; organized groups that have taken a formal position on the abortion issue have generally regarded abortion as a matter for the conscience of the individual and her family. As we have noted, the common law found greater significance in quickening. Physicians and their scientific colleagues have regarded that event with less interest and have tended to focus either upon conception, upon live birth, or upon the interim point at which the fetus becomes "viable," that is, potentially able to live outside the mother's womb, albeit with artificial aid. Viability is usually placed at about seven months (28 weeks) but may occur earlier, even at 24 weeks. The Aristotelian theory of "mediate animation," that held sway throughout the Middle Ages and the Renaissance in Europe, continued to be official Roman Catholic dogma until the nineteenth century, despite opposition to this "ensoulment" theory from those in the Church who would recognize the existence of life from the moment of conception. The latter is now, of course, the official belief of the Catholic Church. As one brief amicus discloses, this is a view strongly held by many non-Catholics as well, and by many physicians. Substantial problems for precise definition of this view are posed, however, by new embryological data that purport to indicate that conception is a "process" over time, rather than an event, and by new medical techniques such as menstrual extraction, the "morning-after" pill, implantation of embryos, artificial insemination, and even artificial wombs.

In areas other than criminal abortion, the law has been reluctant to endorse any theory that life, as we recognize it, begins before live birth or to accord legal rights to the unborn except in narrowly defined situations and except when the rights are contingent upon live birth. For example, the traditional rule of tort law denied recovery for prenatal injuries even though the child was born alive. That rule has been changed in almost every jurisdiction. In most States, recovery is said to be permitted only if the fetus was viable, or at least quick, when the injuries were sustained, though few courts have squarely so held. In a recent development, generally opposed by the commentators, some States permit the parents of a stillborn child to maintain an action for wrongful death because of prenatal injuries. Such an action, however would appear to be one of vindicating the parents' interest and is thus consistent with the view that the fetus, at most, represents only the potentiality of life. Similarly, unborn children have been recognized as acquiring rights or interests by way of inheritance or other devolution of property, and have been represented by guardians ad litem. Perfection of the interests involved, again, has generally been contingent upon live birth. In short, the unborn have never been recognized in the law as persons in the whole sense.

In view of all this, we do not agree that, by adopting one theory of life, Texas may override the rights of the pregnant woman that are at stake. We repeat, however, that the State does have an important and legitimate interest in preserving and protecting the health of the pregnant woman, whether she be a resident of the State or a nonresident who seeks medical consultation and treatment there, and that it has still another important and legitimate interest in protecting the potentiality of human life. These interests are separate and distinct. Each grows in substantiality as the woman approaches term and, at a point during pregnancy, each becomes "compelling."

With respect to the State's important and legitimate interest in the health of the mother, the "compelling" point, in the light of present medical knowledge, is at approximately the end of the first trimester. This is so because of the now-established medical fact...that until the end of the first trimester mortality in abortion may be less than mortality in normal childbirth. It follows that, from and after this point, a State may regulate the abortion procedure to the extent that the regulation is reasonably related to the preservation and protection of maternal health. Examples of permissible state regulation in this area are requirements as to the qualifications of the person who is to perform the abortion; as to the licensure of that person; as to the facility in which the procedure is to be performed, that is, whether it must be a hospital or may be a clinic or some other place of less-than-hospital status; as to the licensing of the facility; and the like.

This means, on the other hand, that, for the period of pregnancy prior to this "compelling" point, the attending physician, in consultation with his patient, is free to determine, without regulation by the State, that, in his medical judgment, the patient's pregnancy should be terminated. If that decision is reached, the judgment may be effectuated by an abortion free of interference by the State.

With respect to the State's important and legitimate interest in potential life, the "compelling" point is at viability. This is so because the fetus then presumably has the capability of meaningful life outside the mother's womb. State regulation protective of fetal life after viability thus has both logical and biological justifications. If the State is interested in protecting fetal life after viability, it may go so far as to proscribe abortion during that period, except when it is necessary to preserve the life or health of the mother....

To summarize and to repeat:

1. A state criminal abortion statute of the current Texas type, that excepts from criminality only a life-saving procedure on behalf of the mother, without regard to pregnancy state and without recognition of the other interests involved, is violative of the Due Process Clause of the Fourteenth Amendment.

(a) For the stage prior to approximately the end of the first trimester, the abortion decision and its effectuation must be left to the medical judgment of the pregnant woman's attending physician.

(b) For the stage subsequent to approximately the end of the first trimester, the State, in promoting its interest in the health of the mother, may, if it chooses, regulate the abortion procedure in ways that are reasonably related to maternal health.

(c) For the stage subsequent to viability, the State in promoting its interest in the potentiality of human life may, if it chooses, regulate, and even proscribe, abortion except where it is necessary, in appropriate medical judgment, for the preservation of the life or health of the mother.

The decision leaves the State free to place increasing restrictions on abortion as the period of pregnancy lengthens, so long as those restrictions are tailored to the recognized state interests. The decision vindicates the right of the physician to administer medical treatment according to his professional judgment up to the points where important state interests provide compelling justifications for intervention. Up to those points, the abortion decision in all its aspects is inherently, and primarily, a medical decision, and basic responsibility for it must rest with the physician. If an individual practitioner abuses the privilege of exercising proper medical judgment, the usual remedies, judicial and intra-professional, are available....

Mr. Justice White, with whom Mr. Justice Rehnquist joins, dissenting.

At the heart of controversy in these cases are those recurring pregnancies that pose no danger whatsoever to the life or health of the mother but are, nevertheless, unwanted for any one or more of a variety of reasons--convenience, family planning, economics, dislike of children, the embarrassment of illegitimacy, etc. The common claim before us is that for any one of such reasons, or for no reason at all, and without asserting or claiming any threat to life or health, any woman is entitled to an abortion at her request if she is able to find a medical advisor willing to undertake the procedure.

The Court for the most part sustains this position: During the period prior to the time the fetus becomes viable, the Constitution of the United States values the convenience, whim, or caprice of the putative mother more than the life or potential life of the fetus; the Constitution, therefore, guarantees the right to an abortion as against any state law or policy seeking to protect the fetus from an abortion not prompted by more compelling reasons of the mother.

With all due respect, I dissent. I find nothing in the language or history of the Constitution to support the Court's judgment. The Court simply fashions and announces a new constitutional right for pregnant mothers and, with scarcely any reason or authority for its action, invests that right with sufficient substance to override most existing state abortion statutes. The upshot is that the people and the legislatures of the fifty States are constitutionally disentitled to weigh the relative importance of the continued existence and development of the fetus, on the one hand, against a spectrum of possible impacts on the mother, on the other hand. As an exercise of raw judicial power, the Court perhaps has authority to do what it does today; but in my view its judgment is an improvident and extravagant exercise of the power of judicial review that the Constitution extends to this Court.

The Court apparently values the convenience of the pregnant mother more than the continued existence and development of the life or potential life that she carries. Whether or not I might agree with that marshalling of values, I can in no event join the Court's judgment, because I find no constitutional warrant for imposing such an order of priorities on the people and legislatures of the States. In a sensitive area such as this, involving as it does issues over which reasonable men may easily and heatedly differ, I cannot accept the Court's exercise of its clear power of choice by interposing a constitutional barrier to state efforts to protect human life and by investing mothers and doctors with the constitutionally protected right to exterminate it. This issue, for the most part, should be left with the people and to the political processes the people have devised to govern their affairs.

It is my view, therefore, that the Texas statute is not constitutionally infirm because it denies abortions to those who seek to serve only their convenience rather than to protect their life or health....

Webster v. Reproductive Health Services

In its decision of July 3, 1989, the United States Supreme Court reversed a decision of the United States Court of Appeals for the Eighth Circuit. The Court of Appeals had itself upheld the decision of a Federal District Court. The case involved a 1986 Missouri law regulating abortion. The preamble to the Missouri statute states that "the life of each human being begins at conception" and that "unborn children have protectable interests in life, health, and well-being." Key provisions of the law (1) prohibit the use of public employees and facilities to perform abortions not necessary to save the life of the mother and (2) specify that the physician, when having reason to believe that the woman is carrying a fetus of at least twenty weeks of gestational age, must adopt procedures necessary to determine the viability of the unborn child. This second provision is the highly controversial section 188.029 of the Missouri law. In the published opinions of the justices, this section is frequently referred to by number. The controversy over section 188.029 concerns the extent to which it mandates medical tests to determine viability of the fetus and the extent to which it modifies the Court's ruling in *Roe v. Wade* (1973).

In the written opinions of the justices, when "court" is written with a lowercase "c," reference is to the District Court or the Eighth Circuit Court of Appeals. When "Court" is written with an uppercase "C," reference is to the Supreme Court.

Chief Justice Rehnquist announced the judgment of the Court and delivered the opinion of the Court....

This appeal concerns the constitutionality of a Missouri statute regulating the performance of abortions. The United States Court of Appeals for the Eighth Circuit struck down several provisions of the statute on the ground that they violated this Court's decision in *Roe v. Wade*....We....now reverse [the decision of the Court of Appeals].

I

In June 1986, the Governor of Missouri signed into law [an act]...which amended existing state law concerning unborn children and abortions. The Act consisted of 20 provisions, 5 of which are now before the Court. The first provision, or preamble, contains "findings" by the state legislature that "[t]he life of each human being begins at conception," and that "unborn children have protectable interests in life, health, and well-being." The Act further requires that all Missouri laws be interpreted to provide unborn children with the same rights enjoyed by other persons, subject to the Federal Constitution and this Court's precedents. Among its other provisions, the Act requires that, prior to performing an abortion on any woman whom a physician has reason to believe is 20 or more weeks pregnant, the physician ascertain whether the fetus is viable by performing "such medical examinations and tests as are necessary to make a finding of the gestational age, weight, and lung maturity of the unborn child" (§ 188.029). The Act also prohibits the use of public employees and facilities for the purpose of "encouraging or counselling" a woman to have an abortion not necessary to save her life (§§ 188.205, 188.210, 188.215).

In July 1986, five health professionals employed by the State and two nonprofit corporations brought this class action in the United States District Court for the Western District of Missouri to challenge the constitutionality of the Missouri statute. Plaintiffs, appellees in this Court, sought declaratory and injunctive relief on the ground that certain statutory provisions violated the First, Fourth, Ninth, and

Fourteenth Amendments to the Federal Constitution. They asserted violations of various rights, including the "privacy rights of pregnant women seeking abortions"; the "woman's right to an abortion"; the "righ[t] to privacy in the physician-patient relationship"; the physician's "righ[t] to practice medicine"; the pregnant woman's "right to life due to inherent risks involved in childbirth"; and the woman's right to "receive...adequate medical advice and treatment" concerning abortions.

Plaintiffs filed this suit "on their own behalf and on behalf of the entire class consisting of facilities and Missouri licensed physicians or other health care professionals offering abortion services or pregnancy counselling and on behalf of the entire class of pregnant females seeking abortion services or pregnancy counselling within the State of Missouri." The two nonprofit corporations are Reproductive Health Services, which offers family planning and gynaecological services to the public, including abortion services up to 22 weeks "gestational age," and Planned Parenthood of Kansas City, which provides abortion services up to 14 weeks gestational age. The individual plaintiffs are three physicians, one nurse, and a social worker. All are "public employees" at "public facilities" in Missouri, and they are paid for their services with "public funds."...The individual plaintiffs, within the scope of their public employment, encourage and counsel pregnant women to have nontherapeutic abortions. Two of the physicians perform abortions....Following a 3-day trial in December 1986, the District Court declared seven provisions of the Act unconstitutional and enjoined their enforcement....The Court of Appeals for the Eighth Circuit affirmed [the judgment of the District Court], with one exception not relevant to this appeal.

II

Decision of this case requires us to address four sections of the Missouri Act: (a) the preamble; (b) the prohibition on the use of public facilities or employees to perform abortions; (c) the prohibition on public funding of abortion counselling; and (d) the requirement that physicians conduct viability tests prior to performing abortions. We address these seriatim.

A

The Act's preamble, as noted, sets forth "findings" by the Missouri legislature that the "[t]he life of each human being begins at conception," and that "[u]nborn children have protectable interests in life, health, and well-being" (Missouri Revised Statute §§ 1.205.1[1],[2][1986]). The Act then mandated the state laws be interpreted to provide unborn children with "all the rights, privileges, and immunities available to other persons, citizens, and residents of this state," subject to the Constitution and this Court's precedents (§ 1.205.2)....

The State contends that the preamble itself is precatory and imposes no substantive restrictions on abortions, and that appellees therefore do not have standing to challenge it. Appellees, on the other hand, insist that the preamble is an operative part of the Act intended to guide the interpretation of other provisions of the Act. They maintain, for example, that the preamble's definition of life may prevent physicians in public hospitals from dispensing certain forms of contraceptives, such as the intrauterine device.

In our view,...the preamble does not by its terms regulate abortion or any other aspect of appellees' medical practice. The Court has emphasized that *Roe v. Wade* "implies no limitation on the authority of a State to make a value judgment favoring childbirth over abortion." The preamble can be read simply to express that sort of value judgment.

We think the extent to which the preamble's language might be used to interpret other state statutes or regulations is something that only the courts of Missouri can definitively decide....It will be time enough for federal courts to address the meaning of the preamble should it be applied to restrict the activities of appellees in some concrete way. Until then, this Court "is not empowered to decide...abstract propositions, or to declare, for the government of future cases, principles or rules of law which cannot affect the result as to the thing in issue in the case before it." We therefore need not pass on the constitutionality of the Act's preamble.

B

Section 188.210 provides that "[i]t shall be unlawful for any public employee within the scope of his employment to perform or assist an abortion, not necessary to save the life of the mother," while § 188.215 makes it "unlawful for any public facility to be used for the purpose of performing or assisting an abortion not necessary to save the life of the mother." The Court of Appeals held that these provisions contravened this Court's abortion decision. We take the contrary view.

As we said earlier this Term in *DeShaney v. Winnebago County Dept. of Social Services*, "our cases have recognized that the Due Process Clauses generally confer no affirmative right to governmental aid, even where such aid may be necessary to secure life, liberty, or property interests of which the government itself may not deprive the individual." In *Maher v. Roe*, the Court upheld a Connecticut welfare regulation under which Medicaid recipients received payments for medical services related to childbirth, but not for nontherapeutic abortions. The Court rejected the claim that this unequal subsidization of childbirth and abortions was impermissible under *Roe v. Wade*. As the Court put it:

> The Connecticut regulation before us is different in kind from the laws invalidated in our previous abortion decisions. The Connecticut regulation places no obstacles-- absolute or otherwise--in the pregnant woman's path to an abortion. An indigent woman who desires an abortion suffers no disadvantage as a consequence of Connecticut's decision to fund childbirth; she continues as before to be dependent on private sources for the service she desires. The State may have made childbirth a more attractive alternative, thereby influencing the woman's decision, but it has imposed no restriction on access to abortions that was not already there. The indigence that may make it difficult- -and in some cases, perhaps, impossible--for some women to have abortions is neither created nor in any way affected by the Connecticut regulation.

Relying on *Maher*, the Court in *Poelker v. Doe*, held that the city of St. Louis committed "no constitutional violation...in electing, as a policy choice, to provide publicly financed hospital services for childbirth without providing corresponding services for nontherapeutic abortions."

More recently, in *Harris v. McRae*, the Court upheld "the most restrictive version of the Hyde Amendment," which withheld from States federal funds under the Medicaid program to reimburse the costs of abortions, "'except where the life of the mother would be endangered if the fetus were carried to term'"...

Missouri's refusal to allow public employees to perform abortions in public hospitals leaves a pregnant woman with the same choices as if the State had chosen not to operate any public hospitals at all. The challenged provisions only restrict a woman's ability to obtain an abortion to the extent that she chooses to use a physician affiliated with a public hospital. This circumstance is more easily remedied, and thus considerably less burdensome, than indigence, which "may make it difficult--and in some cases, perhaps, impossible --for some women to have abortions" without public funding. Having held that the State's refusal to fund abortions does not violate *Roe v. Wade*, it strains logic to reach a contrary result for the use of public facilities and employees. If the State may "make a value judgment favoring childbirth over abortion and ...implement that judgment by the allocation of public funds," surely it may do so through the allocation of other public resources, such as hospitals and medical staff.

...Nothing in the Constitution requires States to enter or remain in the business of performing abortions. Nor, as appellees suggest, do private physicians and their patients have some kind of constitutional right of access to public facilities for the performance of abortions....

Thus we uphold the Act's restrictions on the use of public employees and facilities for the performance or assistance of nontherapeutic abortions.

C

The Missouri Act contains three provisions relating to "encouraging or counselling a woman to have an abortion not necessary to save her life." Section 188.205 states that no public funds can be used for this purpose; § 188.201 states that public employees cannot, within the scope of their employment, engage in such speech; and § 18.215 forbids such speech in public facilities. The Court of Appeals did not consider § 188.205 separately from §§ 188.210 and 188.215. It held that all three of these provisions were unconstitutionally vague, and that "the ban on using public funds, employees, and facilities to encourage or counsel a woman to have an abortion is an unacceptable infringement of the woman's fourteenth amendment right to choose an abortion after receiving the medical information necessary to exercise the right knowingly and intelligently."

Missouri has chosen only to appeal the Court of Appeals' invalidation of the public funding provision, § 188.205. A threshold question is whether this provision reaches primary conduct, or whether it is simply an instruction to the State's fiscal officers not to allocate funds for abortion counselling. We accept, for purposes of decision, the State's claim that § 188.205 "is not directed at the conduct of any physician or health care provider, private or public," but "is directed solely at those persons responsible for expending public funds."...

D

Section 188.029 of the Missouri Act provides:

Before a physician performs an abortion on a woman he has reason to believe is carrying an unborn child of twenty or more weeks gestational age, the physician shall first determine if the unborn child is viable by using and exercising that degree of care, skill, and proficiency commonly exercised by the ordinarily skilful, careful, and prudent physician engaged in similar practice under the same or similar conditions. In making this determination of viability the physician shall perform or cause to be performed such medical examinations and tests as are necessary to make a finding of the gestational age, weight, and lung maturity of the unborn child and shall enter such findings and determination of viability in the medical record of the mother.

As with the preamble, the parties disagree over the meaning of this statutory provision. The State emphasizes the language of the first sentence, which speaks in terms of the physician's determination of viability being made by the standards of ordinary skill in the medical profession. Appellees stress the language of the second sentence, which prescribes such "tests as are necessary" to make a finding of gestational age, fetal weight, and lung maturity.

The Court of Appeals reads § 188.029 as requiring that after 20 weeks "doctors must perform tests to find gestational age, fetal weight, and lung maturity." The court indicated that the tests needed to determine fetal weight at 20 weeks are "unreliable and inaccurate" and would add $125 to $250 to the cost of an abortion. It also states that "amniocentesis, the only method available to determine lung maturity, is contrary to accepted medical practice until 28-30 weeks of gestation, expensive, and imposes significant health risks for both the pregnant woman and the fetus."

We must first determine the meaning of § 188.029 under Missouri law. Our usual practice is to defer to the lower court's construction of a state statute, but we believe the Court of Appeals has "fallen into plain error" in this case....

We think the viability-testing provision makes sense only if the second sentence is read to require only those tests that are useful to making subsidiary findings as to viability. If we construe this provision to require a physician to perform those tests needed to make the three specified findings *in all circumstances*, including when the physician's reasonable professional judgment indicates that the tests would be irrelevant to determining viability or even dangerous to the mother and the fetus, the second sentence of § 188.029 would conflict with the first sentence's *requirement* that a physician apply his reasonable professional skill and judgment. It would also be incongruous to read this provision, especially the word "necessary," to require the performance of tests irrelevant to the expressed statutory purpose of determining viability. It this seems clear to us that the Court of Appeals' construction of § 188.029 violates well-accepted canons of statutory interpretation used in the Missouri courts....

The viability-testing provision of the Missouri Act is concerned with promoting the State's interest in potential human life rather than in maternal health. Section 188.029 creates what is essentially a presumption of viability at 20 weeks, which the physician must rebut with tests indicating that the fetus is *not* viable prior to performing an abortion. It also directs the physician's determination as to viability by specifying consideration, if feasible, of gestational age, fetal weight, and lung capacity. The District Court found that "the medical evidence is uncontradicted that a 20-week fetus is not viable," and that "23 1/2 to 24 weeks gestation is the earliest point in pregnancy where a reasonable possibility of viability exists." But it also found that there may be a 4-week error in estimating the gestational age, which supports testing at 20 weeks.

In *Roe v. Wade*, the Court recognized that the State has "important and legitimate" interests in protecting maternal health and in the potentiality of human life. During the second trimester, the State "may, if it chooses, regulate the abortion procedure in ways that are reasonably related to maternal health." After viability, when the State's interest in potential human life was held to become compelling, the State "may, if it chooses, regulate, and even proscribe, abortion except where it is necessary, in appropriate medical judgment, for the preservation of the life or health of the mother."

...To the extent that § 188.029 regulates the method for determining viability, it undoubtedly does superimpose state regulation on the medical determination of whether a particular fetus is viable. The Court of Appeals and the District Court thought it unconstitutional for this reason. To the extent that the viability tests increase the cost of what are in fact second trimester abortions, their validity may also be questioned under *Akron*, where the Court held that a requirement that second trimester abortions must be performed in hospitals was invalid because it substantially increased the expense of those procedures.

We think that the doubt cast upon the Missouri statute by these cases is not so much a flaw in the statute as it is a reflection of the fact that the rigid trimester analysis of the course of a pregnancy enunciated in *Roe* has resulted in subsequent cases like *Colautti* and

Akron making constitutional law in this area a virtual Procrustean bed....

Stare decisis is a cornerstone of our legal system, but it has less power in constitutional cases, where, save for constitutional amendments, this Court is the only body to make needed changes. We have not refrained from reconsideration of a prior construction of the Constitution that has proved "unsound in principle and unworkable in practice." We think the *Roe* trimester framework falls into this category.

In the first place, the rigid *Roe* framework is hardly consistent with the notion of a Constitution cast in general terms, as ours is, and usually speaking in general principles, as ours does. The key elements of the *Roe* framework--trimesters and viability--are not found in the test of the Constitution or in any place else one would expect to find a constitutional principle. Since the bounds of the inquiry are essentially indeterminate, the result has been a web of legal rules that have become increasingly intricate, resembling a code of regulations rather than a body of constitutional doctrine. As Justice White has put it, the trimester framework has left this Court to serve as the country's "ex officio medical board with powers to approve or disapprove medical and operative practices and standards throughout the United States."

In the second place, we do not see why the State's interest in protecting potential human life should come into existence only at the point of viability, and that there should therefore be a rigid line allowing state regulation after viability but prohibiting it before viability....

The tests that § 188.029 requires the physician to perform are designed to determine viability. The State here has chosen viability as the point at which its interest in potential human life must be safeguarded. See Missouri Revised Statute § 188.030 (1986) "No abortion of a viable unborn child shall be performed unless necessary to preserve the life or health of the woman." It is true that the tests in question increase the expense of abortion, and regulate the discretion of the physician in determining the viability of the fetus. Since the tests will undoubtedly show in any cases that the fetus is not viable, the tests will have been performed for what were in fact second-trimester abortions. But we are satisfied that the requirement of these tests permissibly furthers the State's interest in protecting potential human life, and we therefore believe § 188.029 to be constitutional.

...The Missouri testing requirement here is reasonably designed to ensure that abortions are not performed where the fetus is viable--

an end which all concede is legitimate--and that is sufficient to sustain its constitutionality....

III

Both appellants and the United States as Amicus Curiae have urged that we overrule our decision in *Roe v. Wade*. The facts of the present case, however, differ from those at issue in *Roe*. Here, Missouri has determined that viability is the point at which its interest in potential human life must be safeguarded. In *Roe*, on the other hand, the Texas statute criminalized the performance of all abortions, except when the mother's life was at stake. This case therefore affords us no occasion to visit the holding of *Roe*, which was that the Texas statute unconstitutionally infringed the right to an abortion derived from the Due Process Clause. To the extent indicated in our opinion, we would modify and narrow *Roe* and succeeding cases.

Because none of the challenged provisions of the Missouri Act properly before us conflict with the Constitution, the judgment of the Court of Appeals is reversed.

Justice O'Connor, concurring in part and concurring in the judgment.

I concur in Parts I, II--A, II--B, and II--C of the Court's opinion.

I

Nothing in the record before us...indicates that...the preamble to Missouri's abortion regulation statute will affect a woman's decision to have an abortion. Justice Stevens...suggests that the preamble may also "interfere with contraceptive choices," because certain contraceptive devices act on a female ovum after it has been fertilized by a male sperm. The Missouri Act defines "conception" as "the fertilization of the ovum of a female by a sperm of a male," and invests "unborn children" with "protectable interests in life, health, and well-being," from "the moment of conception...."...Similarly, certain *amici* suggest that the Missouri Act's preamble may prohibit the developing technology of *in vitro* fertilization, a technique used to aid couples otherwise unable to bear children in which a number of ova are removed from the woman and fertilized by male sperm. This process often produces excess fertilized ova ("unborn children" under the Missouri Act's definition) that are discarded rather than reinserted into the woman's uterus. It may be correct that the use of postfertilization contraceptive devices is constitutionally protected by *Griswold* and its progeny but, as with a woman's abortion decision, nothing in the record or the opinions below indicates that the preamble will affect a woman's decision to practice contraception. For that matter, nothing in appellees' original complaint...[indicates] that appellees are sought to enjoin potential violations of *Griswold*. Neither is there any indication of the possibility that the preamble might be applied to prohibit the performance of *in vitro* fertilization. I agree with the Court, therefore, that all of these intimations of unconstitutionality are simply too hypothetical to support the use of declaratory judgment procedures and injunctive remedies in this case....

II

In its interpretation of Missouri's "determination of viability" provision, ...the plurality has proceeded in a manner unnecessary to deciding the question at hand. I agree with the plurality that it was plain error for the Court of Appeals to interpret the second sentence of Missouri Revised Statute § 188.029 as meaning that "doctors must perform tests to find gestational age, fetal weight, and lung maturity."...

Unlike the plurality, I do not understand these viability testing requirements to conflict with any of the Court's past decisions concerning state regulation of abortion. Therefore, there is no necessity to accept the State's invitation to reexamine the constitutional validity of *Roe v. Wade*. Where there is no need to decide a constitutional question, it is a venerable principle of this Court's adjudicatory processes not to do so for "[t]he Court will not 'anticipate a question of constitutional law in advance of the necessity of deciding it.'" Quite simply, "[i]t is not the habit of the court to decide questions of a constitutional nature unless absolutely necessary to a decision of the case." The Court today has accepted the State's every interpretation of its abortion statute and has upheld, under our existing precedents, every reconsideration of *Roe* falls not into any "good-cause exception" to this "fundamental rule of judicial restraint...." When the constitutional invalidity of a State's abortion statute actually turns on the constitutional validity of *Roe v. Wade*, there will be time enough to reexamine *Roe*. And to do so carefully....

Justice Scalia, concurring in part and concurring in the judgment.

I join Parts I, II--A, II--B, and II--C of the opinion of the Chief Justice. As to Part II-d, I share Justice Blackmun's view, that it effectively would overrule *Roe v. Wade*. I think that should be done, but would do it more explicitly. Since today we contrive to avoid doing it, and indeed to avoid almost any decision of national import, I need to set forth my reasons, some of which have been well recited in dissents of my colleagues in other cases.

The outcome of today's case will doubtless be heralded as a triumph of judicial statesmanship. It is not that, unless it is statesmanlike needlessly to prolong this Court's self-awarded sovereignty over a field where it has little proper business since the answers to most of the cruel questions posed are political and not juridical--a sovereignty which therefore quite properly, but to the great damage of the Court, makes it the object of the sort of organized public pressure that political institutions in a democracy ought to receive.

Justice O'Connor's assertion that a "fundamental rule of judicial restraint" requires us to avoid reconsidering *Roe*, cannot be taken seriously, by finessing that we should avoid "'decid[ing] questions of a constitutional nature.'" We have not disposed of this case on some statutory or procedural ground, but have decided, and could not avoid deciding, whether the Missouri statute meets the requirements of the United States Constitution. The only choice available is whether, in deciding that constitutional question, we should use *Roe v. Wade* as the benchmark, or something else. What is involved, therefore, is not the rule of avoiding constitutional issues where possible, but the quite separate principle that we will not "'formulate a rule of constitutional law broader than is required by the precise facts to which it is to be applied.'" The latter is a sound general principle, but one often departed from when good reason exists....

The Court has often spoken more broadly than needed in precisely the fashion at issue here, announcing a new rule of constitutional law....It would be wrong, in any decision, to ignore the reality that our policy not to "formulate a rule of constitutional law broader than is required by the precise facts" has a frequently applied good-cause exception. But it seems particularly perverse to convert the policy into an absolute in the present case, in order to place beyond reach the inexpressibly "broader-than-was-required-by-the-precise-facts" structure established by *Roe v. Wade*.

The real question, then, is whether there are valid reasons to go beyond the most stingy possible holding today. It seems to me there are not only valid but compelling ones. Ordinarily, speaking no more broadly than is absolutely required avoids throwing settled law into confusion; doing so today preserves a chaos that is evident to anyone who can read and count. Alone sufficient to justify a broad holding is the fact that our retaining control through *Roe*, of what I believe to be, and many of our citizens recognize to be, a political issue, continuously distorts the public perception of the role of this Court. We can now look forward to at least another Term with carts full of mail from the public, and streets full of demonstrators, urging us-- their unelected and life-tenured judges who have been awarded those extraordinary, undemocratic characteristics precisely in order that we might follow the law despite the popular will--to follow the popular will. Indeed, I expect we can look forward to even more of that than before, given our indecisive decision today....

It was an arguable question today whether § 188.029 of the Missouri law contravened this Court's understanding of *Roe v. Wade*, and I would have examined *Roe* rather than examining the contravention. Given the Court's newly contracted abstemiousness, what will it take, one must wonder, to permit us to reach that fundamental question? The result of our vote today is that we will not reconsider that prior opinion, even if most of the Justices think it is wrong, unless we have before us a statute that in fact contradicts it-- and even then (under our newly discovered "no-broader-than-necessary" requirement) only minor problematical aspects of *Roe* will be reconsidered, unless one expects State legislatures to adopt provisions whose compliance with *Roe* cannot even be argued with a straight face. It this appears that the mansion of constitutionalized abortion-law, constructed overnight in *Roe v. Wade*, must be disassembled door-jamb by door-jamb, and never entirely brought down, no matter how wrong it may be.

Of the four courses we might have chosen today--to reaffirm *Roe*, to overrule it explicitly, to overrule it sub silentio, or to avoid the question--the last is the least responsible. On the question of the constitutionality of § 188.029, I concur in the judgment of the Court and strongly dissent from the manner in which it has been reached.

Justice Blackmun, with whom Justice Brennan and Justice Marshall join, concurring in part and dissenting in part.

Today, *Roe v. Wade*, and the fundamental constitutional right of women to decide whether to terminate a pregnancy, survive but are not secure. Although the Court extricates itself from this case without making a single, even incremental, change in the law of abortion, the plurality and Justice Scalia would overrule *Roe* (the first silently, the other explicitly) and would return to the States virtually unfettered authority to control the quintessentially intimate, personal, and life-directing decision whether to carry a fetus to term. Although today, no less than yesterday, the Constitution and the decisions of this Court prohibit a State from enacting laws that inhibit women from the meaningful exercise of that right, a plurality of this Court implicitly invites every state legislature to enact more and more restrictive abortion regulations in order to provoke more and more test cases, in the hope that sometime down the line the Court will return the law of procreative freedom to the severe limitations that generally prevailed in this country before January 22, 1973. Never in my memory has a plurality announced a judgment of this Court that so foments disregard for the law and for our standing decisions.

Nor in my memory has a plurality gone about its business in such a deceptive fashion. At every level of its review, from its effort to read the real meaning out of the Missouri statute, to its intended evisceration of precedents and its deafening silence about the constitutional protections that it would jettison, the plurality obscures the portent of its analysis. With feigned restraint, the plurality announces that its analysis leaves Roe "undisturbed," albeit "modif[ied] and narrow[ed]." But this disclaimer is totally meaningless. The plurality opinion is filled with winks, and nods, and knowing glances to those who would do away with *Roe* explicitly, but turns a stone face to anyone in search of what the plurality conceives as the scope of a woman's right under the Due Process Clause to terminate a pregnancy free from the coercive and brooding influence of the State. The simple truth is that *Roe* would not survive the plurality's analysis, and that the plurality provides no substitute for *Roe*'s protective umbrella.

I fear for the future. I fear for the liberty and equality of the millions of women who have lived and come of age in the 16 years since *Roe* was decided. I fear for the integrity of, and public esteem for, this Court.

I dissent.

I

...Although I...am especially disturbed by its misapplication of our past decisions in upholding Missouri's ban on the performance of abortions at "public facilities," the plurality's discussion of these provisions is merely prologue to the consideration of the statute's viability-testing requirement, §188.029--the only section of the Missouri statute that the plurality construes as implicating *Roe* itself. There, tucked away at the end of its opinion, the plurality suggests a radical reversal of the law of abortion; and there, primarily I direct my attention.

In the plurality's view, the viability-testing provision imposes a burden on second-trimester abortions as a way of furthering the State's interest in protecting the potential life of the fetus. Since under the Roe framework, the State may not fully regulate abortion in the interest of potential life (as opposed to maternal health) until the third trimester, the plurality finds it necessary, in order to save the Missouri testing provision, to throw out *Roe*'s trimester framework. In flat contradiction to *Roe*, the plurality concludes that the State's interest in potential life is compelling before viability, and upholds the testing provision because it "permissibly furthers" that state interest....

Having set up the conflict between § 188.029 and the *Roe* trimester framework, the plurality summarily discards *Roe*'s analytic core as "unsound in principle and unworkable in practice."...

The plurality opinion is far more remarkable for the arguments that it does not advance than for those that it does. The plurality does not even mention, much less join, the true jurisprudential debate underlying this case: whether the Constitution includes an "unenumerated" general right to privacy as recognized in many of our decisions, most notably *Griswold v. Connecticut*, and *Roe*, and, more specifically, whether and to what extent such a right to privacy extends to matters of childbearing and family life, including abortion....

But rather than arguing that the text of the Constitution makes no mention of the right to privacy, the plurality complains that the critical elements of the *Roe* framework--trimesters and viability--do not appear in the Constitution and are, therefore, somehow inconsistent with a Constitution cast in general terms. Were this a true concern, we would have to abandon most of our constitutional jurisprudence. As the plurality well knows, or should know, the "critical elements" of countless constitutional doctrines nowhere appear in the Constitution's text....

With respect to the *Roe* framework, the general right, for which it was developed is the right to privacy....It is this general principle, the "'moral fact that a person belongs to himself and not to others nor to society as a whole,'"...that is found in the Constitution. The trimester framework simply defines and limits that right to privacy in the abortion context to accommodate, not destroy, a State's legitimate interest in protecting the health of pregnant women and in preserving potential human life. Fashioning such accommodations between individual rights and the legitimate interests of government, establishing benchmarks and standards with which to evaluate the competing claims of individuals and government, lies at the very heart of constitutional adjudication. To the extent that the trimester framework is useful in this enterprise, it is not only consistent with constitutional interpretation, but necessary to the wise and just exercise of this Court's paramount authority to define the scope of constitutional rights.

The plurality next alleges that the result of the trimester framework has "been a web of legal rules that have become increasingly intricate, resembling a code of regulations rather than a body of constitutional doctrine." Again, if this were a true and genuine concern, we would have to abandon vast areas of our constitutional jurisprudence....

Finally, the plurality asserts that the trimester framework cannot stand because the State's interest in potential life is compelling throughout pregnancy, not merely after viability. The opinion contains not one word of rationale for its view of the State's interest. This "it-is-so-because-we-say-so" jurisprudence constitutes nothing, other than an attempted exercise of brute force; reason, much less persuasion, has no place.

In answering the plurality's claim that the State's interest in the fetus is uniform and compelling throughout pregnancy, I cannot improve upon what Justice Stevens has written [in *Thornburgh*]:

> I should think it obvious that the State's interest in the protection of an embryo--even if that interest is defined as "protecting those who will be citizens"...--increases progressively and dramatically as the organism's capacity to feel pain, to experience pleasure, to survive, and to react to its surroundings increases day by day. The development of a fetus--and pregnancy itself--are not static conditions, and the assertion that the government's interest is static simply ignores this reality....[U]nless the religious view that a fetus is a "person" is adopted...there is a fundamental and well-recognized difference between a fetus and a human being; indeed, if there is not such a difference, the permissibility of terminating the life of a fetus could scarcely be left to the will of the state legislatures. And if distinctions may be drawn between a fetus and a human being in terms of the state interest in their protection--even though the fetus represents one of "those who will be citizens"--it seems to me quite odd to argue that distinctions may not also be drawn between the state interest in protecting the freshly fertilized egg and the state interest in protecting the 9-month-gestated, fully sentient fetus on the eve of birth. Recognition of this distinction is supported not only by logic, but also by history and by our shared experiences.

For my own part, I remain convinced, as six other Members of this Court 16 years ago were convinced, that the *Roe* framework, and the viability standard in particular, fairly, sensibly, and effectively functions to safeguard the constitutional liberties of pregnant women while recognizing and accommodating the State's interest in potential human life. The viability line reflects the biological facts and truths of fetal development; it marks that threshold moment prior to which a fetus cannot survive separate from the woman and cannot reasonably and objectively be regarded as a subject of rights or interests distinct from, or paramount to, those of the pregnant woman. At the same time, the viability standard takes account of the undeniable fact that as the fetus evolves into its postnatal form, and as it loses its dependence on the uterine environment, the State's interest in the fetus' potential human life, and in fostering a regard for human life in general, becomes compelling. As a practical matter, because viability follows "quickening"--the point at which a woman feels movement in her womb--and because viability occurs no earlier than 23 weeks gestational age, it establishes an easily applicable standard for regulating abortion while providing a pregnant woman ample time to exercise her fundamental right with her responsible physician to terminate her pregnancy. Although I have stated previously for a majority of this Court that "[c]onstitutional rights do not always have easily ascertainable boundaries," to seek and establish those boundaries remains the special responsibility of this Court. In *Roe*, we discharged that responsibility as logic and science compelled. The plurality today advances not one reasonable argument as to why our judgment in that case was wrong and should be abandoned.

Having contrived an opportunity to reconsider the *Roe* framework, and then having discarded that framework, the plurality finds the testing provision unobjectionable because it "permissibly furthers the State's interest in protecting potential human life."...

The "permissibly furthers" standard completely disregards the irreducible minimum of *Roe*: the Court's recognition that a woman has a limited fundamental constitutional right to decide whether to terminate a pregnancy. That right receives no meaningful recognition in the plurality's written opinion. Since, in the plurality's view, the State's interest in potential life is compelling as of the moment of conception, and is therefore served only if abortion is abolished, every hindrance to a woman's ability to obtain an abortion must be "permissible." Indeed, the more severe the hindrance, the more effectively (and permissibly) the State's interest would be furthered. A tax on abortions or a criminal prohibition would both satisfy the plurality's standard. So, for that matter, would a requirement that a pregnant woman memorize and recite today's plurality opinion before seeking an abortion.

The plurality pretends that *Roe* survives, explaining that the facts of this case differ from those in *Roe*: here, Missouri has chosen to assert its interest in potential life only at the point of viability, whereas, in *Roe*, Texas has asserted that interest from the point of conception, criminalizing all abortions, except where the life of the mother was at stake. This, of course, is a distinction without a difference. The plurality repudiates every principle for which *Roe* stands; in good conscience, it cannot possibly believe that *Roe* lies "undisturbed" merely because this case does not call upon the Court to reconsider the Texas statute, or one like it. If the Constitution permits a State to enact any statute that reasonably furthers its interest in potential life, and if that interest arises as of conception, why would the Texas statute fail to pass muster? One suspects that the plurality agrees. It is impossible to read the plurality opinion and especially its final paragraph, without recognizing its implicit invitation to every State to enact more and more restrictive abortion laws, and to assert their interest in potential life as of the moment of conception. All these laws will satisfy the plurality's nonscrutiny, until sometime, a new regime of old dissenters and new appointees will declare what the plurality intends: that *Roe* is no longer good law.

Thus, "not with a bang, but a whimper," the plurality discards a landmark case of the last generation, and casts into darkness the hopes and visions of every woman in this country who had come to believe that the Constitution guaranteed her the right to exercise some control over her unique ability to bear children. The plurality does so either oblivious or insensitive to the fact that millions of women, and their families, have ordered their lives around the right to reproductive choice, and that this right has become vital to the full participation of women in the economic and political walks of American life. The plurality would clear the way once again for government to force upon women the physical labor and specific and direct medical and psychological harms that may accompany carrying a fetus to term. The plurality would clear the way again for the State to conscript a woman's body and to force upon her a "distressful life and future."

The result, as we know from experience, would be that every year hundreds of thousands of women, in desperation, wold defy the law, and place their health and safety in the unclean and unsympathetic hands of back-alley abortionists, or they would attempt to perform abortions upon themselves, with disastrous results. Every year, many women, especially poor and minority women, would die or suffer debilitating physical trauma, all in the name of enforced morality or religious dictates or lack of compassion, as it may be.

Of the aspirations and settled understandings of American women, of the inevitable and brutal consequences of what it is doing, the tough-approach plurality utters not a word. This silence is callous. It is also profoundly destructive of the Court as an institution. To overturn a constitutional decision is a rare and grave undertaking. To overturn a constitutional decision that secured a fundamental personal liberty to millions of persons would be unprecedented in our 200 years of constitutional history. Although the doctrine of stare decisis applies with somewhat diminished force in constitutional cases generally, even in ordinary constitutional cases "any departure from stare decisis demands special justification." This requirement of justification applies with unique force where, as here, the Court's abrogation of precedent would destroy people's firm belief, based on past decisions of this Court, that they possess an unabridgeable right to undertake certain conduct.

As discussed at perhaps too great length above, the plurality makes no serious attempt to carry "the heavy burden of persuading...that changes in society or in the law dictate: the abandonment of *Roe* and its numerous progeny, much less the greater burden of explaining the abrogation of a fundamental personal freedom." Instead, the plurality pretends that it leaves *Roe* standing, and refuses even to discuss the real issue underlying this case: whether the Constitution includes an unenumerated right to privacy that encompasses a woman's right to decide whether to terminate a pregnancy. To the extent that the plurality does criticize the *Roe* framework, these criticisms are pure ipse dixit.

This comes at a cost. The doctrine of *stare decisis* "permits society to assume that bedrock principles are founded in the law rather than in the proclivities of individuals, and thereby contributes to the integrity of our constitutional system of government, both in appearance and in fact." Today's decision involves the most politically divisive domestic legal issue of our time. By refusing to explain or to justify its proposed revolutionary revision in the law of abortion, and by refusing to abide not only by our precedents, but also by our canons for reconsidering those precedents, the plurality invites charges of cowardice and illegitimacy to our door. I cannot say that these would be undeserved.

For today, at least, the law of abortion stands undisturbed. For today, the women of this Nation still retain the liberty to control their destinies. But the signs are evident and very ominous, and a chill wind blows.

I dissent.

Justice Stevens, concurring in part and dissenting in part.

Having joined Part II-C of the Court's opinion, I shall not comment on § 188.205 of the Missouri statute. With respect to the challenged portions of §§ 188.210 and 188.215, I agree with Justice Blackmun that the record identifies a sufficient number of unconstitutional applications to support the Court of Appeals' judgment invalidating those provisions. The reasons why I would also affirm that court's invalidation of § 188.029, the viability testing provision, and §§ 1.205.1(1)(2) of the preamble, require separate explanation.

It seems to me that in Part II-D of its opinion, the plurality strains to place a construction of § 188.029 that enables it to conclude, "[W]e would modify and narrow *Roe* and succeeding cases." ...I agree with the Court of Appeals and the District Court that the meaning of the second sentence of § 188.029 is too plain to be ignored. The sentence twice uses the mandatory term "shall," and contains no qualifying language. If it is implicitly limited to tests that are useful in determining viability, it adds nothing to the requirement imposed by the preceding sentence.

My interpretation of the plain language is supported by the structure of the statute as a whole, particularly the preamble, which "finds" that life "begins at conception" and further commands that state laws shall be construed to provide the maximum protection to "the unborn child at every stage of development." I agree with the District Court that "[o]bviously, the purpose of this law is to protect the potential life of the fetus, rather than safeguard maternal health." A literal reading of the statute tends to accomplish that goal. Thus it is not "incongruous" to assume that the Missouri Legislature was trying to protect the potential human life of nonviable fetuses by making the abortion decision more costly. On the contrary, I am satisfied that the Court of Appeals, as well as the District Court, correctly concluded that the Missouri Legislature meant exactly what it said in the second sentence of § 188.029. I am also satisfied, for the reasons stated by Justice Blackmun, that the testing provision is manifestly unconstitutional under *Williams* v. *Lee Optical Co.*, "irrespective of the *Roe* framework." ...

To the extent that the Missouri statute interferes with contraceptive choices, I have no doubt that it is unconstitutional under the Court's holdings in *Griswold* v. *Connecticut, Eisenstadt* v. *Baird,* and *Carey* v. *Population Services International.* ...

Indeed, I am persuaded that the absence of any secular purpose for the legislative declarations that life begins at contraception or occurs at fertilization makes the relevant portion of the preamble invalid under the Establishment Clause of the First Amendment to the Federal Constitution. This conclusion does not, and could not, rest on the fact that the statement happens to coincide with the tenets of certain religions, or on the fact that the legislators who voted to enact it may have been motivated by religious considerations. Rather, it rests on the fact that the preamble, an unequivocal endorsement of a religious tenet of some but by no means all Christian faiths, serves no identifiable secular purpose. That fact alone compels a conclusion that the statute violates the Establishment Clause. ...

...The preamble to the Missouri statute endorses the theological position that there is the same secular interest in preserving the life of a fetus during the first 40 or 80 days of pregnancy as there is after viability--indeed, after the time when the fetus has become a "person" with legal rights protected by the Constitution. To sustain that position as a matter of law, I believe Missouri has the burden of identifying the secular interests that differentiate the first 40 days of pregnancy from the period immediately before or after fertilization when, as *Griswold* and related cases establish, the Constitution allows the use of contraceptive procedures to prevent potential life from developing into full personhood. Focusing our attention on the first several weeks of pregnancy is especially appropriate because that is the period when the vast majority of abortions are actually performed.

As a secular matter, there is an obvious difference between the state interest in protecting the freshly fertilized egg and the state interest in protecting a 9-month-gestated, fully sentient fetus on the eve of birth. There can be no interest in protecting the newly fertilized egg from physical pain or mental anguish, because the capacity for such suffering does not yet exist; respecting a developed fetus, however, that interest is valid. ... The State's suggestion that the "finding" in the preamble to its abortion statute is, in effect, an amendment to its tort, property, and criminal law is not persuasive. The Court of Appeals concluded that the preamble "is simply an impermissible state adoption of a theory of when life begins to justify its abortion regulations." ....

In my opinion the preamble to the Missouri statute is unconstitutional for two reasons. To the extent that it has substantive impact on the freedom to use contraceptive procedures, it is inconsistent with the central holding in *Griswold*. To the extent that it merely makes "legislative findings without operative effect," as the State argues, it violates the Establishment Clause of the First Amendment. ...

CANADA

The House of Commons of Canada
BILL C-43
Second Session, Thirty-fourth Parliament, 1989

First reading, November 3, 1989

Her Majesty, by and with the advice and consent of the Senate and House of Commons of Canada, enacts as follows:

1. Sections 287 and 288 of the *Criminal Code* are repealed and the following substituted therefore:

287. (1) Every person who induces an abortion on a female person is guilty of an indictable offence and liable to imprisonment for a term not exceeding two years, unless the abortion is induced by or under the direction of a medical practitioner who is of the opinion that, if the abortion were not induced, the health or life of the female person would be likely to be threatened.

(2) For the purposes of this section,

"health" includes, for greater certainty, physical, mental and psychological health;

"medical practitioner," in respect of an abortion induced in a province, means a person who is entitled to practise medicine under the laws of that province;

"opinion" means an opinion formed using generally accepted standards of the medical profession.

(3) For the purposes of this section and section 288, inducing an abortion does not include using a drug, device or other means on a female person that is likely to prevent implantation of a fertilized ovum.

288. Every one who unlawfully supplies or procures a drug or other noxious thing or an instrument or thing, knowing that it is intended to be used or employed to induce an abortion on a female person, is guilty of an indictable offence and liable to imprisonment for a term not exceeding two years."

2. This Act shall come into force on a day to be fixed by order of the Governor in Council.

EXPLANATORY NOTES

Clause 1: The substance of the proposed section 287 is new. The proposed amendments to section 288 are consequential on the amendments proposed to section 287.

Sections 287 and 288 at present read as follows:

287. (1) Every one who, with intent to procure the miscarriage of a female person, whether or not she is pregnant, uses any means for the purpose of carrying out his intention is guilty of an indictable offence and liable to imprisonment for life.

(2) Every female person who, being pregnant, with intent to procure her own miscarriage, uses any means or permits any means to be used for the purpose of carrying out her intention is guilty of an indictable offence and liable to imprisonment for a term not exceeding two years.

(3) In this section, "means" includes
   (a) the administration of a drug or other noxious thing;
   (b) the use of an instrument; and
   (c) manipulation of any kind.

(4) Subsections (1) and (2) do not apply to

   (a) a qualified medical practitioner, other than a member of a therapeutic abortion committee for any hospital, who in good faith uses in an accredited or approved hospital any means for the purpose of carrying out his intention to procure the miscarriage of a female person, or

   (b) a female person who, being pregnant, permits a qualified medical practitioner to use in an accredited or approved hospital any means for the purpose of carrying out her intention to procure her own miscarriage, if, before, the use of those means, the therapeutic abortion committee for that accredited or approved hospital, by a majority of the members of the committee and at a meeting of the committee at which the case of the female person has been reviewed,

(c) has by certificate in writing stated that in its opinion the continuation of the pregnancy of the female person would or would be likely to endanger her life or health, and

(d) has caused a copy of such certificate to be given to the qualified medical practitioner.

(5) The Minister of Health of a province may by order

(a) require a therapeutic abortion committee for any hospital in that province, or any member thereof, to furnish him with a copy of any certificate described in paragraph (4)(c) issued by that committee, together with such other information relating to the circumstances surrounding the issue of that certificate as he may require, or

(b) require a medical practitioner who, in that province, has procured the miscarriage of any female person named in a certificate described in paragraph (4)(c), to furnish him with a copy of that certificate, together with such other information relating to the procuring of the miscarriage as he may require.

(6) For the purposes of subsections (4) and (5) and this subsection,

"accredited hospital" means a hospital accredited by the Canadian Council on Hospital Accreditation in which diagnostic services and medical, surgical and obstetrical treatment are provided;

"approved hospital" means a hospital in a province approved for the purposes of this section by the Minister of Health of that province;

"board" means the board of governors, management or directors, or the trustees, commission or other person or group of persons having the control and management of an accredited or approved hospital;

"Minister of Health" means
(a) in the Provinces of Ontario, Quebec, New Brunswick, Prince Edward Island, Manitoba and Newfoundland, the Minister of Health,
(b) in the Provinces of Nova Scotia and Saskatchewan, the Minister of Public Health,

(c) in the Province of British Columbia, the Minister of Health Services and Hospital Insurance,

(d) in the Province of Alberta, the Minister of Hospitals and Medical Care,

(e) in the Yukon Territory and the Northwest Territories, the Minister of National Health and Welfare;

"qualified medical practitioner" means a person entitled to engage in the practice of medicine under the laws of the province in which the hospital referred to in subsection (4) is situated;

"therapeutic abortion committee" for any hospital means a committee, comprised of not less than three members each of whom is a qualified medical practitioner, appointed by the board of that hospital for the purpose of considering and determining questions relating to terminations of pregnancy within that hospital.

(7) Nothing in subsection (4) shall be construed as making unnecessary the obtaining of any authorization or consent that is or may be required, otherwise than under this Act, before any means are used for the purpose of carrying out an intention to procure the miscarriage of a female person.

288. Every one who unlawfully supplies or procures a drug or other noxious thing or an instrument or thing, knowing that it is intended to be used or employed to procure the miscarriage of a female person, whether or not she is pregnant, is guilty of an indictable offence and liable to imprisonment for a term not exceeding two years.

R. v. MORGENTALER

The judgment of Dickson C. J. and Lamer J. was delivered by

THE CHIEF JUSTICE--The principal issue raised by this appeal is whether the abortion provisions of the *Criminal Code*, R.S.C. 1970, c. C-34, infringe the "right to life, liberty and security of the person and the right not to be deprived thereof except in accordance with the principles of fundamental justice" as formulated in s. 7 of the *Canadian Charter of Rights and Freedoms*. The appellants, Dr. Henry Morgentaler, Dr. Leslie Frank Smoling and Dr. Robert Scott, have raised thirteen distinct grounds of appeal. During oral submissions, however, it became apparent that the primary focus of the case was upon the s. 7 argument. It is submitted by the appellants that s. 251 of the *Criminal Code* contravenes s. 7 of the *Canadian Charter of Rights and Freedoms* and that s. 251 should be struck down. Counsel for the Crown admitted during the course of her submissions that s. 7 of the *Charter* was indeed "the key" to the entire appeal. As for the remaining grounds of appeal, only a few brief comments are necessary. First of all, I agree with the disposition made by the Court of Appeal of the non-*Charter* issues, many of which have already been adequately dealt with in earlier cases by this Court. I am also of the view that the arguments concerning the alleged invalidity of s. 605 under ss. 7 and 11 of the *Charter* are unfounded. In view of my resolution of the s. 7 issue, it will not be necessary for me to address the appellants' other *Charter* arguments and I expressly refrain from commenting upon their merits.

During argument before this Court, counsel for the Crown emphasized repeatedly that it is not the role of the judiciary in Canada to evaluate the wisdom of legislation enacted by our democratically elected representatives, or to second-guess difficult policy choices that confront all governments. In *Morgentaler v. The Queen*, [1976] 1 S.C.R. 616, at p. 671, [hereinafter "*Morgentaler* (1975)"] I stressed that the Court had "not been called upon to decide, or even to enter, the loud and continuous public debate on abortion." Eleven years later, the controversy persists, and it remains true that this Court cannot presume to resolve all of the competing claims advanced in vigorous and healthy public debate. Courts and legislators in other democratic societies have reached completely contradictory decisions when asked to weigh the competing values relevant to the abortion question. See, e.g., *Roe v. Wade*, 410 U.S. 113 (1973); *Paton v. United Kingdom* (1980), 3 E.H.R.R. (European Court of Human Rights); *The Abortion Decision of the Federal Constitutional Court--First Senate--of the Federal Republic of Germany*, February 25, 1975, translated and reprinted in (1976), 9 John Marshall J. Prac. and Proc. 605; and the *Abortion Act*, 1967, c. 87 (U.K.)

But since 1975, and the first *Morgentaler* decision, the Court has been given added responsibilities. I stated in *Morgentaler* (1975), at p. 671, that:

The values we must accept for the purposes of this appeal are those expressed by Parliament which holds the view that the desire of a woman to be relieved of her pregnancy is not, of itself, justification for performing an abortion.

Although no doubt it is still fair to say that courts are not the appropriate forum for articulating complex and controversial programmes of public policy, Canadian courts are now charged with the crucial obligation of ensuring that the legislative initiatives pursued by our Parliament and legislatures conform to the democratic values expressed in the *Canadian Charter of Rights and Freedoms*. As Justice McIntyre states in his reasons for judgment, at p. 138, "the task of the Court in this case is not to solve nor seek to solve what might be called the abortion issue, but simply to measure the content of s. 251 against the *Charter*." It is in this latter sense that the current *Morgentaler* appeal differs from the one we heard a decade ago.

I

The Court stated the following constitutional questions:

1. Does section 251 of the *Criminal Code* of Canada infringe or deny the rights and freedoms guaranteed by ss. 2(a), 7, 12, 15, 27 and 28 of the *Canadian Charter of Rights and Freedoms*?

2. If section 251 of the *Criminal Code* of Canada infringes or denies the rights and freedoms guaranteed by ss. 2(a), 7, 12, 15, 27 and 28 of the *Canadian Charter of Rights and Freedoms*, is s. 251 justified by s. 1 of the *Canadian Charter of Rights and Freedoms* and therefore not inconsistent with the *Constitution Act*, 1982?

3. Is section 251 of the *Criminal Code* of Canada *ultra vires* the Parliament of Canada?

4. Does section 251 of the *Criminal Code* of Canada violate s. 96 of the *Constitution Act*, 1867?

5. Does section 251 of the *Criminal Code* of Canada unlawfully delegate federal criminal power to provincial Ministers of Health or Therapeutic Abortion Committees, and in doing so, has the Federal Government abdicated its authority in this area?

6. Do sections 605 and 610(3) of the *Criminal Code* of Canada infringe or deny the rights and freedoms guaranteed by ss. 7, 11(d), 11(f), 11(h) and 24(1) of the *Canadian Charter of Rights and Freedoms*?

7.   If sections 605 and 610(3) of the *Criminal Code* of Canada
infringe or deny the rights and freedoms guaranteed by ss. 7,
11(d), 11(f), 11(h) and 24(1) of the *Canadian Charter of Rights
and Freedoms*, are ss. 605 and 610(3) justified by s. 1 of the
Canadian Charter of Rights and Freedoms and therefore not
inconsistent with the *Constitution Act*, 1982?

The Attorney General of Canada intervened to support the respondent
Crown.

II

Relevant Statutory and Constitutional Provisions

Criminal Code

251. (1) Every one who, with intent to procure the miscarriage of a
female person, whether or not she is pregnant, uses any means for the
purpose of carrying out his intention is guilty of an indictable offence
and is liable to imprisonment for life.

(2) Every female person who, being pregnant, with intent to
procure her own miscarriage, uses any means or permits any means
to be used for the purpose of carrying out her intention is guilty of
an indictable offence and is liable to imprisonment for two years.

(3) In this section, "means" includes
   (a) the administration of a drug or other noxious thing,
   (b) the use of an instrument, and
   (c) manipulation of any kind.

(4) Subsections (1) and (2) do not apply to
   (a) a qualified medical practitioner, other than a member of a
therapeutic abortion committee for any hospital, who in good faith
uses in an accredited or approved hospital any means for the purpose
of carrying out his intention to procure the miscarriage of a female
person, or
   (b) a female person who, being pregnant, permits a qualified
medical practitioner to use in an accredited or approved hospital any
means described in paragraph (a) for the purpose of carrying out her
intention to procure her own miscarriage, if, before the use of those
means, the therapeutic abortion committee for that accredited or
approved hospital, by a majority of the members of the committee

and at a meeting of the committee at which the case of such female person has been reviewed,

(c) has by certificate in writing stated that in its opinion the continuation of the pregnancy of such female person would or would be likely to endanger her life or health, and

(d) has caused a copy of such certificate to be given to the qualified medical practitioner.

(5) The Minister of Health of a province may by order

(a) require a therapeutic abortion committee for any hospital in that province, or any member thereof, to furnish to him a copy of any certificate described in paragraph (4)(c) issued, by that committee, together with such other information relating to the circumstances surrounding the issue of that certificate as he may require, or

(b) require a medical practitioner who, in that province, has procured the miscarriage of any female person named in a certificate described in paragraph (4)(c), to furnish to him a copy of that certificate, together with such other information relating to the procuring of the miscarriage as he may require.

(6) For the purposes of subsections (4) and (5) and this subsection

"accredited hospital" means a hospital accredited by the Canadian Council on Hospital Accreditation in which diagnostic services and medical, surgical and obstetrical treatment are provided;

"approved hospital" means a hospital in a province approved for the purposes of this section by the Minister of Health of that province;

"board" means the board of governors, management or directors, or the trustees, commission or other person or group of persons having the control and management of an accredited or approved hospital;

"Minister of Health" means

(a) in the Provinces of Ontario, Quebec, New Brunswick, Manitoba, Newfoundland and Prince Edward Island, the Minister of Health,

(a.1) in the Province of Alberta, the Minister of Hospitals and Medical Care,

(b) in the Province of British Columbia, the Minister of Health Services and Hospital Insurance,

(c) in the Provinces of Nova Scotia and Saskatchewan, the Minister of Public Health, and

(d) in the Yukon Territory and the Northwest Territories, the Minister of National Health and Welfare;

"qualified medical practitioner" means a person entitled to engage in the practice of medicine under the laws of the province in which the hospital referred to in subsection (4) is situated;

"therapeutic abortion committee" for any hospital means a committee, comprised of not less than three members each of whom is a qualified medical practitioner, appointed by the board of that hospital for the purpose of considering and determining questions relating to terminations of pregnancy within that hospital.

(7) Nothing in subsection (4) shall be construed as making unnecessary the obtaining of any authorization or consent that is or may be required, otherwise than under this Act, before any means are used for the purpose of carrying out an intention to procure the miscarriage of a female person.

The Canadian Charter of Rights and Freedoms

1. The *Canadian Charter of Rights and Freedoms* guarantees the rights and freedoms set out in it subject only to such reasonable limits prescribed by law as can be demonstrably justified in a free and democratic society.

...

7. Everyone has the right to life, liberty and security of the person and the right not to be deprived thereof except in accordance with the principles of fundamental justice.

VII

Conclusion of The Chief Justice

Section 251 of the *Criminal Code* infringes the right to security of the person of many pregnant women. The procedures and administrative structures established in the section to provide for therapeutic abortions do not comply with the principles of fundamental justice. Section 7 of the *Charter* is infringed and that infringement cannot be saved under s. 1.

In oral argument, counsel for the Crown submitted that if the Court were to hold that procedural aspects of s. 251 infringed the *Charter*, only the procedures set out in the section should be struck down, that is subss. (4) and (5). After being pressed with questions from the bench, Ms. Wein conceded that the whole of s. 251 should fall if it infringed s. 7. Mr. Blacklock for the Attorney General of Canada took the same position. This was a wise approach, for in *Morgentaler* (1975), at p. 676, the Court held that "s. 251 contains a comprehensive code on the subject of abortions, unitary and complete within itself." Having found that this "comprehensive code" infringes the *Charter*, it is not the role of the Court to pick and choose among the various aspects of s. 251 so as effectively to re-draft the section. The appeal should therefore be allowed and s. 251 as a whole struck down under s. 52(1) of the *Constitution Act, 1982*.

The first constitutional question is therefore answered in the affirmative as regards s. 7 of the *Charter* only. The second question, as regards s. 7 of the *Charter* only, is answered in the negative. Questions 3, 4 and 5 are answered in the negative. I answer question 6 in the manner proposed by Beetz J. It is not necessary to answer question 7.

Conclusion of Beetz and Estey JJ.

The constitutional questions should be answered as follows:

1. The first constitutional question is answered in the affirmative in respect of the right of a pregnant woman to "security of the person" in s. 7 of the *Charter*.

2. In respect of the violation of the right of a pregnant woman to "security of the person" in s. 7 caused by s. 251 of the *Criminal Code*, s. 251 is not justified by s. 1 of the *Charter*.

3. No, in the sense that s. 251 is within the proper jurisdiction of Parliament on the basis of s. 91(27) of the *Constitution Act, 1867*.

4. No.

5. No.

6. With respect to s. 605, the answer is no. Whether or not s. 610(3) of the *Criminal Code* violates a *Charter* right, I agree with the Court of Appeal that, whatever this Court's power to award costs in appeals such as this one, costs should not be awarded in this case.

7. Given the answer to question 6, this question does not call for an answer.

On the basis of my answers to the first two constitutional questions, I would allow the appeal.

McIntyre and La Forest JJ. would answer the constitutional questions as follows:

1. No.

2. No answer is required.

3. No.

4. No.

5. No.

6. With respect to s. 605, the answer is No. As to s. 610(3), I adopt the reasons of the Court of Appeal and say that no costs should be awarded.

7. No answer is required.

Disposition of Wilson J.

I would allow the appeal. I would strike down s. 251 of the *Criminal Code* as having no force or effect under s. 52(1) of the *Constitution Act*, 1982. I would answer the first constitutional question in the affirmative as regards s. 7 of the *Charter* and the second constitutional question in the negative. I would answer questions 3, 4 and 5 in the negative and question 6 in the manner proposed by Beetz J. It is not necessary to answer question 7.

3. **Bibliography**

General

"A Comparison of United States and Canadian Approaches to the Rights of Privacy and Abortion." *Brooklyn Journal of International Law* 15 (1989): 759-799.

Beschle, D. L. "Judicial Review and Abortion in Canada: Lessons for the United States in the Wake of *Webster v. Reproductive Health Services* [109 S. Ct. 3040]. *University of Colorado Law Review* 61 (Summer 1990): 537-565.

Cook, Rebecca K. "Abortion Laws and Policies: Challenges and Opportunities." *International Journal of Obstetrics and Gynecology* Supplement 3, (1989): 61-89.

Cook, Rebecca K. and Bernard Dickens M. "International Developments in Abortion Laws: 1977-88." *American Journal of Public Health* (October 1988): 1301-1311.

Henshaw, Stanley K. "Induce Abortion: A World Review, 1990." *Family Planning Perspectives* (March-April 1990): 76-89.

Jacobson, Jody. *The Global Politics of Abortion.* Paper 97 Washington DC: Worldwatch Institute, 1990.

United States

"Abortions and the Court": "An Egalitarian View," Mary Segers (5-6); "An Anti-Abortion View," Sidney Callahan (7-9);"A Legal View," George Annas (8-9). *The Hastings Center Report* 7 (August 1977).

Annas, George. "Four-One-Four." *Hastings Center Report* 19 (September-October 1989): 27-29.

_____. "*Roe v. Wade* Reaffirmed." *Hastings Center Report* 13 (August 1983): 20-28.

_____. "*Roe v. Wade* Reaffirmed Again." *Hastings Center Report* 16 (October 1986): 26-27.

_____. "The Supreme Court and Abortion: The Irrelevance of Medical Judgment." *Hastings Center Report* 10 (October 1980): 23-24.

_____. "*Webster* and the Politics of Abortion." *Hastings Center Report* 19 (March-April 1989): 36-38.

Annas, George J., Leonard Glantz and Wendy K. Mariner. "Brief for Bioethicists for Privacy as Supporting Appellees." (The *Webster*

Amicus Curiae Briefs: Perspectives on the Abortion Controversy and the Role of the Supreme Court) *American Journal of Law and Medicine* 15 (Summer-Fall 1989): 169-177.

Blaustein, Albert P., Edward Grant, Ann-Louise Lohr and Kevin Todd. "The Role of stare decisis in the Reconsideration of *Roe v. Wade*." (The *Webster* Amicus Curiae Briefs: Perspectives on the Abortion Controversy and the Role of the Supreme Court) *American Journal of Law and Medicine* 15 (Summer-Fall 1989): 404-210.

Bopp, James Jr., and Richard E. Coleson. "Judicial Standard of Review and *Webster*." (The *Webster* Amicus Curiae Briefs: Perspectives on the Abortion Controversy and the Role of the Supreme Court) *American Journal of Law and Medicine* 15 (Summer-Fall 1989): 211-216.

------. "*Webster* and the Future of Substantive Due Process." *Duquesne Law Review* 28 (Winter 1990): 271-294.

------. "*Webster*, Vagueness and the First Amendment." (The *Webster* Amicus Curiae Briefs: Perspectives on the Abortion Controversy and the Role of the Supreme Court) *American Journal of Law and Medicine* 15 (Summer-Fall 1989): 217-222.

------."What Does *Webster* Mean?" (Colloquy: *Webster v. Reproductive Health Services*) *University of Pennsylvania Law Review* 138 (November 1989): 157-177.

Brown, Kristen J. "*Bellotti v. Baird*: The Impropriety of Extending the Invalid Assumptions of *Bellotti* to Determine the Constitutionality of Pure Notification Statutes." *Capital University Law Review* 18 (Summer 1989): 297-312.

DeBenedictis. "Abortion Battles; State Legislatures Wrestle With Proposed Restrictions." *ABA Journal* (American Bar Association) 76 (February 1990): 30.

Cole, Leonard A. "The End of the Abortion Debate." (Colloquy: *Webster v. Reproductive Health Services*) *University of Pennsylvania Law Review* 138 (November 1989): 217-223.

Dellinger, Walter, and Gene Sperling. "Abortion and the Supreme Court: Retreat From *Roe v. Wade*." (Colloquy: *Webster v. Reproductive Health Services*) *University of Pennsylvania Law Review* 138 (November 1989): 83-118.

Drucker, Dan. *Abortion Decisions of the Supreme Court, 1973 Through 1989*. Jefferson, NC: McFarland and Co., 1990.

Estrich, Susan R. and Kathleen M. Sullivan. "Abortion Politics: Writing for an Audience of One." (Colloquy: *Webster v. Reproductive Health Services*) *University of Pennsylvania Law Review* 138 (November 1989): 119-155.

Farber, Daniel A. "Abortion After *Webster.*" *Constitutional Commentary* 6 (Summer 1989): 225-230.

Ganske, Graziano and Robert Holmes. "Ohio Parental Notification Law For a Minor's Abortion: Akron 11." *Ohio Northern University Law Review* 15 (Summer 1989): 543-561.

Garfield, Jay L., and Patricia Hennessey. Ed. *Abortion: Moral and Legal Perspectives.* Amherst, MA: University of Massachuetts Press, 1984.

Gerard, Jules B. "*Roe v. Wade* is Constitutionally Unprincipled and Logically Incoherent: A Brief in Support of Judicial Restraint." (The *Webster* Amicus Curiae Briefs: Perspectives on the Abortion Controversy and the Role of the Supreme Court) *American Journal of Law and Medicine* 15 (Summer-Fall 1989): 222-226.

Givens, Richard A. "Status of Pre-Webster Abortion Statutes." *New York State Bar Journal* 62 (February, 1990): 55.

Grant, Edward R. "Conclusion: The Future of Abortion as a Private Choice." (The *Webster* Amicus Curiae Briefs: Perspectives on the Abortion Controversy and the Role of the Supreme Court) *American Journal of Law and Medicine* 15 (Summer-Fall 1989): 233-243.

Halatyn, Susan M. "Sandra Day O'Connor, Abortion, and the Compromise for the Court." *Touro Law Review* 5 (Spring 1989): 327-349.

Johnsen, Dawn. "From Driving to Drugs: Governmental Regulation of Pregnant Women's Lives after *Webster.*" (Colloquy: *Webster v. Reproductive Health Services*) *University of Pennsylvania Law Review* 138 (November 1989): 179-215.

Johnsen, Dawn and Marcy J. Wilder. "*Webster* and Women's Equality." (The *Webster* Amicus Curiae Briefs: Perspectives on the Abortion Controversy and the Role of the Supreme Court) *American Journal of Law and Medicine* 15 (Summer-Fall 1989): 178-184.

Kolbert, Kathryn. "Introduction: Did the Amici Effort Make a Difference?" (The *Webster* Amicus Curiae Briefs: Perspectives on the Abortion Controversy and the Role of the Supreme Court) *American Journal of Law and Medicine* 15 (Summer-Fall 1989): 153-168.

------. "*Webster v. Reproductive Health Services* [109 S. Ct. 3040]: Reproductive Freedom Hanging From a Thread." *Women's Rights Law Reporter* 11 (Fall-Winter 1989): 153-536. (Double Issue)

Linton, Paul Benjamin. "*Roe v. Wade* and the History of Abortion Regulation." (The *Webster* Amicus Curiae Briefs: Perspectives on the Abortion Controversy and the Role of the Supreme Court) *American Journal of Law and Medicine* 15 (Summer-Fall 1989): 227-233.

------. "Enforcement of State Abortion Statutes After *Roe* [*Roe v. Wade*, 93 S. Ct. 705]: A State by State Analysis." *University of Detroit Law Review* 67 (Winter 1990): 157-259.

Maddox, Robert L. and Blaine Bortnick. "*Webster v. Reproductive Health Services*: Do Legislative Declarations that Life Begins at Conception Violate the Establishment Clause?" *Campbell Law Review* 12 (Winter 1989): 1-21.

Marcus, Ruth. "Supreme Court Accepts Abortion-Counseling Case." *Washington Post* (May 30, 1990).

Marks, Deborah. "*Webster* versus Florida's Constitutional Right to Privacy." *Florida Bar Journal* 62 (October 1989): 63-67.

McCormick, Richard et al. "Abortion: What Does Webster Mean?" *Commonweal* (August 11, 1989): 425-428.

Michelman, Frank I., Norman Redlich, Stephen R. Neuwirth and Denise Carty-Bennia. "Brief for 885 Law Professors in Support of Maintaining Adherence to the *Roe* Decision." (The *Webster* Amicus Curiae Briefs: Perspectives on the Abortion Controversy and the Role of the Supreme Court) *American Journal of Law and Medicine* 15 (Summer-Fall 1989): 197-203.

Miller, Hal. *The Abandoned Middle: The Ethics and Politics of Abortion in America.* Salem, MA: Penumbra Press, 1989.

"Minors' Rights to Abortion--Are Parental Notice and Consent Laws Justified?" *University of Detroit Law Review* 66 (Summer 1989): 691-712.

Moore, Kathryn G., Ed. *Public Health Policy Implications of Abortion.* Washington, DC: American College of Obstetricians and Gynecologists, 1990.

Naville, Timothy J. "Abortion--In a Class Action Suit Three Illinois Statutes and Regulations Promulgated Under Said Statutes Were Held to Violate the Constitutional Right to Privacy in Seeking an Abortion." *Journal of Family Law* 27 (October 1989): 883-888.

Novick, Sheldon M. "Justice Holmes and *Roe v. Wade*." (The Constitution and Direction) *Trial* 25 (December 1989): 58-64.

Orentlicher, Davis. "*Webster* and the Fundamental Right to Make Medical Decisions." (The *Webster* Amicus Curiae Briefs: Perspectives on the Abortion Controversy and the Role of the Supreme Court) *American Journal of Law and Medicine* 15 (Summer-Fall 1989): 184-188.

Paul, Eve W. and Dara Kassel. "Minor's Right to Confidential Contraceptive Services: The Limits of State Powers." *Women's Rights Law Reporter* 10 (Spring 1987): 45-63.

Pine, Rachel N. "Abortion Counselling and the First Amendment: Open Questions After Webster. " (The *Webster* Amicus Curiae Briefs: Perspectives on the Abortion Controversy and the Role of the Supreme Court) *American Journal of Law and Medicine* 15 (Summer-Fall 1989): 189-197.

Plave, Erica Frohman. "The Phenomenon of Antique Laws: Can a State Revive Old Abortion Laws in a New Era?" *George Washington Law Review* 58 (November 1989): 111-124.

Rhoden, Nancy K. "Trimesters and Technology: Revamping *Roe v. Wade*." *Yale Law Journal* 94 (March 1986): 639-697.

Rice, Charles. "Issues Raised by the Abortion Rescue Movement." *Suffolk University Law Review* 23 (Spring 1989): 15-40.

Rotterman, Debra. "Forced Cesarean Kills Mother." *Off Our Backs* 18 (January 1988).

Secrest, Sandra M. "Minor's Rights to Abortion--Are Parental Notice and Consent Laws Justified?" *University of Detroit Law Review* 66 (Summer 1989): 691-712.

Shaw, Patricia Swearingen. "Constitutional Law-Abortion Protest-First Amendment Speech Rights Outweigh Privacy Rights of Women Seeking Abortions." (case note) *Mississippi Women's Medical Clinic v. McMillan*, 866 F. 2d 788 (5th Cir. 1989) *Cumberland Law Review* 20 (Winter 1990): 183-194.

Smith, Philip A. "Abortion: From *Roe* to *Webster*." *Law and Justice* (Summer-Fall 1989): 6-29.

Smolen, D. M. "Abortion Legislation After *Webster v. Reproductive Health Services* [109 S.Ct. 3040]: Model Statutes and Commentaries." Cumberland Law Review 20 (1989-1990): 71-163.

Starke, J.G. "The United States Supreme Court and the Constitutionality of Anti-Abortion Measures." *Australian Law Journal* 63 (October 1989):660-665.

Strictland, Ruth Ann, and Marcia Lunn Whicker. "Banning Abortion: An Analysis of Senate Votes on a Bimodal Issue." *Women and Politics* 6 (Spring 1986):41-56.

"The Supreme Court and Abortion": "Upholding Constitutional Principles," John Noonan (14-16); "Side-Stepping Social Realities," David Mechanic (14-19). *Hastings Center Report* 10 (December 1980).

Warwick, Donal. "Foreign Aid to Abortion." *Hastings Center Report* 10 (April 1980).

Wohl, Alexander. "The Abortion Cases." *ABA Journal* (American Bar Association) 76 (February 1990): 68.

Canada

"Abortion Law in Canada: A Need for Reform." *Saskatchewan Law Review* 42 (1977): 221, 229-232. [legislative history]
"Abortion Ruling in Quebec." *Medico-Legal Journal* 57 (Fall 1989): 233-235.
L'Avortement: Sources Jurisprudentielles." *Le Monde Juridique* 5 (1989): 23-25.
Benson, I.T. "An Examination of Certain ‹Pro-choice› Abortion Arguments: Permanent Concerns about a ‹Temporary› Problem." *Canadian Journal of Family Law* 7 (1988): 146-165.
British Columbia. *Abortion Clinic Investigation.* Victoria, B.C.: The Ombudsman, 1988.
Bouffard, Martin. "Pour une Reforme du Droit a L'Avortement." Les *Cahiers de Droit* 31 (June 1990): 575-597.
Conkle, D. O. "Canada's *Roe*: The Canadian Abortion Decision and Its Implications for American Constitutional Law and Theory." *Constitutional Commentary* 6 (Summer 1989): 299-318.
Crann, G.P. "*Morgentaler* and American Theories of Judicial Review: The *Roe v. Wade* Debate in Canadian Disguise?" *Faculty of Law Review* (University of Toronto) 47 (1989): 499-525.
Dickens, Bernard M. "Eugenic Recognition in Canadian Law." *Osgoode Hall Law Review* 13 (1975): 547, 562-65 (1975).
_____. "The *Morgentaler* Case: Criminal Process and Abortion Law." *Osgoode Hall Law Journal* 14 (1976): 229.
Fox, L.M. "*Canadian Abortion Rights Action League Inc. v. A.G. of Nova Scotia,* 39 (1990) Administrative Law Reports." *Administrative Law Reports* 39 (1990): 249-254.
Gavigan, Shelley A. M. "On 'Bringing on the menses': The Criminal Liability of Women and Therapeutic Exception in Canadian Abortion Law." *Canadian Journal of Women and the Law* 1 (1986): 279-312.
Gentiles, Ian. Ed. *A Time to Choose Life: Women, Abortion, and Human Rights.* Toronto: Stoddard, 1990.
Goldberg, Edward. "The ‹Bad Law› Argument in *Morgentaler v. The Queen.*" *R. v. Morgentaler* (1988), 44 D.L.R. (4th) 385 (Q.B.) (S.C.C.). *Canadian Journal of Women and the Law* 3 (1989-90): 584-591.
Grant, I. "Forced Obstetrical Intervention: A Charter Analysis." *University of Toronto Law Journal* 39 (1989): 217-257.

Grant, S. "The Non-Human Child." *Canadian Journal of Family Law* 7 (1988): 176-182.

Greschner, Donna. "Abortion and Democracy for Women: A Critique of *Tremblay v. Daigle.*" *McGill Law Journal* 35 (May 1990): 633-669.

Hartney, M. *R. v. Morgentaler* [1988] 1 R.C.S. 30. *Cahiers de Droit* 29 (1988): 775-793.

Hébert, M. "L'Application des *Chartes* Canadiennes et Québecoises en Droit Medical." *Cahiers de Droit* 30 (1989): 495-523.

Hovins, B. "The *Morgentaler* Decision: Parliament's Options." *Canadian Family Law Quarterly* 3 (1988): 137-165.

Hunter, I.A. "The Canadian Abortion Quagmire: The Way In and a Way Out." *Canadian Family Law Quarterly* 6 (1990): 57-78.

Jodouin Andre. "Reflexion sur l'arret Morgentaler, sur la criminalisation de l'avortement et sur certaines consequences logiques qui semblent decouler, pour la redaction legislative en matiere criminelle, de la notion de principes de justice fondamentale." *Revue Juridique Thémis* 24 (Spring 1990): 177-197.

Martin, Sheilah L. "Canada's Abortion Law and the *Canadian Charter of Rights and Freedoms.*" *Canadian Journal of Women and the Law* 1 (1986): 339-384.

------. "Is There a *Borowski* Case after the *Morgentaler* Decision?" *Canadian Journal of Family Law* 7 (1988): 131-145.

------. *R v. Morgentaler et al.* [1988] 82 N.R.1. *Canadian Journal of Women and the Law* 1 (1985): 194-205.

------. "*Morgentaler v. The Queen* in the Supreme Court of Canada." *Canadian Journal of Women and the Law* 2 (1987-88): 422-431.

------. "The New Abortion Legislation." *Constitutional Forum* 1 (1990): 5-7, 20.

------. "The Reluctance of the Judiciary to Balance Competing Interests: *R. v. Morgentaler.*" *Canadian Journal of Women and the Law* 1 (1986): 537-546.

------. "Using the Courts to Stop Abortion by Injunction." *Mock v. Brandanburg* (1988), 61 Alta. L.R. (2d) 235 (Q.B.) *Canadian Journal of Women and the Law* 3 (1989-90): 569-583.

MacAlister, D. "*R. v. Morgentaler*: Access to Abortion and Section 7 of the Charter." *Canadian Journal of Family Law* 7 (1988): 166-175.

McConnell, M.L. "Abortion and Human Rights: An Important Canadian Decision." *International and Comparative Law Quarterly* 38 (October, 1989): 905-913.

------. "Even by Commonsense Morality *Morgentaler, Borowski* and the Constitution of Canada." *Canadian Bar Review* 68 (1989): 765-796.

McCourt, K.M. and D. J. Love. "Abortion and Section 7 of the *Charter*: Proposing a Constitutionally Valid Foetal Protection Law." *Manitoba Law Journal* 18 (1989): 365-394.

McLellan, A.A. "Abortion Injunction Vacated: *Daigle v. Tremblay.*" *Constitutional Forum* 2 (1990):9-11.

Overall, C. "Mother/Fetus/State Conflicts." *Health Law In Canada* 9 (1989): 101-103.

Poirier, S. "L'Avortement et la liberté de conscience du médecin." *Cahiers de Droit* 31 (1990): 287-305.

Ryan, H. R. S. "Reflections on *Morgentaler.*" *Criminal Reports* (3d) 62 (1988): 118-123.

Shumiatcher, M.C. "The *Borowski* Case." *Revue Générale* 20 (1989); 299-324.

Somerville, M. "Reflections on Canadian Abortion Law: Evacuation and Destruction--Two Separate Issues." 31 *University of Toronto Law Journal* 1 (1981).

Tateishi, S. A. "Apprehending the Fetus en Ventre de sa Mère: A Study in Judicial Sleight of Hand." *Saskatchewan Law Review* 53 (1989): 113-141.

Tolton, C. "Medicolegal Implications of Constitutional Status for the Unborn: ‹Ambulatory Chalices› or ‹Priorities and Aspirations.›" *Faculty of Law Review* (University of Toronto) 47 (1988): 3-57.

Viau, L. "L'Arrêt Morgentaler: une Nouvelle Page Dans L'Histoire du Droit des Femmes." *La Revue Juridique Thémis* 22 (1988): 259-264.

------. *R. v. Morgentaler* [1988] 1 R.C.S. 30. *La Revue Juridique Thémis* 22 (1988): 259-264.

Weiler, K. M. "Of Courts and Constitutional Review." *Criminal Law Quarterly* 31 (1989): 121-141.

Notes

1. J. Mohr, *Abortion in America: The Origins and Evolution of National Policy* (Oxford: Oxford University Press, 1978), 3.
2. Sharon Marmon and Howard A. Palley, "The Decade After *Roe Versus Wade*: Ideology, Political Cleavage, and the Policy Process," *Research in Politics and Society*, Vol. 2 (JAI Press, Inc., 1986), 182.
3. Ibid., 183.
4. R. Polenburg, "The Second Victory of Anthony Comstock?" *Society* 19: 32-38.
5. *Griswold v. Connecticut* 381 U.S. 479 (1965).
6. *U.S. v. Vuitch* 305 F. 1032 (1969).
7. Polenberg, 32.
8. *Roe v. Wade* 410 U.S. 113 (1973).
9. *Doe v. Bolton* 410 U.S. 179 (1974).
10. See B.J. George for an analysis of state abortion laws before 1967, between 1968 and 1973, and after 1973. "State Legislatures Versus the Supreme Court: Abortion Legislation in the 1980's," ed. J. Douglas Butler and David F. Walbert, *Abortion, Medicine and the Law* 3rd. ed. (New York: Facts on File, 1986), 23-105.
11. See *Roe v. Wade: Briefs, Oral Arguments and Opinions* (Frederick, MD: University Publications of America, forthcoming).
12. Marmon and Palley, 185.
13. Albert Pearson and Paul Kurtz, "The Abortion Controversy: A Study in Law and Politics," in J. Douglas Butler and David Walbert, eds., *Abortion, Medicine and the Law* (New York: Facts on File, 1984), 107-135.
14. Ibid., 116.
15. *Planned Parenthood of Central Missouri v. Danforth* 428 U.S. 52 (1976).
16. *Bellotti v. Baird* 443 U.S. 622 (1979); *Bellotti v. Baird* 428 U.S. 132 (1976).
17. Id. at 643 n. 22.
18. Pearson and Kurtz, 111-16.
19. *Collautti v. Franklin* 439 U.S. (1979).
20. H.C.S., House Bill No. 1211 (appr'd June 14, 1974), quoted in 428 U.S. at 76, 86-88.
21. Id. at 78.
22. *Akron v. Akron Center for Reproductive Health* 103 S.Ct. 2481, 2488 n.3 (1983).

23. *Deerfield Medical Center v. Deerfield Beach* 661 F. 2d 328 5th Cir. (1981).
24. Pearson and Kurtz, 113.
25. *Planned Parenthood Association v. Ashcroft* 103 S.Ct. 2517 (1983).
26. Pearson and Kurtz (115) describe another case of procedural process which may have the effect of deterring abortion. In *Scheinburg v. Smith*, the state argued that an abortion posed a threat to the procreational potentiality of the marriage. Therefore, spousal notification should be required. The Court struck down the statute on the basis that a properly conducted abortion did not pose more than a minimal threat to the procreational potential and did not vindicate a legitimate state interest. 550 F. Supp. 1112 (S.D. Fla. 1982).
27. *H.L. v. Matheson* 450 U.S. 398 (1981).
28. Joan Biskupic, "‹Right to Die,› Abortion Rulings Spur Calls for Hill Action," *Congressional Quarterly* (June 30, 1990): 2058.
29. In 1987, the court reviewed parental notification in *Hartigan v. Zbaraz* 108 S. Ct. 479 (1987). At this time there was one court vacancy and the justices split 4-4 on an Illinois statute requiring that parents be told before a physician performs an abortion on a minor. In *Bellotti v. Baird* 443 U.S. 622 (1979), the court struck down a Massachusetts parental-consent statute. It argued that a minor must have access to a confidential, expeditious proceeding before a judge.
30. *Planned Parenthood of Central Missouri v. Danforth* 428 U.S. at 65-66. See also *Akron v. Akron Center for Reproductive Health* with regard to the detailed informed consent requirement. This portion of the ordinance was rejected by the Court on the grounds that the actual purpose was to dissuade women from having abortions. 103 S. Ct. at 2502-03.
31. *Planned Parenthood of Central Missouri v. Danforth* 428 U.S. at 80.
32. *Mather v. Roe* 432 U.S. 464 (1977).
33. *Harris v. McRae* 448 U.S. 297 (1980). For a discussion of the reasoning with regard to the due process and equal protection challenges, see Pearson and Kurtz, 117-18.
34. Pearson and Kurtz, 119.
35. S.J. Res. 119, 93rd Cong., 1st Sess. (1973).
36. Pearson and Kurtz, 120.
37. S.J. Res. 17, 97th Cong., 1st Sess. (1981).
38. S.J. Res. 3, 98th Cong., 1st Sess. (1977).
39. Pearson and Kurtz, 121.
40. Ibid., 122.

41. See, e.g., S.J. Res. 17, 97th Cong., 1st Sess. (1981); H.J. Res. 17, 96th Cong., 1st Sess. (1979).
42. H.J. Res. 115, 95th Cong., 1st Sess. (1977).
43. Pearson and Kurtz, 123.
44. See H.R. 867, 97th Cong., 1st Sess. (1981); H.R. 73, 97th Cong., 1st Sess. 1981).
45. See S. 2646, 85th Cong., 1st Sess. (1975).
46. *Human Life Bill* S. 158, 97th Cong., 1st Sess. (1981).
47. Pearson and Kurtz, 127.
48. *Thornburgh v. American College of Obstetricians and Gynaecologists* 106 S. Ct. 2169 (1976).
49. Dennis Horan, Edward Grant, and Paige Cunningham, eds., *Abortion and the Constitution: Reversing Roe v. Wade Through the Courts* (Washington, D.C.: Georgetown University Press, 1986), 268.
50. *Webster v. Reproductive Health Services* 109 S.Ct. 3040 (1989).
51. See *Webster v. Reproductive Health Services, Inc.: Briefs, Oral Arguments, and Opinions* (Frederick, MD: University Publications of America, 1989).
52. "U.S. Supreme Court Guts *Roe v. Wade*, Inviting State Battles Over Limits," *Hospital Ethics* 5 (September/October, 1989): 4.
53. Biskupic, "‹Right to Die,› Abortion Rulings Spur Calls for Hill Action," 2056, 2057.
54. Joan Biskupic, "New Limits on Abortion Rights are Upheld by 5-4 Majority," *Congressional Quarterly* (July 8, 1989): 1699.
55. Law Reform Commission of Canada, *Crimes against the Foetus*, Working Paper 58 (Ottawa: Law Reform Commission, 1989), 7.
56. Ibid., 7.
57. *Criminal Code, Revised Statutes of Canada*, 1970, Chapter C-34, Section 251.
58. Mildred Morton, "The Morgentaler Judgment: How the Decisions Differ," *Backgrounder*, Library of Parliament (February 9, 1988), 2.
59. For an account of the parliamentary debate preceding the passage of the 1969 abortion law, see Alphonse de Valk, *Morality and Law in Canadian Politics: The Abortion Controversy* (Montreal: Palm Publishers, 1974), 99-126.
60. Law Reform Commission, *Crimes against the Foetus*, 8.
61. *Hansard*, May 6, 1969, 8397.
62. *R v. Morgentaler* [1988] 1 S.C.R. 30, reversing 1985 (1985), 22 D.L.R. (4th) 641 (Ont. C.A.).
63. Part I of the *Constitution Act*, 1982, Schedule B of the *Canada Act* 1982 (U.K.), 1982, c. 11.

64. For a description of the position taken by each of the judges and an analysis, see Morton, *The Morgentaler Judgment: How the Decisions Differ*, 3-12. She notes two reports which were used as a source of information crucial to the reasoning of two of the majority decisions. These are: the *Report of the Committee on the Operation of the Abortion Law*, (*Badgley Report*) (Ottawa: Minister of Supply and Services, 1977); and the *Report on Therapeutic Abortion Services in Ontario* (The Powell Report), (Toronto: The Ministry, 1987).
65. Morton, 4.
66. Francois Baylis, "Abortion: Recent Canadian History," *Westminster Affairs* 2 (Summer 1989): 1-2.
67. Canada, House of Commons, *Order Paper and Notices*, no. 357 (July 27, 1988), 20-22.
68. "Emotional Abortion Debate Inconclusive." *Ottawa Letter* XVIII, no. 83 (August 2, 1988): 666.
69. "Abortion Issue Back in the PM's Lap: Top Court Refuses to Rule," *Halifax Mail-Star*, March 10, 1989, 1, 2.
70. *Borowski v. Canada* (Attorney General) [1989] 1 S.C.R. 342.
71. Canada, House of Commons, Bill C-43, 2nd sess., 34th Parliament, s. 287 and s. 288.
72. Christie McLaren, "MDs and the New Abortion Law," *The Globe and Mail*, June 16, 1990, D2.
73. Richard Mackie, "Commons Restricts Abortions," *Globe and Mail*, May 30, 1990, A2.
74. Geoffrey York, "Senators Kill Abortion Bill with Tied Vote," *Globe and Mail*, February 1, 1991, A1, A6.
75. Lynda Hurst, "Abortion," *Toronto Star*, July 15, 1989, D1, D5.
76. Ibid., D1.
77. *Quebec Charter of Human Rights and Freedoms* R.S.Q. 1977 Chap-12.
78. "Abortion on Trial," *Maclean's*, July 31, 1989, 16.
79. Danielle Crittenen, "Whose fetus is it, anyway?" *Chatelaine* (November, 1989): 146.
80. *Tremblay v. Daigle* [1989] S. C. J. 79, 56.
81. Ibid., 70.
82. "Abortion and the Law," *The Globe and Mail*, July 6, 1989, A6.
83. Glen Alan, "A Crusader's Challenge," *Maclean's*, November 6, 1989, 14-5.
84. Kevin Cox, *The Globe and Mail*, October 20, 1990, A1, 2.

Index